FASTALLIANCES™

FASTALLIANCES™

POWER YOUR E-BUSINESS

LARRAINE SEGIL

John Wiley & Sons, Inc.

New York • Chichester • Weinheim • Brisbane • Singapore • Toronto

This book is printed on acid-free paper.♾

Published by John Wiley & Sons, Inc.

Published simultaneously in Canada.

Library of Congress Cataloging-in-Publication Data:
Segil, Larraine.
FastAlliances : power your E-business / Larraine Segil.
p. cm.
Includes index.
ISBN 0-471-39683-4 (cloth : alk. paper)
1. Strategic alliances (Business) 2. Electronic commerce—Management.
I. Title.

HD69.S8 S437 2001
658.8'4—dc21

00-064916

Printed in the United States of America.

10 9 8 7 6 5 4 3 2 1

To my son, James Segil, who has been my inspiration for this book

TO THE READER

E-business is serious stuff. So is life. But taking yourself too seriously is a flaw that will impede success no matter the extent of your talents. For this reason, I have found the funny bone of e-business in the marvelous characters that have crept out of my head and onto the page as I observed, analyzed, commented on, and celebrated the challenges and joys of FastAlliances. One of these characters is a young lady, fictional of course (although she bears a faint resemblance to what I see in the mirror), with the unusual name of (yes, you guessed it) Fast Alli. She has the newly created job of e-business liaison in a company that could be yours. She must interrelate with everyone in the company—crossing divisional silos and encountering strange and wonderful personalities as she learns the particular preferences (and peeves) of her colleagues. I hope you enjoy Fast Alli and the comic strips that trace her journey through the book.

Larraine Segil

CONTENTS

INTRODUCTION

The announcement of the acquisition of Time Warner by AOL changed the rules of the business development game. What has happened since then has been a "net real estate grab"[1] that has made the Wild West look tame. Not-yet-Net companies have been evaluating their business development and alliance options with those already established in the Internet world.

Business development in the e-economy is a critical management function. It is both strategic and tactical and fundamental to Internet success. Business development and alliances are interconnected as never before. Both have morphed into different, sleeker, swifter, corporate and operating functions. I call them *FastAlliances*™ (FastAlliances is a trademark of Larraine Segil). Companies in all industries must learn how to develop effective alliances or slip into oblivion, and that could happen faster than any strategic plan could predict. Although these alliances may sound familiar (acquisitions, licensing, comarketing and promotion, outsourcing, joint development, constellations and networks of interconnected corporations), the way they must occur in the Internet environment is very different: There is no time to fail and recover. When the market matures, the winners will be those who have perfected the art of managing FastAlliances, which means this is not a fad. It's an essential management skill for the present and future.

This book is the first one to slice and dice the deliverables for business development and alliances in the Internet world and present the tools to create these swift and decisive relationships. This book will show you how to take the short experience of the new economy and combine it with selected experiences from traditional alliances. Flexibility and change must be woven into your actions, because the field is too new to have well-oiled lessons. You will learn to create your own customized formula that works, tailored (like everything else in this world) especially *by* you and *for* you. These are targeted approaches to the alliance world, different from the methodology examined in my first book *Intelligent Business Alliances* (Times Business, Random House, 1996).

There is no "business as usual." The e-commerce business world has turned many old rules on their heads.

First, with the onset of e-business, there was the prediction of the death of *bricks-and-mortar companies,* the name webheads[2] gave to the pre-Internet world. The general feeling was that the web ruled. But, that has not happened. Instead, the *click* and *brick* worlds[3] are becoming more intertwined. For example, as Amazon.com exploded in the click world, it rushed to acquire and build warehouses and logistics assembly lines in the brick world; as Intel pushed harder to increase its already impressive percentage of sales to net-based orders (keep in mind the company has relatively few large customers as opposed to Amazon.com's millions), it's embarked on an acquisition frenzy to acquire Internet-related chip manufacturers with all their accompanying bricks and mortar.

The second prediction was that valuations would change and never go back to previous levels. That happened, but only temporarily. What's different about the way the analysts and shareholder communities view the e-commerce world? This change in approach accounts for one of the most breathtaking increases in market valuations (and corrections) the stock market has ever seen (except for the year preceding 1929, as ominous as that may sound). Yet many of the most respected brands in business have lagged (Eastman Kodak, Mattel), and their stock has not reached the appreciation levels of those companies who have barely been around long enough to file name reservation requests.

Why? What's different?

Old-line companies are judged on earnings. Until recently, Internet space companies were judged on revenues. The difference in these business models is that it makes it extraordinarily difficult for large companies to incubate Internet opportunities in-house without underinvesting in them. If they allocate the appropriate amount of investment in order to build the revenues in that aspect of their business, it hurts their earnings. The solutions are not simple and have far-reaching effects, not only on valuations but also on employees and other stakeholders (e.g., supply chain and shareholders).

Here's a case in point. Stamps.com signed a $56 million exclusive marketing alliance with America Online. If Pitney Bowes had made that deal, with 275 million shares outstanding, the impact on its shares with an AOL deal would be about 10 cents pretax. This would impact its earnings. The analysts would hate it. The stock would go down since it is an earnings-based valuation. However Stamps.com makes that announcement and the stock goes up 8 points, even though its estimates were reduced by 50 cents per share. Why? Because Stamps.com is an Internet company and the perception is that the deal will accelerate revenues and increase its potential for winning long term in the marketplace. E-Stamps cuts a deal with eBay to offer stamps online when a purchase is made and the buyer/seller clicks the Shipping icon. Same result—the stock goes up. Is it fair? No. Is it reality? Absolutely. Can you leverage this reality for your company? Indeed.

There's another way that analysts traditionally value companies—through cash flow and supply and demand. Since Internet companies have broken into new territories, there has been great demand and not enough supply. (Adam Smith, the father of capitalistic demand/supply theory, would be proud.) The lack of supply (scarcity) of Internet equity fueled a huge appreciation in valuation. But as more Internet stocks fed at the shareholder trough and competition loomed on the horizon for existing Internet companies, scarcity became plenty and a series of corrections have ensued.

What does this mean for you? You have to be ahead of the players in this game. FastAlliances can be the tool—the approach that helps you reinvent a small part of your organizational structure if you are a traditional (not new Internet) company. If you are a new Internet company, the challenge will be to apply some level of discipline while maintaining the velocity you have already created.

I have created a formula that you can adapt to your company and industry. One size does not fit all in the Net space. In fact, one size fits *one*—the very model of mass customization. And that is why the traditional approach to alliances is faulty in the Internet world—it cannot flex or move nimbly enough to meet a speed of change that no one can totally comprehend.

I have spent the past 20 years creating traditional alliances, as CEO in a number of companies and as a consultant and teacher of alliance methodology worldwide. My first book, *Intelligent Business Alliances* (Times Business, Random House, 1996), was devoted to the art and practice of alliances. Traditional alliances involve extensive analysis, a clear understanding of partner characteristics and priorities, corporate commitment and resources, remediation, and conflict resolution.

The new economy requires a different approach to creating, managing, and evaluating alliances, making them into FastAlliances—faster, cleaner, and able to cope with relationships that, in many ways, are more complex and flexible than those of the past. This book will lay out the essentials and provide a frame-breaking model that can be adapted to meet your ongoing and ever changing needs.

This unique model presents a seven-step approach. (You will be able to state on seven laminated cards the essence of a strategy, plan, process, and metrics for your FastAlliances approach.) It will be concise, clear, and communicable. Examples are given of companies that have applied these principles and succeeded, companies such as Compaq, Sun Microsystems, Kodak, Flextronics, Office Depot Online, Intuit, Cisco, Stamps.com, Chubb (United Kingdom), Praxair (formerly Union Carbide), newer companies such as Ninth House (web-based intranet distance learning), Virtualis, and BigStep.com (web-hosting application service providers), venture capital firms such as W.R. Hambrecht, incubators like Garage.com and Guy Kawasaki, and others. Case illustrations are from interviews with those who have succeeded and failed. The key is for you to make it work for your company, industry, market, and culture. The secret to success lies in taking the approach and making it your own.

The reality is that no one really knows what to do and how to do it—everyone I spoke to and worked with is making it up as they go along (no matter what they tell the analysts!). The approach presented in this book is a *change* mechanism that will fit all situations—but the adaptation will make it relevant only for you and only in your situation. Here is a summary of the seven-step approach and the issues that are addressed:

Chapter 1. Step 1: Diagnosis of Your Company, Competitors, and Industry Players. What's different now in business development—the new value proposition; when FastAlliances work and when traditional alliances are the right choice; the Spider Network.

Chapter 2. Step 2: The Up-Front Work in the Creation of FastAlliances. How business is transacted on the computer screen, not in meetings; doing business on the web; FastStrategy, branding, and tools.

Chapter 3. Step 3: Define the Deliverables for FastAlliances. Key deliverables every FastAlliances *must* have—and how you can find them quickly; more tools of FastAlliances.

Chapter 4. Step 4: Managing Stakeholder Expectations. The lawyers, angels, venture capitalists (VCs), investment bankers (IBs), executive search, consultants, and government (yes, I do mean government!).

Chapter 5. Step 5: The Essential Characteristics for Business Development. Traits that make up the business development competency; creating and adding to your FastAlliances business development team.

Chapter 6. Step 6: Leveraging the Global E-Space. Cross-border FastAlliances—the must-have success factors and approaches to test and create them.

Chapter 7. Step 7: Employing the E-Mindshift System. The life-cycle stages of e-businesses and the corporate cultures, personalities, and individual managerial personalities that fit within them.

Chapter 8. Step 8: The Deals—Making, Managing, Adding Value, and Terminating Them. The nitty-gritty of creating and managing FastAlliances—metrics, ongoing change mechanisms, and knowledge transfer; tools, tools, tools!

Chapter 9. Pitfalls and Opportunities—Summing Up. Growing the company in the e-space by using traditional alliances along with FastAlliances.

Have alliances been a successful tool in the past 20 years? I've done surveys on hundreds of companies—over 235 for my book *Intelligent Business Alliances* and, more recently, 250 global companies, each of whom had multiple alliances. The result? Close to 60 percent have not been successful.

What is different about FastAlliances that makes them worth doing? Two reasons: *cost-efficiency* and *accelerated growth.* I will address these themes throughout every chapter of the book since they are all-pervasive. Here is a short illustration of their importance.

Cost Efficiency of Alliances

There is no way that Stamps.com could penetrate the market depth accessible to America Online (AOL) in the same amount of time without an alliance. Is the Stamps.com investment worth it? That depends on the customer acquisition cost without it. It is doubtful whether within the time available to gain market leadership (in the early stages of the dot-com revolution—that is always the key issue), Stamps.com could ever gain similar exposure to the specific market it is targeting through advertising alone. Its targets are small to medium-sized businesses, individuals, sole proprietors, and even large businesses. The only way for Stamps.com to reach its targets speedily is through an alliance with a dominant player (e.g., AOL) for *eyeball acquisition* (i.e., the number of consumers who visit a site) in the online market. Analyzing customer acquisition costs, this becomes the more cost-effective way for Stamps.com to go. Now that E-Stamps has announced an alliance with eBay, the Net real estate grab is on for both of these companies, with Pitney Bowes still planning its own entry. The early life-cycle stages of FastAlliances are *the* critical time for choosing the right partner. Making the wrong choice (a company who could be a brilliant partner in a later stage) could be an irretrievable mistake. (See Chapter 7 on life-cycle stages for FastAlliances—the E-Mindshift approach).

History has already presented a lesson regarding branding. During the 1999–2000 holiday season, many dot-com companies chose not to use the partnering approach to promote their brands but to go it alone with traditional advertising. They were disappointed in their return on advertising dollars. Some canceled campaigns. Others announced miserable revenue projections. Value America Inc., a consumer electronics gear company, spent huge amounts on print-based ads. Nevertheless, its revenue projections came in close to 9 percent below previous projections and caused the company to lay off about 50 percent of its staff. Given the cluttered advertising channels, customers are numb to many of the messages and are now looking to brands they know and trust to help them make purchasing decisions on the web.

Hallelujah! The moment for the brick-and-mortar companies (BAMs) is here. Solid well-respected brands have a chance to evolve their web presence and web-customer market share. By using FastAlliances, they can move into winning positions in *customer stickiness* (traffic and transaction flow).

With the shakeout of dot-coms upon us, we now see a phenomenon that will become all too common—dot-coms for sale as the market consolidates, especially in some of the crowded consumer-products arenas (toys and pet products). For those companies, splurging on

FastAlli, by Larraine Segil

alliances rather than on ad campaigns would have been money well spent, leveraging their dollars further in a more cost-efficient way.

Growth through Alliances

This is the name of the dot-com game. Growth in revenues, growth in eyeballs, growth in stickiness, growth in back-end support and infrastructure, growth in talent, growth in brand—and on and on. The competition is unlike anything before or since. Why? Because the very nature of the medium means that scouring the web for competitors is a full-time job, and the dissemination of information is so universal that keeping ahead of the curve of innovation is increasingly difficult. Today's innovation is yesterday's news.

Innovation is probably one of the more essential areas of growth. New ways of executing every part of the business are as important as the new technology and products and services. Amazon's amazing logistical prowess in warehousing, inventory management, and customer service (learned at Mach speed) enabled the company to do better than most e-tailers during the holiday season of 1999–2000.

Growth in talent is another area of breathtaking change. Finding people who can learn fast and combine flexibility, creativity, and dot-com self-esteem (see page 144ff) is one of the ongoing and most difficult challenges of all companies in this area. Revenue and market share growth is key—dot-com valuations are closely related to revenue increase, so growth in that traditional sense is critical for all players.

Impacting this trend is the growth in expectations, which is quite daunting to those in traditional jobs in non-dot-com companies. Often, senior dot-com management salaries start at $200,000, and options give 1 to 2 percent of the company to employees, whose average age is 28. This trend in the United States has affected cultures worldwide. At a recent Singapore conference on the Internet sponsored by the Silicon Valley Bank, the Singapore American Chamber, and the Singapore government, I addressed more than 500 companies (most of them start-ups) looking to make a place in the e-commerce money pit for themselves, their compatriots, and their country. They were hungry for FastAlliances, wanting not only to tap into the over $1 billion that the Singaporean government has designated for investment in e-business, but the expertise and experience of those in other parts of the world who are already in this space. The presence of venture capitalists, investment bankers, and consultants from all over the world at that meeting was evidence enough of the mutuality of interest. I have spoken in the past year about Fast-Alliances in Asia, Latin America, and Europe—the overwhelming interest and concern is that *now* is the moment to grab e-business opportunities.

Cost-efficiency and growth are topics that permeate this book. They are the key issues to address whenever a FastAlliance choice is being made: Does this decision add to our growth (defining growth for that application)? Will it be cost-effective (in the context of other comparable options)?

Growth, which can be leveraged cost-effectively, will be a mandate for you and your company. To be successful, you need a checklist and a formula in your pocket on how to do business development in the Internet world. The new reality for the analyst and investor community has impacted the old reality for employees. Making it work requires a well-thought-out approach. The good news is that even though it seems that everyone is doing it, we are in the early stages of the dot-com revolution. There is still time to join the game—but not everyone who plays will survive.

In this book, I give you a set of survival tools and a winning strategy for the new economy.

CHAPTER 1

Step 1: Diagnosis of Your Company, Competitors, and Industry Players

There is a new value proposition at work, a fresh approach to business development that must be understood.

When people want information about the silent disease of depression, they don't visit Eli Lilly's web site to find out about it, even though that company manufactures the popular antidepressant Prozac. The web visitor looks for a solution to a problem. The problem is depression. The web site they are most likely to access is www.depression.com. There they will find information about the condition, multiple solutions (including information about Prozac), and access to a community of patients and professionals offered by PlanetRX.com, a satellite health channel. The site offers much more than just information about a particular drug. The goal of this site is to create *stickiness* (the ability to keep a visitor at a web site due to its depth of information, attractiveness for transactions, or other valuable benefits). Visitors will find so much value that they will linger to gather information and find multiple solutions to their problems. Some of what makes this possible are chat rooms, access to medical databases and articles, and online dialogue with experts. In creating a

FastAlli, by Larraine Segil

sticky web site, the company must associate and co-brand marketing partners who form a kind of chamber of commerce for the web visitor, thus creating perceived value. (It's so much more than the pitch-and-sell technique.) The value of those alliances is critical in giving the web visitor access to many ways of deriving value, or value streams, and not just the one leading to the Eli Lilly home page.

James Segil,[1] who is running an Internet company with its founder, stated the strategy that creates the desired web-site results: "Delight your visitor with information, services, and products that solve their problems quicker, cheaper, and more effectively than they could ever have imagined. This is what keeps a site dynamic. And partnerships are a key component since they give visitors access to information they can use or they didn't know was available or even relevant before you showed it to them. That is how you make your web site sticky!" James's approach has been hugely successful—in the 10 months since he entered the company (after a Harvard MBA and six years as product manager at a Fortune 500 consumer products company), he and the founder reorganized, tripled revenues, and positioned the company for resale. (It was recently acquired by a telecommunications company.)

The desired results of such a strategy will be as follows:

- Stickiness to your site and content
- New eyeballs and increased market share
- Revenues from related commercial transactions
- Advertising revenues from increased value of your site
- Brand growth that increases company value and blocks your competitors

Online versus Offline Alliances

So, what is different in business development for the Internet world? The new value proposition means that partners—large and small—can come together with components of the solution. Those involved in creating the chamber of commerce must understand the speed, the negotiation of value contributions, and the metrics (measurement or size) of these relationships. Since e-commerce is causing a transformational event in business, many factors are affecting the traditional business development role. For many traditional or offline companies that are in transition, their initial efforts in business development have been in partnering to create and deepen their online presence, whereas for dot-com companies, business development deals have been used to leverage their growth and go public.

Keith Butler, who was vice president responsible for Office Depot Online when we spoke, put it this way: "Business development doesn't have only to create e-business opportunities, but must expand the scope once the deal has been done. The business development role has to permeate many aspects of the organization—for example, ensuring that decision processes are not hierarchical or multilayered. That takes too long and speed is essential in e-business." This leads to a discussion of the change that is happening to the definitions of traditional roles in management.

It is helpful to categorize organizations into three large groups:

1. *Dot-coms.* These are companies whose entire business is on the Internet.

2. *Traditional companies.* These are companies that don't have a web presence beyond a home page and some initial customer contact on the web.
3. *Transitional companies.* These are companies that have made a significant commitment to creating a web presence (e.g., have an e-business group, initiative that is well funded, and a strategy to grow this part of their business into a core capability—potentially transforming the entire organization).

This categorization is not meant to be a limiting factor. However, it can be used as a diagnostic to understand the intent and resources of a partner who talks the e-business talk but may not have put significant resources into making it happen. In creating FastAlliances, understanding where your partner is will enable a more effective management of expectations.

Changing Management Roles

Detailed here are how the roles of members of senior management teams have changed.

The Chief Executive Officer (CEO)

Normally, the CEO is the ultimate business development contact, playing a variety of roles either as the opener who goes in to get the potential partner's attention and then lets the vice president and director-level people take over or as the big gun who comes in to close the deal. When a high level of support is needed by the organization, the CEO may show up to play an appropriate role or to make the deal happen fast if there is a personal relationship. For example, the founder of Register.com and one of the founders of Stamps.com were old friends who simply got together and made a deal following Register.com's initial public offering. In the FastAlliances world, the CEO of the smaller organization will often find him- or herself sitting across from a business development person from a larger company. This is not very different from the way things have always been. Only the approach is different. The potential and leverage of the small company may well exceed its relative size. Again, Stamps.com is a classic example of this. Just past the start-up stage the company partnered with industry giant AOL. Likewise, CEO Bo Ewald of E-Stamps has developed alliances with eBay, Microsoft, and Intuit.

The Chief Financial Officer (CFO)

In 2000, I took part in an executive report on alliances developed by the Corporate Executive Board for the Working Council for Chief Financial Officers, CFOs of the Fortune 1,000 firms.[2] As part of this study, we looked at the changing role of CFOs, who are now often concerned with the lack of measurable, quantifiable metrics and results for the alliances of their firms and have now involved themselves in the alliance process. As the dot-com valuations and market perceptions become more attractive to CFOs, we can expect them to be even more involved. This means that instead of the huge deals that would normally cross the CFO's desk, much smaller yet still strategically significant deals may now catch the CFO's attention, and his or her business development skills could be critical to success. The ability to engage the imagination of a smaller company in the financial opportunities and leverage available to all organizations could be the deal closer that makes it all happen. There is no doubt that someone in the organization has to calculate a reasonable return on investment (ROI) for FastAlliances, and that role is increasingly delegated to the CFO and his or her staff.

Other senior managers may also be involved in the business development activity if they are stakeholders in the outcome—operationally, strategically, or both.

The Chief Information Officer (CIO)

This management role has perhaps undergone the most dramatic change, especially in companies that are serious about e-business. The CIO is not only the one who should be in the forefront of understanding the strategic importance of information technology (IT) needs and capabilities as part of the company's competitive advantage, but this executive should be a key player in external alliances with suppliers of technology and should be aware of any joint development or license relationships for technology and expertise. The dot-com may be an attractive acquisition or equity investment for the company, and here the CIO may be involved in working with business development and the corporate or divisional strategy teams to review the strategic opportunities, helping with the early research of what's hot or not, performing due diligence regarding potential partners, leading evaluation, and finally executing the FastAlliances deals.

The Chief Technology Officer (CTO)

The chief technology officer's role has also increased. In some dot-com companies, this is the spot the founder assumes in the end—sometimes happily, sometimes not. Keeping the company functional and creating innovation is the competitive role that the CTO must play—often presenting the company's unique advantages to venture capitalists and investment bankers. The roles of CIO and CTO are sometimes combined, especially in smaller companies.

The Chief Administrative Officer (CAO), Chief Marketing Officer (CMO), and Chief Operating Officer (COO)

These executives are all team players contributing to the business development role, supporting or spearheading with the implementation team brought together from various areas of the company.

Chief E-business Officer

An important player is the newest position: chief e-business officer. Kodak, for example, has appointed a chief e-business officer for every division in the company. Doug Pileri (now VP of e-business for Thomson Consumer Electronics) recently held this role for Kodak's Entertainment Division. "There is a change in the business model now—it is more than just e-commerce. It affects all aspects of the company—research, marketing, and supply chain. The business as a whole has to understand the transformational change that is happening—it's not incremental change." This could be seen as a transitional role—namely, when the company moves from being traditional to being fully e-business (if indeed that is its goal), this position may be blended into another (CIO, CTO, or even CMO). In other companies it may remain as a contributive and facilitative position.

Under the e-business model, mass customization has reached its zenith. Marketing and selling is being done on a one-on-one basis with the customer, meaning that the value to the customer is constantly being measured. This affects the entire value chain of suppliers and all business processes both inside and outside the organization. The role of the chief e-business officer is to facilitate, educate, and change all functional processes and capabilities in order to deliver the result to the customer. That reaches into shipping, inventory control, service, IT—every part of the business—which is why e-business is transformational, not incremental. Pileri describes his perspective: "It means looking always at your services and products from the customer's point of view. And that means not just your company, but your 'chamber of commerce,' too. For example, everything a customer could possibly want in entertainment should be offered in value streams available and accessible from the Kodak web site. This is fundamentally different from the way business has been done in the past. It is a much broader view to deliver a much more targeted result."

The role of the chief e-business officer is divided between internal and external activities. He or she must facilitate the functional capabilities of the whole organization to ensure it is responsive to e-business requirements. Otherwise, no matter the effectiveness of the web message and information, the execution of the promise will fail. Chapters 2 and 5 focus on tools to make this happen.

Vice President of Customer Service

This is an increasingly important role in dot-com companies. With data centers, call centers, and customer service centers as the only point of human contact for many e-commerce transactions, these people and teams are becoming critical points of connection for an otherwise personality-less brand. In addition, a troublesome trend is the outsourcing of the customer management process, or customer resource and relationship management (CRM) solutions, by many dot-coms, who are increasingly losing touch with their customers. Technical prowess, people skills, product/service knowledge, and conflict-resolution skills are essential tools in combination with speedy systems to analyze and correct customer-oriented demands. The huge change that is coming about in CRM, however, is that many companies are looking to these groups to reinvent themselves as profit centers, *not* cost centers. They are charged with the tasks of upselling customers, charging for support services, and other value-added roles.

E-economy Categories

A number of categories are evolving in the e-economy. For many offline businesses, the disconcerting experience of operating two entirely different business models simultaneously can be compared to growing another head.

For example, *e-tailers* such as E-toys and Amazon.com are causing the evolution of second heads for traditional retailers like Wal-Mart (Walmart.com) and Barnes & Noble (BarnesandNoble.com).

Services now manifest from E-loan to priceline.com and democratize information for the consumer. Price shopping has never been easier.

Portals, an entirely e-economy device, such as AskJeeves and Yahoo!, represent an aggregation of customer eyeballs. They themselves are now linked to communities and financial and value streams so that they are no longer just *the way in,* but also *the road to* a defined destination for the web visitor. This has given rise to the *affinity portal* for the web visitor. For example, if someone needs information on photography, he or she can go to the Kodak affinity portal, which optimizes information on photography, not just on Kodak products. *Vertical portals* evolved based on vertical industries. Kodak, using the same example, is both an *affinity portal,* where you can gain information on photography, and a *vertical portal,* where you can get industry information. There are also *country portals,* such as India.com or China.com.

Then there are the *auction sites* such as eBay and Egghead.com; *communities* like iVillage; *content providers* as seen in Theglobe.com and hundreds of others; *software e-companies* such as Healtheon; e-marketers like DoubleClick; and, of course, the *infrastructure providers* such as Cisco. Now add the *exchanges*—Chemdex is one, and Chevron recently announced an exchange to link buyers and sellers in the global energy market, which was developed in an alliance with electronic commerce software developer Ariba Inc.

And don't forget the application service providers (ASPs) who develop software and are often combined with web-hosting companies as well as the Internet service providers (ISPs) like Earthlink. These are the business-to-business (b2b) companies offering services and products to other businesses, such as Bigstep.com and Virtualis.com.

We know the e-business world is different. Offline companies are now competing with entirely online businesses and offline double-headed businesses while trying to grow another head themselves. Many of them could use both the traditional alliances approach and FastAlliances as their competitive growth strategy.

Key Factors in Choosing the Right Alliance Approach—Traditional or FastAlliances

In this section I address the strategies necessary for large and/or traditional companies (what I call the *transitional companies*) who are creating an online activity—the how, where, why, and what of integrating the Internet into the organization—and for the dot-coms who may have to partner with them.

There is great value in understanding the approach being used not only by your own company, but also your partner—especially if one is a traditional company and the other a dot-com or e-business organization. A clear understanding of the motivations, management commitment and experience, and financial support or lack thereof will lead to more effective alliance relationships.

A good approach for more conservative companies is to take the concepts of the past for alliance building and business development and adapt them to fit the e-business environment. Then select the appropriate approach: FastAlliances, traditional alliances, or a combination of both.

Using the traditional approach to alliances must, however, be placed in the context of increased speed of competition. Some companies can start, come to market, and go public in the same time that it takes certain large organizations to examine and develop a business opportunity. For Internet opportunities, the FastAlliances approach must be used. It does not mean that the traditional processes have no value. On the contrary, their value is augmented if applied appropriately. And if the FastAlliances approach is applied to the wrong situation, it could diminish value, not add to it.

The threshold questions are as follows:

- Where will the e-business effort be positioned within the company?
- Is it a separate division?
- Is it an initiative that permeates the whole company?
- Will it be spun off into a new company?

Until the answers are clear, it is difficult to select the right alliance methodology—the one for non-dot-coms and companies in transition to e-business or the one for dot-coms.

For Non-dot-coms and Companies in Transition to E-business

If you are from a traditional company, not a dot-com, one solution is to differentiate the e-business activity from the management processes of your company's mainstream activities if private, or to build it and spin it off into a separate (not consolidated) entity if it is public. This way the necessary funding needed to acquire market share and revenues can be financed without impacting the earnings potential of the mainstream business. The companies that are now in the Internet space (as it's referred to by people in the Internet economy) will be long-term winners only if they win the short-term race for critical mass. This kind of thinking has evolved from the logic (or illogic) of revenues-based valuations versus earnings-based valuations. Until recently, companies in the Net space were valued by the amount and growth of revenues, not earnings, as old-line companies are traditionally valued. Are some valuations still at nosebleed levels? They are. Risks undoubtedly go with them, but you are either in the game or out of it. There is no standing on the sidelines hoping for an available opportunity at this stage of the new economy. The kinds of stock market corrections that happened in early April of 2000 are to be expected, as are consolidations of industry players in which the competitive advantages of multiple players are unclear. It is early in this game, and therein lies the opportunity—no one has real experience, and everyone is making it up as they go along.

Midsized companies (e.g., Synopsys, the $1 billion-plus Silicon Valley company whose groundbreaking work in the semiconductor industry through innovative software and services is the backbone of the manufacture of the very microchips that make the Internet economy and its players effective) have adopted a web strategy that is evolving carefully, taking into account their internal stakeholder issues as well as the external market opportunities. The web group of Synopsys is headed by Dave Burow, senior vice president. "Dave is taking care to communicate throughout the organization as changes are happening," comments Synposys's president and COO, Chi-Foon Chan. "It's neither simple nor straightforward, but we are very aware of all the stakeholders inside the company as well as external partners."

Many companies will do well to adopt this approach so that they co-opt the support of those within the organization who can accelerate or slow down the movement into the e-business world.

There is a downside when the e-business group is separated from the rest of the operations. This kind of action can cause mutterings of discontent in the rest of the organization that is not part of the new concern and its accompanying rewards (and risks). Sun Microsystems knew this when it considered a structure for its e-commerce group. The company had to deal with the fact that other divisions not part of the designated dot-commers would feel devalued if it created a separate group for this function, especially since the Sun advertising slogan was "the dot in dot-com." To prevent this, the company designated E-Sun as a project, not as a separate group. It became a major corporate initiative that would transform the entire company. Terry Keeley, vice president of the E-Sun Architecture and Technology Solutions at Sun,[3] described the activity to me: "E-Sun is a program, across all the divisions, with 400 people who are focused on changing all the business processes at Sun. The goal is to position ourselves to increase revenue without linear growth in expense." Through technology, E-Sun is looking to deliver a variety of different audience portals with interest groups as well as service functions that will enable customers to do any type of business online with Sun. This will enable the sales force to be relationship-focused rather than placing orders and validating configurations. Keeley explains, "We are building a high-performance electronic commerce store environment as well as information containers and news containers and desirable services that customers, resellers, suppliers, and employees will want." Keeley's job (and that of his team) is to deliver the technology that enables all this to happen. This program, which provides an overarching view of changes that must occur, is implemented by cross-organizational teams. Adds Keeley, "We want to be so good at this that we can share it with customers—so that our change model becomes the reference to share, and in that way we will lead the industry. We call it Venus's-flytrap. . . . [T]he Sun portal is so great that when you visit it, you like it so much that you stay a long time!"

Sun created a web strategy called MySun portal with three segments:

1. *Services.* These are transactions in which customers place orders, get billed, and configure the products. There are also tailorable sets of services that are optional to the user. In this way

the desktop can be tailored to have the services the customer wants and also productivity enhancements such as e-mail and a calendar, which are not directly related to selling or servicing. Again, the idea is to make the customer want to stay.

2. *Information.* This segment provides tailored information to a particular user. Sun's customers are generally interested in systems information and high-end servers as well as system information tools. This segment has key reference areas.
3. *News.* This is similar to the information segment, but here any newsfeeds are related to the areas in which customers are interested.

"These segments are anchors to attract people to the site," Keeley adds. "But this requires that the information and news is fresh all the time. The cost is well worth it due to the leverage of the numbers of people that can be reached through this medium."

No comment about Sun would be complete without mention of Java. The magic behind Sun—its currency—has been Java. It could be said that the stickiest part of Sun's web presence is Java, since over 1.5 million software developers visit Sun's Java site daily. It could be said they practically *live* on it. Java is free, and because of its accessibility, Sun has a huge network of software developers creating applications for their servers. Java was and is a key contributor of the "dot in dot-com" strategy of Sun.

Another approach for traditional companies is to implant the e-business role into the mainstream organization as a facilitator and message carrier to all functions and groups within the company. That is what Kodak did in creating the chief e-business officer role and placing it on the division level where it can be most effective on a day-to-day basis. Of course, that can work only when the vision for the transformational aspects of e-business has been communicated from senior management throughout the entire organization. (Chapter 2 discusses ways to facilitate that.)

There is a downside to this approach: When the company is slow and bureaucratic, the creation of an internal e-business approach to supposedly permeate the whole company is tantamount to a massive culture change and corporate transformation—and we all know how difficult that is. Even though that goal is achievable, can it happen fast enough to lay some stakes in the game, or will faster-moving players take market share?

For Dot-Coms

The FastAlliances approach will most often be the approach you will use in the early stages of your company. It is explained in detail, along with the tools to implement it, throughout the book. However, it is critical that you understand the mind-set of the larger and traditional companies with whom you may need to partner: What have they done in their alliances in the past? What expectations do they may have for the present? How can they educate themselves (maybe with your help!) regarding the need for FastAlliances for the future?

Approaches Best Used for Traditional Alliances

For the past 15 years, I have been creating, refining, and applying a series of processes to the alliance field.[4] Companies like Federal Express, Sun Microsystems, Compaq, Kodak, and others have applied them with great success. Although many companies are overprocessed and others are resistant, it has always been a challenge to adapt and insert a new set of processes with regard to alliance management. The traditional alliance processes have included the following:

1. *Strategy and analysis.* This takes time—sometimes a long time. In many ways, time can work in the favor of the partnering organizations: They can learn to understand each other, examine multiple options, test for the most qualified partner, and develop a due diligence that will be thorough. This requires development and alignment of an *alliances strategic plan* interlinked to the overall *corporate strategic plan.*
2. *Partner selection and relationship development.* Since many traditional alliances take from 6 to 12 months to develop (cross-border may take even longer), a greater emphasis has been placed on the up-front partner analysis and criteria development stages, analysis for appropriateness, and strategic and cultural fit. Companies that are moderately to greatly risk-averse have chosen legal structures (e.g., distribution, licensing, OEM, private label) that allow for some level of failure and adjustment without resorting to acquisitions.

3. *Alliance management and metrics.* This involves the following methodology.
   - A variety of flowcharts and measurements
   - A model for a center of excellence for alliances (a group at corporate or in the senior management team of each division who advise on alliance competency and maintain the database of alliance activity of the company/division; if divisional, all centers of excellence must collaborate with each other to share data)
   - Tools and training programs for increasing alliance competency throughout the organization
   - Supervision of the staff versus line issues
   - Metrics and remediation of the alliance over time
   - The development of second-stage reinventions of existing alliances in order to add continuing value[5]

Characteristics of an Alliance Opportunity That Will Fit into the FastAlliances Approach

1. Internet-related businesses are ripe for this approach—that is, information, selling, buying, or any activity that uses the Internet as its *primary* vehicle.
2. Your competition is operating (or beginning to) in an Internet model.
3. The customer wants value and the Internet information/chamber of commerce model is the best solution. The customer valuation model has changed so that number of eyeballs, stickiness, how long they stay, click-through rate, and amount actually purchased (including purchase behavior and a multitude of other metrics that are evolving daily) are key.
4. The trend is toward large numbers of alliances that are nonexclusive rather than small numbers of alliances that are exclusive. The reason is that the evolution of e-business is so dramatic, new players and ideas so prevalent, and markets so unstable that all opportunities must be investigated and attempted. However, there is a place for preemptive alliances that attempt to be first

into a particular space (see page 134). Those who garner a preemptive position, however, are in many cases those who already have market share rather than those who tie up partners with exclusive relationships.

In most dot-com companies, or even in divisions of larger companies, *process* is a dirty word—and for good reason: The time constraints in that space prevent adherence to a sequential process. The FastAlliances.com approach takes that into account. It is directive, not detailed. In other words, the overriding goals are described, but the way you interpret and apply them to your situation can be customized, modified on the run, and parallel to implementation.

First, you must decide whether the opportunity fits the preceding characteristics. If it does, you are in the FastAlliances world. Whether you are a dot-com partnering with a company transitioning to e-business or with another dot-com, or whether you are the transitioning company, here are some questions you will need to answer:

- Where is responsibility for the e-business effort within the company? Is it the spin-off choice (focused on one area of the company), or is it the disseminated approach (chief e-business officers at the business unit level)? This will establish the accountability and authority profiles that will fundamentally affect application of the Strategy Playbook Tool as well as the Cool Decision Tree (fast approach to getting decisions made) in Chapter 2. The answer to both these questions could be yes—that is, the accountability is matrixed. It's complex, but at least you'll know where the responsibility lies.
- How is the e-business initiative being implemented? The two main approaches follow.

Effective Implementation of Net Systems

This is often seen in those companies that supply e-commerce companies with services and products. Cisco is the classic prototype, but Intel follows closely. Cisco Systems hardware is critical to the Internet. Almost every bit of data on the Net moves through a Cisco router, or switch. Cisco follows its own advice to its customers regarding net operations. Over 80 percent of its orders are handled online, and every day it sells products worth more than $32 million (and growing) on the Net. Cisco is far larger than Amazon.com as an e-commerce company! It has integrated the web into all of its operations, using it to handle all internal employee communications as well as its accounting and finance activities—even its manufacturing. It has also perfected use of the Net for hiring employees, the side benefit being that you can track where they came from (and, indirectly, how many employees your competitors might be losing!).

Complete Revitalization

Many offline companies are cautiously beginning to do this in order to retrofit themselves to compete in the e-commerce world. Intel now receives over 50 percent of its revenues from online sales of products, over $1 billion per month. Remember, however, that Intel has relatively few, but large, customers as opposed to Amazon.com, who has millions of small ones. With Intel's acquisitions of Internet-related chip makers such as Level One Communications and DSP Communications (costing over $6 billion), the company is investing heavily to increase its weight as a player in Internet products and services. AT&T has, until recently, received only about 20 percent of its revenues from data traffic. But its bold and expensive moves into cable TV are expected to change that and reinvent the company into a genuine e-business. The jury is still out on this one! Other companies are taking this step more cautiously. They are struggling to deal with, or maybe even redesign, distribution relationships and channel conflict, and they face the costs and logistics of reeducating huge numbers of employees to the new online versus offline mentality.

Understanding this will contribute to your success by telling you how swiftly (and cleanly *with* appropriate resourcing but *without* internal second guessing of decision making) you or your partner will be able to make the FastAlliances happen or whether the e-business initiative is all talk and no action.

The Spider Network: FastAlliances Tool #1

It is important to constantly evaluate opportunities to build a network of partners rather than simply bilateral relationships. Look at each e-business opportunity from the perspective that rarely is a single partner going to be the total solution. Every partner you bring in has a series of interlocking relationships that could impact your activities. In this way, the network is a web of opportunities. The Spider Network is a methodology for creating and managing the complex, fast-moving relationships of the new economy. Consider it an issue to be managed.

For example, the announcement of the acquisition of Time Warner by AOL had a far-reaching effect on AT&T, which is now faced with the AOL/Time Warner pledge to provide open access on its broadband networks. Since AT&T has a 26 percent investment in Excite@Home, a company that provides Internet services over the cable television infrastructure and leases digital telecommunications lines to consumers and businesses, the game will change for the telecommunications giant. Even though AT&T has resisted open access that would require allowing all online services to use its cable pipes on the same terms as Excite@home, the company will probably be compelled to go along with the idea. Also, AOL's joint venture with Bertelsmann to roll out AOL in Europe has been permanently affected because AOL/Time Warner competes strongly with Bertelsmann in Europe in magazine and book publishing. To add to the complication, the Time Warner–EMI deal also competes with Bertelsmann in the music arena. Interestingly, Bertelsmann has decided to use the spin-out approach to increase the value of its e-business strategy. Chairman and CEO Thomas Middelhoff has stated, "Bertelsmann intends to increase sharply its budget for acquisitions—in part by spinning off more of its Internet properties, giving the company some of the cyberstock that is today's media-deal currency."[6] In anticipation of this conflict, Bertelsmann's chairman has resigned from the AOL board.

The decision to create a partner network requires looking at these interlocking relationships. They can add leverage or cause conflict. Adding partners with a portfolio approach is a method to handle this challenge—by identifying and gaining access to the value and identifying the conflicts well in advance.

To accomplish this, answer these questions early in your investigation:

1. Do your partners compete with each other?
2. How can you leverage the strengths of the partners as a consortium?

3. What information barriers have to be put up between partners who are competitors in order to prevent the seeping of proprietary information from one to the other?
4. Can you add value to your network of partners as well as to yourself? Will doing so make you even more competitive in the marketplace?
5. Do your partners have partnering relationships that can benefit you, thus making them more likely than another company to be chosen as your partner?
6. Can you benefit from association with a particular partner? Or would association with a specific partner preclude you from partnering with others?

Another aspect to gathering partners depends on whether your company is public or private. Public stock can play the useful role of being used as currency for acquisitions. For example, WorldCom morphed into MCIWorldCom by using its stock as currency to make huge acquisitions.

Amazon.com is another example. In 1999, Amazon acquired three small Internet businesses, paying most of the acquisition price with stock by issuing about 8 million shares. The value of those shares was then added to the company's equity. It's perfectly legal and in accordance with the Financial Accounting Standards Board (FASB) rules. If Amazon had paid cash, the story would have been quite different. The amount would have been *subtracted* from the equity. The result of buying with stock: Amazon's shareholder equity jumped *up* to the mind-boggling level of $571 million in June 1999. As for its profits, there weren't any. In fact, Amazon lost an equally mind-boggling amount of $161 million that same quarter. How can a company continue like this? Well, it can't, certainly not forever. But for the immediate future (one year in Internet life), the company will be fine since it has a pot of cash (close to $1 billion) and has registered with the government to raise another $2 billion. But now, because of the revenues-to-earnings valuation shift—the pressure on Amazon to show profits is mounting. The point is, you can't play the revenue game forever: Eventually, the earnings rules *will* apply. But if you are public and can take advantage of the FASB rules, the best legal structure for your alliances might be acquisition.

If you are a privately held company, your alliances are best created around alliance structures that are less costly than acquisitions (joint marketing, licensing, joint research, outsourcing, private label, co-branding) unless you have access to large amounts of capital. Acquisitions will generally be too costly and will use up scarce and precious capital that is necessary for operations and to fund the human resource buildup. However, joint marketing, outsourcing, and joint research could defray some of the costs involved in the start-up or market launch mode. It could speed the time to market, gaining many of the benefits that accrue to public companies from acquisitions. Of course, these options are also available to public companies. By the same token, private companies should not turn away from great acquisition targets at reasonable valuations. As with everything in this space, there are no hard-and-fast rules. It's all a matter of managing uncertainty and ambiguity, the key facets of dot-com self-esteem (more in Chapter 3).

Yet another interesting play has been the hallmark of an unusual Japanese entrepreneur named Masayoshi Son, whose Internet empire is centered in a holding company, Softbank, in Tokyo.[7] He is fast implementing his 300-year plan to invest in as many Internet companies as possible so that no matter what country you are in, you are likely to be dealing with a company that he partially owns.

For example, Softbank owns 23 percent of Yahoo! and is part owner of E*Trade, Global Sports, 1-800-Flowers.com, Buy.com in the United States, Viso (a joint venture with Vivendi) in France and Japan, as well as insurance, finance, car sales, and shopping companies. In all, about 10 to 15 percent of the companies that do business on the web (130 companies and growing) is part of the Softbank family. Masayoshi's plan is to have 780 companies within five years.

Can others play this game too? What about you?

The way to do it is to accumulate partners into a constellation as part of building your network. Having cross-equity stakes in companies that could enhance your strategy—not just suppliers or distributors, but those that strategically position your company in a more competitive position than other players—is a worthwhile strategy. Masayoshi Son started early and has amassed a huge fortune that has enabled him to be a major participant in Silicon Valley with his venture capital firm and incubator. The philosophy behind his strategy is equally applicable to others with less capital. Ronald Fisher, who arrived in the United States from my place of birth, South Africa, around the time I did about 30 years ago, runs Softbank's global ventures group. He told me recently that this is one of the most exciting moments of his life:

> Our philosophy at Softbank is based on three beliefs. The first is strategic. Softbank was originally a software company that went public in Japan and made acquisitions where they controlled either all or a significant portion of equity of companies whose mission was to provide the infrastructure and support services to technology providers and their consumers. About four years ago we saw that this was all going to change due to the Internet. So we changed our business model and became a minority investor in many promising companies where our value-added could be synergy and access. Now we are invested in over 300 Internet companies and can help all of them with their strategies because of the magnitude of our reach in these industries. The second part of our approach is the active family synergy [The Spider Network]. We don't dictate the terms of alliances between our portfolio companies, but we actively support them and facilitate introductions. Our third differentiator is perhaps the greatest—that is, providing our portfolio companies with global access.

There is no doubt that Softbank, through its portfolio of companies, is having an effect on the world in which we live. The power of its Spider Network cannot be underestimated. The way the company leverages it is as important as the players. The best Spider Network is one that is implemented with as much excellence as it is created. Ron Fisher explains:

> Although we have regular meetings to which we invite the portfolio company management, by market segment as well as for all companies in a two- to three-day session in which they talk about how to interconnect with each other and add value, we also function as the sponsor of the companies. For each portfolio company, we designate a person whose role it is to develop these interconnected relationships as we bring new companies into the family. These people figure out who the likely partners could be and

actively work the relationships on a daily basis. We also have interim meetings of companies in our portfolio who are in the same business arenas.

Even private companies can exchange their stock in a stock-for-stock transaction with a partner who could add significant competitive strength. This is another way of looking at the financing of alliances in a cost-effective way where cash is not flowing freely. And once public, this approach falls into the acquisition strategy previously described. Many of the factors affecting these structural decisions are handled in Chapter 5. They are particularly affected by the life-cycle stages of the FastAlliances described in Chapter 2.

Used appropriately, the Spider Network will create Connectivity Velocity (speed of being connected), which could be a competitive advantage in preempting others from getting there first. It is a constellation/network of interlocking relationships between potential partners and the points of leverage between them, including sensitive areas where they could compete. It is a living document that informs the business development team about new partner candidates and interlocking or conflicting areas of competency, business, and, of course, points of leverage. Capitalizing on the opportunities in the points of leverage can then be assigned to team members to be investigated for value. Otherwise, these points of opportunity will fade away, just like many good ideas that come up and are never acted on in the endless meetings that occur in all companies (even the dot-com type). The Spider Network chart should be displayed in a war room–type environment so that new partners can be added as they come into the network and their networks are examined. The velocity that the added partners contribute to the network adds excitement, fueling even more good ideas and execution. (See Figure 1.1.)

Some companies I have worked with who have used this tool keep a column on one side of the chart for summarizing ideas on how to leverage the interlocking network of companies. Making the whiteboard accessible generates great creativity and insights from those with knowledge about network members. Those who control the marker pen control the thought documentation. In meetings, tossing the pen to anyone who wants it frees the control of ideas and makes them flow easier. This enables all team members to become vested in out-of-the-box solutions as well as the obvious ideas.

In some respects, this book is one way that I am able to share my Spider Network with you. The insights and tools, perspectives and opinions, contact information and web addresses of all those quoted in the book, who willingly shared their information, are part of my Spider Network. My hope is that you will incorporate their wisdom into your own.

The Spider Network Characteristics

The 10 main characteristics of the Spider Network are as follows:

1. It is fragile but flexible.
2. It takes real commitment to create.
3. It often hangs from tenuous precipices.
4. It is a thing of beauty when it can be used cleanly.
5. It is transparent except to educated eyes.
6. It can easily be broken (can cause destruction if treated roughly).
7. Its creation is ongoing and never ends.
8. It is acutely aware of and intertwined with its environment—and must respond accordingly.
9. It is driven by a single vision.
10. Implementation adapts constantly.

The Spider Network is an interconnected group of entities and individuals who are connected directly and indirectly to each other. They are at one time competitors, at another collaborators, and sometimes both at the same time. At one time a partner may be the market leader and at another, a follower or, even worse, an also-ran (no longer in the game). Constant change and complexity mean that time and resources produce certain benefits from the Spider Network that are often different from those of the traditional constellation network common in the traditional economy. Many of the Spider Network members will be equity partners, ensuring their longer-term relationship with the network; but just as many others will have an indirect connection (e.g., through an existing relationship with a partner that is directly joined to the network through equity). All the Spider Network characteristics discussed are valid regardless of the legal

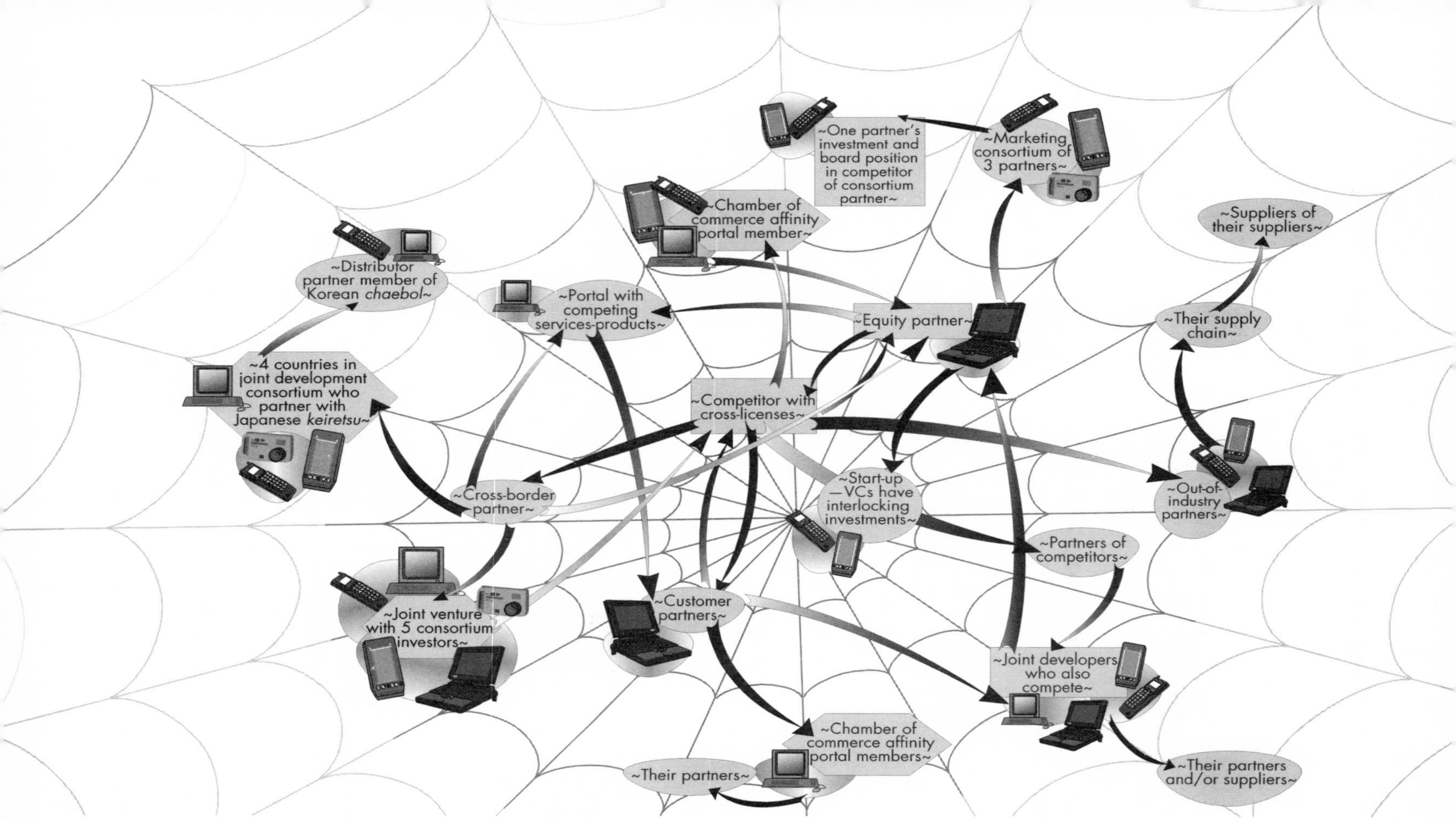

Figure 1.1 The Spider Network: FastAlliances Tool #1

structure used, but they will vary in intensity. And, depending on the project and the direct or indirect nature of the network members, the Connectivity Velocity will also vary. Spider Network partners must be continually ranked for risk and reward relative to your organization. Only then will you be able to allocate the right resources to manage these relationships.

How the Spider Network Works

The partners in the Spider Network must be evaluated according to the 10 characteristics that follow.

1. It is fragile but flexible.

Network partners are seen as perishable. That means that their value may be short-lived. Metrics must take this into account. Creating a FastAlliances with a new network member means setting the expectations clearly and quickly up front. It also requires understanding that, since the life cycles of FastAlliances relationships can be short, the network relationship is a fragile situation. It requires high levels of communication and constant awareness of a changing marketplace that may make the alliance either irrelevant or much more important within a short period of time. This requires judgment and risk taking—hence the need for the dot-com self-esteem described in Chapter 3. Setting specific milestones that are short and defined is a key to success. Since a FastAlliances could start, reach its peak, and end all in the space of six months or a year, the deliverables must be visible and measurable within a very short period of time. Setting up communication systems that are efficient means breaking into very small teams—no more than three people—and having a traffic cop. This is a team coordinator from each alliance partner who is responsible for coordinating the timeliness and delivery of all team commitments. This team and its coordinators will eventually hand off to the worker bee alliance managers, who make sure the alliance implementation lives by the words of commitment given by each side. That handoff must include the high-level stamp of approval that accompanies this approach. If the Spider Network member is an equity participant, the fragility of the relationship will *decrease*. However, due to rapid market changes, the need for flexibility remains. The following tale offers a good illustration.

The Story of the Giant and the Gazelle[8]

Once upon a time, there was a giant—a large, well-respected, but staid technology company known for slow decisions and frustrating bureaucracy. Sadly, some of the giant's employees (especially those who had been there for a while) remembered its nimble and quick days, times when it would jump on opportunities and run joyously with them until satisfactory completion.

Lately, new blood had come into the giant's establishment. The mission of the new team was to create a fast-track methodology for FastAlliances creation. One day, the reality of their intent was tested. Along came a gazelle—an e-business company that was fleet of foot and very seductive. Needless to say, along with its beauty (and the fact that everyone praised its looks and accomplishments) went a healthy (or maybe unhealthy) dose of arrogance. As the gazelle charmed the giant, it also probed for personal gain. It was clear that although its words spoke of mutual benefit, the gazelle was young, self-involved, used to flattery, and in need of a gentle nudge toward compromise.

Compromise means that no one is really completely happy, but that mutual benefit could still exist for all sides. The giant pulled together all the key people who would be able to deal with this alluring but troublesome seduction. "We want what the gazelle brings—but can we deliver?" the giant's team wondered. The solution was a fast-track combination traditional/e-team creation. The giant looked deeply and seriously at the competencies of the people within its massive body and requested a team that could fit the speed and creativity (and, of course, the attractive enthusiasm) of the gazelle. The group came together. The common mission began to bind them into a special team and the giant viewed with wonder the transformation of giantism into gazellism. "Ah yes," thought the giant, "what if I could take the characteristics of this group and make the whole company behave like a gazelle!"

The gazelle and the giant's "gazellized" team met for the first time to test the giant's team. The group might look like a gazelle (sort of a large one since giantism is hard to hide), but could it act like one? The alliance goals were outlined (of course, the giant had thought hard about this before entering the first meeting), and the giant and gazelle group divided into minigroups to work on various issues.

A ranger (the traffic cop) was appointed by each partner to coordinate and organize the outputs of each minigroup. The two rangers spoke often and candidly with each other. The giant's CEO and top executives stayed close to the project, willing to make immediate decisions and compromise. The gazelle was equally available.

One issue was dealing with the arrogance of the gazelle (see Chapter 5 on dot-com self-esteem). The giant had to change some team members in order to match the energy and arrogance of the gazelle and, more important, to soften its impact. After all, if the gazelle partner's arrogance made the giant defensive, that would get in the way of the ultimate transformation of the giant and the creation of a really good alliance. With major compromise on both sides, the deal was done. In the process, the giant transformed the behavior of a key group of managers into gazellism—whether it will last throughout the entire alliance remains to be seen, but the first six months achieved the success hoped for, and in a FastAlliances that could be enough. Added value would be a bonus.

2. It takes real commitment to create.

There is no possibility for a FastAlliances in a Spider Network to succeed without real commitment. This will be reflected in the people resources necessary to make the relationship happen. Although financial resources are important, they are next to useless without the right people to implement the alliance. The characteristics of these people are discussed in Chapters 2 and 3, but the real commitment is indicated by the presence of senior managers in the alliance creation stages and their overall sponsorship and endorsement of the FastAlliances. Bringing real commitment into the Spider Network when not all members have it will accentuate the fragility of this structure. The following threshold questions should be asked of all potential network members:

- What is the level of executive sponsorship?
- Who are the team members who will be involved?
- What resources will be committed to the project—where, how much, when, how long, who?

3. It often hangs from tenuous precipices.

The tenuous nature of the Spider Network cannot be overemphasized. Partner participants are networked to each other as they are to other partners not part of the original network. This means that there is a constant change in positioning among the network members from partner and collaborator to competitor and also-ran. Yet the creation of the network can mean the difference between success and failure in the new economy.

According to Dennis Walsh, vice president and chief technology officer for OnStar, the GM service for security and safety information delivery to the automobile, "Without a network of alliances we are unable to make change happen on a routine basis. For example the first Internet-connected car will be voice-activated and hands-free, and further changes have to happen incredibly fast. The auto industry is focused on relationships—350,000 suppliers and over 8,500 dealers—and all of these relationships have to now reflect the new environment." Although OnStar has been created to operate independently of the rest of GM, it is accountable for its own results and services. OnStar is part of the newly formed e-GM group set up to pull all the e-commerce activities of GM worldwide into one group. And e-GM's mission, over time, is to disappear. In short, the processes established by e-GM will be absorbed by the whole of GM and will reinvent the entire company. Will the new way be adopted by the whole company including those who have spent a lifetime in the old way? The risks are mitigated by encapsulating the e-GM group into a separate division so that the change will not be seen as a dive over a precipice into a deep abyss but rather as a soft and carefully executed landing on dry land.

The speed of change in the identity of the members within a network means that managing the relationships requires a software program to efficiently track and change the dynamics as new partners enter and their coordinates and characteristics are included in the Spider mix.[9]

4. It is a thing of beauty when it can be used cleanly.

The Spider Network is a remarkable but necessary achievement. It requires vision. It requires a whiteboard and a free-floating marker pen at minimum or, better yet, a software program to maximize efficiency. Moreover, it requires awareness of the benefits that come from virtual organizational structures, shared goals and responsibilities, and a level of integrity. It has to be clean—not dirtied by back-door politics and underhanded dealings. Dishonesty is easily and quickly visible in the Spider Network. Because it is fragile, network members can come and go, and unethical behavior will reach to the far corners of the network and be communicated like wildfire.

Ethics in the old economy have been found lacking in many aspects of business. However, in the new economy, instant information transfer among lateral and flat organization structures means that it is hard to keep secrets in the Spider Network. Less-than-honest behavior will put all network members on guard.

Another part of the challenge is the protection of proprietary information, especially when competitors enter into the network or partners turn into competitors. This requires the identification and protection of *embedded knowledge*[10] (information that may be your company's competitive advantage but is not protected from observation or use by others). Instead of hardware or even software knowledge, it could be the knowledge of how to sell to a particular customer.

Ninth House Network Inc. is a living embodiment of embedded knowledge at work. This company[11] is what Paul Allen calls a "brave new idea," not just a reiteration of the same idea through a different vehicle. Paul Allen (cofounder of Microsoft) has a stellar reputation and is held in some awe by latecomers to the Internet space. His words are often repeated throughout the venture capital and investee community. The "brave new idea" comment has been passed on from start-up to start-up. Indeed, many companies (E-Toys is an example) don't qualify as brave new ideas. These companies simply provide another channel for selling the same old stuff (or even the same new stuff). The telephone, however, was a brave new idea. It changed the way people communicate. Ninth House is also a brave new idea—that rare opportunity to create something entirely different. Hence, one of the more discerning venture firms, Chase Capital Group, has bet on this opportunity.

The idea is to take the *thought leaders* of the world—those who have written best-selling books and created a new paradigm of management thinking such as Ken Blanchard and Tom Peters (I consider myself fortunate to have been chosen as their thought leader in Alliances)—and to create a way of learning for executives that breaks all the rules. Jeff Snipes, CEO of Ninth House puts it this way:

> Working with movie producers and directors, screen writers, educational curriculum designers, sound experts, editors from the publishing industry, computer game designers, software developers, video designers and marketers, production designers, and others enables us to translate your thoughts and ideas and those of other thought leaders into "edutainment"—a way of learning encompassed in a learning network offered on corporate intranets in a way that immediately implements into the workplace.

The Spider Network created by Ninth House involved enormous complexity—many different ways of thinking and conceptualizing and building the infrastructure to meet the needs of customers and of those who will distribute these amazing products and services. All of it creates a learning environment that makes executives and middle managers *want* to learn. Ninth House's Spider Network has the collaborative goal of making the customers more valuable to *their* customers in real time and despite the bureaucracy of most management structures. That vision is constant. The result is a thing of beauty. Snipes adds,

> There is a lot of passion and creativity in our organization. The only way to make it all work has been a sense of inquiry, not a sense of advocacy, asking questions, not convincing people, and a high degree of trust. The trust is not only within the team, it's between me, as CEO, and the investors. There is not enough time to tell the investors everything that is going on—they just have to trust my judgment and the people around me, since the pace of the way things happen is breakneck.

5. It is transparent except to educated eyes.

One of the interesting phenomena evolving from the Spider Network is that the actual partners are not visible to those who don't know what they are looking for. That can be good news or bad news. The good news is that speed in partner participation and contribution can give a competitive advantage, especially if you build your Spider Network early. If you know what and whom you want, what you want from them and are willing to give to them in the short and long term, the lack of visibility could work to your advantage. The bad news is that unless the team involved in network building and management is astute and good at research (i.e., knowing who is in whose network and who could be ready for a change) and at managing partner communication, partners may be creating their own networks to your disadvantage, especially if they are not abreast of all your strategic intents. However, it is part of Spider Network management skills that the opportunities and risks of the network are continually being evaluated and discussed by the team network managers. Small SWAT[12] teams must be sent to explore network ideas and translate them into opportunities as soon as they arise. This will require a commitment to setting up the network in the first place; otherwise, the resources needed to take advantage of network opportunities won't be there.

One of the advantages Ninth House employees have is that they learn on the job from the thought leaders of the world. In a session with Ninth House employees, Tom Peters said, "This could apply to you in the future—as much as it does now to your large organizational customers and network partners. If you are big and fat, you're dead. Give the entrepreneurs in your organization freedom, or the individuals will take flight and the start-ups are going to eat away at your products one by one."

6. It can be easily broken (can cause destruction if treated roughly).

The Spider Network is not meant to be permanent, but the sad end of a Spider Network is one that occurs too soon. Some level of loyalty is expected—a loyalty that requires some defined deliverables. However, no network will survive forever—nor should it. More-permanent networks move into the traditional methodology of alliance constellations—with all their careful planning and exclusionary expectations. Spider Network members require shorter commitments, but expect loyalty while in the group. Since many participants will have entered the network as *preemptive partners* (those that look to prevent other competitors from usurping that place or partnership), their long-term commitment could be limited.

7. Its creation is ongoing and never ends.

There is no end to a Spider Network. The network creation will never be completed. The satisfaction from this undertaking is in the very creation of a changing environment rather than a finished one. Microsoft's Spider Network is so extensive that it cannot be charted on one page. The industries, legal structures, countries, and players that make up the Microsoft Spider Network defy definition and are expanding minute by minute. Regardless of any action taken to break up the company structurally, the Spider Network connections will remain hugely powerful. There is no finite end to a truly comprehensive Spider Network.

Isabel Maxwell is president of Commtouch.com, an Israeli-founded company and recent investment of Microsoft that has 10 million active mailboxes in 18 languages and 300 partners in its Spider Network worldwide. Microsoft sees Commtouch as a distribution network. Maxwell told me recently, "We will have Microsoft Messenger on our network, enabling Microsoft to be on our network without their name on it—as a private label. Microsoft's investment in us put us on the map. It gave us instant credibility, validated our technology and service in the marketplace."

8. The Spider Network is acutely aware of and intertwined with its environment—and must respond accordingly.

The physical environment that houses the constantly changing and moving activity of the Spider Network is one of the enabling or restricting elements. Namely, putting the team that is working on the Spider Network creation or management into a connected environment is essential in order to make it seamless and workable.

Gensler Architecture Design and Planning Worldwide is a forward-thinking organization that is examining how to meet the needs of clients who are trying to create and maintain Spider Networks. For example, one client of Gensler was trying to break the mold of the old-economy traditional organization, which was partially hierarchical. The new setting had to allow for collaboration. As Jordan Goldstein, an energetic young member of the Gensler team explains:

> The design industry has changed dramatically. The conventional architectural process typically broke design down into three phases, with key milestone points leading from early schematic phases to more detailed construction documentation. Increasingly, the design process is consolidated into one design development phase. Currently, we are seeing a trickle-down effect in our industry. As the market pace increases, we are asked to deliver high-design space in record time. This means that traditional lead times for furniture products and building materials are no longer acceptable. The industry is looking for fast-track delivery, durable materials, high flexibility, and low cost as primary criteria. Manufacturers are responding by introducing new product lines that are modular, durable, and cheaper than conventional workplace furniture. Mobility and connectivity are now standard with many major manufacturers. On the construction side, contractors are integrated into the process earlier as core team members. For example, for one client, the problem was that the physical did not match the intellectual learning environment. Individuals want to work in cross-functional teams; thus the space must encourage this. It must be large with open ceilings and a comfortable feel. Desks are not cubicles but are flexible and mobile. You can pull two or eight together and have a miniconference in seconds. There are spaces off to the side, which are war rooms with whiteboards for freewheeling thought and discussion. Walls are flexible, as are data connections, and they can move with the laptop and create semiprivate small groupings for a short period of time if necessary.

Goldstein and his colleague Walter Trujillo, senior associates in the Washington, D.C., office of Gensler,[13] have done in-depth studies for their brick-and-mortar clients and have developed a set of criteria for physically transforming brick-and-mortar companies into e-business organizations. Their findings have been re-created into a FastAlliances Tool #2, the Brick-to-Click Culture Change Process. Gensler's two-part process requires a diagnostic first: Match the characteristics of your company's environment (both culture and workplace) and the workplace/work culture facts with the space, furniture, and technology issues. Both pieces work together in transforming traditional companies into e-business-ready companies.

Brick-to-Click Culture Change Process: FastAlliances Tool #2 Part 1

Work Culture

BRICKS AND MORTAR	E-BUSINESS
Thing as product	Information as product
Slow growth	Fast track
Space as perk	Technology as perk
Hierarchical/top-down	Horizontal organization
Centralized	Decentralized decision making
Discipline-based organization	Cross-functional teaming
Diversified resources	Consolidating into less space
Larger space standards based on title	Universal space standards regardless of title
Concern for individual workspace	Concern for total workplace
Companywide goals	Team and project goals
Work at desk	Work all day long at multiple venues
Promotion and advancement	Recruitment and retention
Mergers and acquisitions	Strategic alliances

Workplace

BRICKS AND MORTAR	E-BUSINESS
Reception/vestibule	Orientation zone
Boardroom	War room
Small conference room	Touchdown space
Kitchen	Cybercafé
Pantry	Coffee/copy
Library	Resource area
Phone closet	Zen room
Back of house	Central support
Training room	Desktop learning
Staff room	Town square
High-paneled cubicles	Modular, mobile team furniture
Private office	Open, collaborative work area

Brick-to-Click Culture Change Process: FastAlliances Tool #2 Part 2

Redefining the Workplace

FACTOR 1: SPACE

Integrate universal office planning concept by developing space standards that can provide long-term flexibility.

- A designated size for individual workstations
- A standard size for private offices regardless of title
- A standard zoning of critical support spaces regardless of department

Create shared community spaces throughout the office.

- Lounge areas that allow employees to interact informally with one another
- Retreat zones as quiet spaces where individuals can step away from the action and collect their thoughts
- Resource space that functions as a consolidated library within the workplace
- Town square as an activity area encouraging face-to-face contact

Use reception areas as an opportunity for orientation to your business services.

- Introducing clients, vendors, and visitors to your organization through interactive media displays, video kiosks, print graphics, and product display
- Opportunity to reinforce your brand
- Recognizing your work process as your image—putting your workplace on display

FACTOR 2: HARD TOOLS

Use flexible furniture systems that can be easily reconfigured.

- Teaming furniture that fosters communication
- Mobile, modular desk systems that can be added onto with ease
- Loose fit furniture that can adapt to varying room size and configuration
- Technology-savvy furniture that fosters a plug and play environment
- Mobile white boards, tackable wall surfaces and smart boards to easily record concepts and ideas

(continued)

Brick-to-Click Culture Change Process: FastAlliances Tool #2 Part 2

Integrate wired spaces.

- Seamless integration of technology
- Power, voice, data interfaces throughout the workplace and at each desktop
- Pull-down power access from ceiling and floor-based connection points
- Mobile A/V carts, videoconference, and net-based meeting systems that allow presentation to happen anywhere within the office

FACTOR 3: SOFT TOOLS

Work Patterns

Integrate different types of meeting and conference spaces.

- Touchdown spaces for quick meetings
- Breakout meeting space adjacent to larger conference areas
- Curtained teaming areas that offer semiprivate interaction zones
- Capturing underutilized space, introducing teaming areas and work-pods
- Movable, pivoting, or sliding wall panels that allow the room to flex and grow on demand

Create opportunities for informal interaction. High-level decisions can happen in the most informal of spaces.

- Coffee/copy spaces that integrate traditional pantry functions and shared technology equipment (copy machine, communal fax machines, and printers)
- Café spaces that redefine the traditional employee lunchroom; a wired space that doubles as a lounge and informal meeting space
- Corridors with informal lounge seating strategically placed to foster interaction

Recognize different workflow patterns and workplace cultures.

- *Hoteling:* home bases, places to plug in and work, for telecommuters
- Pod configurations for group and team interaction
- Different work areas balanced throughout the office: private, project, and shared spaces for individuals to work, each with different character and context

The concept of plug and play is core to the collaborative environment. This is something that Ericsson has done well. Its offices worldwide are all plug and play. Conference rooms are for quiet working, open office spaces for collaborative get-togethers. All Ericsson executives are equipped and wireless and travel fully modular, able to be globally effective wherever they are in the world.

This factor is key in effective Spider Network implementation: *The Spider Network will be limited by the lowest level of portability of its least mobile member.*

It is a critical element of Spider Network success that compatibility of communication systems and modes is a high priority and must be resolved quickly and early in the relationship-building process. If not, it will hinder leverage of network opportunities.

One client, a highly networked and sophisticated company, was partnered in a Spider Network with two other partners, each of whom had their own Spider Networks and disciples of partners interconnected in three groupings. Each grouping had its own communication protocol and compatibility problems. The FastAlliances has slowed to a halt. Few of the benefits that were predicted from the three spider networks coming together have been realized. New management is now running the venture. The creators of the original Spider Network have been moved aside. The new management asked for my advice. "There is no way to get there from here," I told them. "Change the communication protocol to a single standard to take into account the new combined environment or die. Time is running out—do it now and do it clean or your competitors will create a Spider Network to compete. All of what you are doing is now in the public domain even if you think it isn't, since the attrition rate of employees in that space is huge. Theirs, yours, and ours are all the same. Put aside the barriers and differences or lose your opportunity." The jury is still out on this one.

9. It is driven by a single vision.

No question about this one: a single vision communicated clearly and often does wonders for Spider Networks. Look at DirecTV. The last place one would expect to find a virtual organization in a Spider Network is in Hughes Satellite Division. But there it is—and in the cap-rate environment of dot-coms, the tracking stock of Hughes (General Motors Class H stock) was greatly enhanced by DirecTV as opposed to other cable companies in 1999 to 2000. This service, started in 1994, transmits over 200 channels of digital television to over 8.1 million subscribers and is now the third largest provider of pay television in the United States, behind AT&T and Time Warner. As the nation's largest distributor of pay-per-view movies, it is now a force to be reckoned with in Hollywood. It also distributes more programming created by Time Warner than does Time Warner Cable. This is a clear example of the *invisible competitor*[14] (i.e., an outsider company that enters an industry and becomes a substantial player and competitor before others in the industry understand the competitive threat). This division has been the catalyst to transform Hughes from a military contractor to a consumer and business services company. DirecTV now contributes more than two-thirds of the overall company revenues.

Michael T. Smith, chairman and CEO of Hughes, stated recently, "Cable's spending all kinds of money to catch up and when they catch up we want to be 10 steps ahead of them."[15] Hughes is now moving into content, taking stakes in programming ventures, and making acquisitions—a clear movement to firm up its Spider Network, as indeed AOL and Time Warner and others have done. However, the biggest challenge for Hughes lies ahead—in its race to the Internet access field. In this arena, growing internally may be a challenge. It is time for Hughes to identify its direct and indirect Spider Network partners in order to accelerate its reach for speedy Internet access for its customers while waiting for its three-satellite $1.4 billion system to come into play in 2003. Will anyone (e.g., Echostar Communications or Teledesic or start-up iSky) create a competing and viable Spider Network before that?

10. Implementation adapts constantly.

It's not enough to have the Spider Network in place. Efforts must be applied constantly to change the implementation of the network interactions and ventures. It is difficult to comprehend the actual speed of change on the Internet. In the United Kingdom, it is estimated that 1.25 new pages are created on the Net every second. Worldwide, the numbers are staggering. Deal making is on fast-forward in every industry.

It is essential to have a good research team who can communicate what they find to those who are in the FastAlliances partner discovery group, who in turn can communicate it to those managing the relationships already in place, who in turn can communicate it to senior management, who in turn can communicate the changed vision (if relevant) to the group empowered to make the fast alliances happen, and so on.

This flowing communication system is not for the purposes of buy-in—although that can be one of the side benefits. Nor is it to build consensus. Consensus building takes too long, requires too many face-to-face meetings, and often wastes huge amounts of money on outside consultants. FastAlliances must happen after consensus has been built on the vision. And the vision comes from senior managers, with input from the top team members who report directly to them.

They are what I call the *head of the dog*. The organization is in the *body of the dog*, and the trick is to communicate clearly from the head to the body. If an acquisition has taken place, often there is either a double-headed and/or a double-bodied dog. Nasty thought. Requires radical surgery. Poor results. The best approach is to combine both heads or cut one off. Then show the bodies by clear and simple repetitive example where the head is going. The bodies get to join forces and go along with the program. If they don't, they get chopped up, too. Unfortunately, many senior managers have great difficulty either locating the body and joining it to the head or in communicating the direction of the head so that the body can follow it. In many acquisitions, there is a perception of democracy—often communicated by senior managers who talk about "mergers of equals," which rarely if ever happen. This is not a situation where there is one-person, one-vote. Although input is encouraged, at a certain point in time there will be a dominant culture. In the meantime, confusion gives alert competitive Spider Networks a grand opportunity to step in and create a preemptive relationship with one of the partners you cannot afford to lose. And the game continues.

The best way to ensure that you are not managing a double-headed or double-bodied dog in the Spider Network environment is in the *articulation* of the Spider Network vision and the *behavior* that supports it—whether compensation systems, recognition, or promotion. Rewards must be consistent with the achievement of the vision. If not, it's all talk, and nothing will lose employee commitment faster than all talk and no walk. For a Spider Network to be implemented, senior management must clarify the vision. Once it is clearly defined, implementing it should be left to those with the skills, the resources, and the team to manage the evolving and ever changing demands of the web—the Spider Web.

For example, Microsoft's Spider Network vision might be (I am hypothesizing since no one from the company has articulated it to me): "To be a significant player in every industry that could touch a potential or actual Microsoft customer." This vision could ensure that Spider Network members were market-share leaders, innovators, entrepreneurs, thought leaders, and revenue/profit generators in just about anything. After all, who would not potentially be a Microsoft customer? Those who implement the vision could interpret this in a number of ways as they drill down into the specifics of a business and operating plan to create, manage, leverage, and take advantage of present and future network opportunities.

A Spider Network can fulfill many purposes:

- It can be used to illustrate the growth of FastAlliances members—and as a communication tool among team members.
- It can be an opportunity diagnostic to identify the partners of your partners in the Spider Network to see how to better leverage your existing partner relationships by using them to facilitate high-level introductions to their partners. This enables you to position your company in a favorable way and do it fast. I have seen this become a competitive advantage continuously when companies have a strong network that positions them as more valuable than they would be on their own to a potential partner. The key is whether the ability to leverage and the willingness to do so is *built into* the fast alliance up front. The way to do that is to *ask* for it, bring it up as one of the negotiating points, make it overt, and, if necessary, pay for it if it has real value. Again, speed and access mean everything in the e-business space. The Spider Network is one of the tools that will give you these advantages.
- It can be an analytical tool to present a vertical Spider Network, which is a mapping of the players in a particular industry. By seeing the interconnections of companies in a

particular industry (and their connections to companies in *other* industries that can be leveraged to your benefit or detriment), your company can understand some of the competitive or opportunistic pressures in the environment.

- It can be an analytical tool to present a horizontal Spider Network, which is the expansion of a single company's overall network across many industries and companies—a way to analyze the prospective value of a potential partner or competitor.
- It can be used to to differentiate between two partner candidates in terms of their short- and longer-term benefits to your company.
- It can be a visual method of displaying the interlocking relationship between suppliers and subsequently to leverage those suppliers and their networks. This can augment the tiering approach often used by the automobile and software industries for rating some suppliers as critically or strategically more important than others.
- Interestingly, I have also used the Spider Network as a tool to look at internal alliance issues between individuals and groups within the same company and as a supporting tool in a stakeholder analysis and definition of new internal services that can be provided or are lacking.

The goal of this chapter has been to differentiate between the traditional approach to alliances in the non-Internet world and the new-economy FastAlliances, as well as to set up terminology and context. Understanding the two new principles of business development and its players, as well as the Spider Network (a critical tool for playing by the new rules of the FastAlliances game), is of value to traditional offline companies, transitional companies, and dot-coms, since all will have to face each other across the partnering table at one time or another.

Now let's move to the idea of strategy. Is strategy dead? There is not a lot of time for analysis in the creation of a FastAlliances. You need a way to create strategy *fast* and to make it *flexible*. The FastStrategy capability is the tool to use, as Chapter 2 demonstrates.

CHAPTER 2

Step 2: The Up-Front Work in the Creation of FastAlliances

In this chapter you will learn how to adapt strategy to Internet time. In addition, you will be introduced to a number of tools that will assist you in both creating and implementing the strategy. Some real-life examples will explain how executives implement and use the tools in start-up, traditional, and transitional companies.

The FastStrategy: FastAlliances Tool #3

Strategy is defined as the activities that design the direction and goal of the organization before the creation of the FastAlliances. The difference is that strategy is on a roller coaster in e-business alliances. It is developed by the month, sometimes by the week, and will be as reactive as it is proactive since the environment is in a mode of permanent flux. Very often there is a new value proposition (the value that is expected to come from the strategy and its resulting FastAlliances), and often this includes enhancement of existing products with added services. While many traditional and transitional companies need to create the flexibility to change direction, many Internet companies lack *focus* (which is, in large part, the company's vision). Focus translates into knowing what you do, how you do it, and for whom. Only with focus will you be able to create and implement a business development strategy that targets the right partners at the right time. Your focus is what will impress *all* stakeholders, whether venture capitalists, investment bankers, or your partners. You become a more desirable partner if you have clear focus. The Internet environment tends to create a gold-rush atmosphere (grab as much as you can and sort it out later), and your focus can attract others to follow you or connect with you while others are still scrambling.

What Is FastStrategy™?

FastStrategy is what happens when thinking and idea creation occur *before* engagement, with the added component that when active engagement (implementation) occurs, the *feedback is speedily translated* into further thinking and idea creation that can modify the strategy quickly.

Traditional strategic planning, which might have taken place in groups or as separate functions, is integrated into a more flexible approach that enables brainstorming and input sessions to be inserted into a normal operating environment. In this way, strategy development becomes an integral part of day-to-day activities and is not a static function that happens quarterly or annually—nor is it the purview of a small group or an off-site session.

FastStrategy™ as a process is conceptualized in Figure 2.1.

For dot-coms, strategy development will happen fast anyway—their problem will be focus and vision and the continuous and consistent communication of that focus/vision so that their strategy (even as it changes) can be translated into action. Traditional and transitional companies have the added challenge of changing the place where strategy is developed, the people who develop it, and the speed with which it is created. The key differences in creating a FastStrategy environment are the speed of the decision making and the people who are empowered to make those decisions (and their rela-

Figure 2.1 The FastStrategy: FastAlliances Tool #3

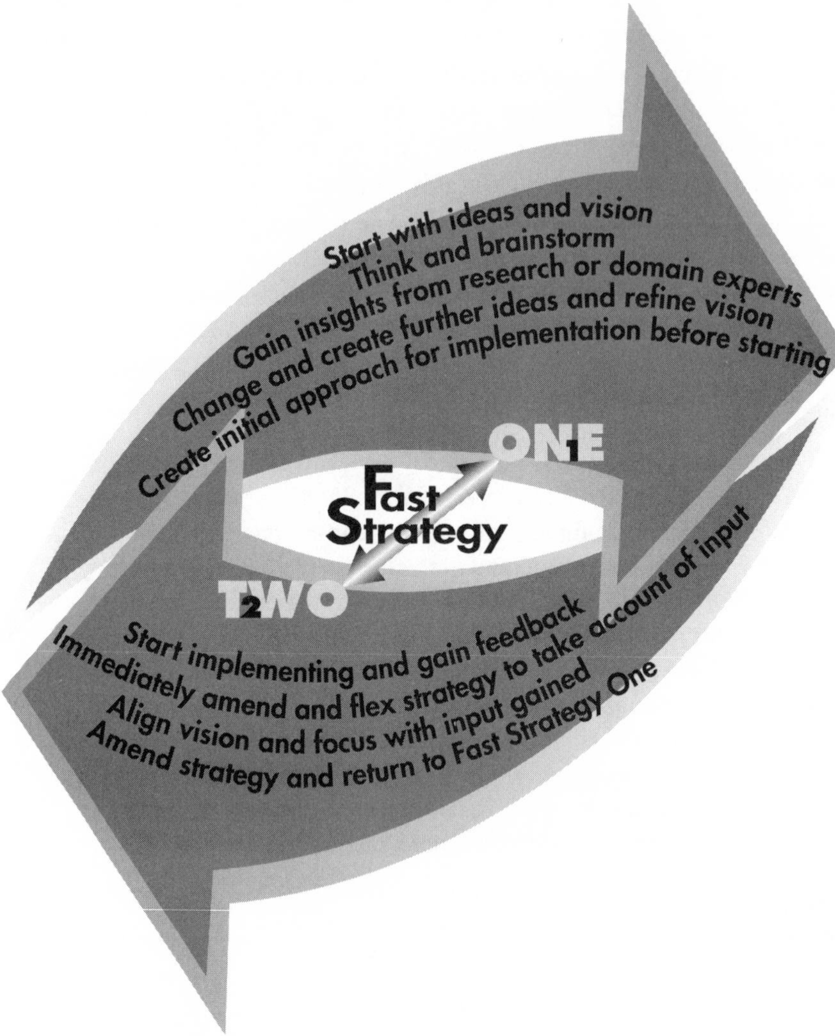

tive positions within the organization). This is addressed in the Cool Decision Process on page 83 ff.

The focus and vision of the organization must be set at the top regardless of whether the company is dot-com, traditional, or transitional. The founders or senior managers will create focus and vision and are responsible for communicating it. The strategy that will make that vision happen, however, cannot be isolated within a small group or relegated to a staff function. Strategy must be foremost in the minds of everyone in the company who could conceivably have contact with the customer (electronically, directly, or indirectly)—and that means everyone. The market (i.e., the customers) will give many insights and feedback about whether the strategy is valid or needs further thought and change. Big business may now be carried out from a computer screen—it is no longer the exclusive domain of boardrooms and closed-door meetings. FastStrategy is fluid and flexible as the market grows or reinvents itself in an evolving e-economy. If your strategy includes changing the rules in an existing industry, you will be even more attractive as a partner.

For example, in business-to-consumer (b2c) provider Webvan has created a service business offering delivery, convenience, and efficiency in a low-margin commodity industry—namely, supermarkets. Webvan has changed the rules. Supermarkets are scrambling to catch up, changing the rules of grocery shopping to include education and entertainment. Now some chains are even including freshly prepared gourmet meals, cooking lessons, and boutique-type services to enhance the shopping experience. Others are looking to invest in (or potentially acquire) companies like Webvan and other players who are similarly changing the rules.

It is the business-to-business (b2b) and mobile-to-mobile (m2m) arenas that hold the greatest potential and also where the strategy change must be deeply understood and flexible.

In order to understand why flexibility and a FastStrategy approach are needed, let's look at the new players that are changing the rules for everyone in the e-business game.

Doing Business on the Computer Screen: The New Players

Although *portals* were defined in Chapter 1, it's helpful to expand on that definition here, especially in the context of the evolution of exchanges and aggregators.

Your business development strategy will evolve within the context of the Internet business environment. It is therefore important to understand how web business works and where opportunities for deal making exist today and tomorrow.

Many companies have taken the first step in playing the Internet game by digitizing their catalogs in such a way that they become portals. As Doug Pileri of Kodak puts it, becoming a "chamber of commerce" means more than being just a place where products can be ordered. Instead of presenting a catalog that says, "Here is what we sell and how much costs," the portal says, "Here's lots of stuff, including products, services, information, and access to other resources, and you can use our portal to find what you want. Solve your problem *here* (and we won't presume to identify it for you). We give you the broadest [or narrowest, however you wish to define it] access and information to satisfy your needs. Should you run into trouble, call our customer service center and we'll take care of you. By the way, here are some of our partners [incorporate banner ads or click-through opportunities] who can offer additional help (financing, logistics, delivery, and lots of other services). Stick around for a while—there's lots to be had on our portal."

Amazon.com took the portal idea to the next step—offering a customized web page that *learns* from your behavior to offer books of interest to you personally (unlike the brick-and-mortar way). As Jeff Bezos, CEO of Amazon.com, said in an interview on Primedia Satellite Television, "The paradigm shift that we made that changed the rules was that for every book you buy, there are another 100 books that you will be interested in. Its our job to bring them onto your web page so that you can buy them easily."[1]

To illustrate, I have created an imaginary web page conversation that a b2b company in a chamber of commerce paradigm might have with you, the customer. It could go like this:

> Well, hi there again, Jane, it's me, e-Kit. [*ID and security*] We remember your name since we had a short registration requirement for a b2b buyer to qualify you as an official representative of your company (with authorization to make purchases), and we issued a password to you. When you ordered last time we processed that order through to lots of our databases, some of which were connected to our partners [*value-added alliances*] to get your delivery there on time with the correct financing arrangement.
>
> We know that you like copies of the invoice e-mailed to three other people in the organization for digital sign-off since our registration form told us that you are not the only one with responsi-

bility on this account. Consider it done! [*Customization and decreased switching costs*]

Incidentally, if you need help at any time while using this page, we have a whole roomful of customer service people who are lonely. They'd love to hear from you—so call us! Don't be a stranger! [*Customer service call centers*]

By the way, would you like more stuff like this? What we mean is, it may be difficult for you to describe by keywords exactly what you want, but if it is more stuff like this, we can help. The next time you access this page it will offer you similar products. We learned from you and now we understand you. Honest! A promise is a promise! [*Intelligence adds to customization*]

Oh, forgot to tell you. We've been told [*intelligent links—here are a few customer references to link to*] that using this product with another one [*here's a demo*] adds 30 percent more value. [*Upselling*] Thought you might like to know. [*Market research done on web, results in one hour, different iterations of offerings repeated daily for one week, best results incorporated in modified web page offerings on ongoing basis*] Also, a number of customers [*another link*] use our friends at JoeConsult to ensure good installation. It will cost you just a few dollars to add that service, but it could help you avoid getting extra help down the road. Of course, JoeConsult always adds a long-term service agreement at no extra charge. [*Bundling services with product and selling at higher price*]

If you prefer not to come back to our site, we'll miss you, of course, and you might miss all the extra goodies we will be adding as we get to know you better, especially if you are a good customer and eligible for our special benefits [*reduces switching costs, increases loyalty*]. Still, we won't lose touch with you. In fact, give us a site where you'd like us to meet you and we will be there! [*Convenience and customization*]

We will never ask for the same information twice. Once we have your preferences, we have them forever. We save you time and money—we are so much more than a catalog. And if you'd like to chat with other folks who use this portal, feel free to join the chat room. We know you'll tell others about your good experience with us—in fact, we depend on that! [*Viral marketing*] We hope to see you soon, Jane.

It can be seen from the preceding imaginary conversation (showing the business deliverables in brackets) that web interaction is not just generating e-commerce. It also adds the component of content and a sense of community (chat room). Many other possibilities for revenues come from assisting the portal's vendors to mine data from the information they get there, or even by helping them design the best site and image for inclusion in your portal. The potential for new revenue streams is unlimited. If something isn't working, you'll know within minutes or hours. Changes can be made on the fly—not after months of painstaking focus groups and expensive reports. Jeff Bezos noted in his satellite interview on Primedia, "Research is in real time. We can try things out and see almost immediately if they are working or not." The most difficult question to answer becomes simple: Is our advertising working? Banner ads can be changed and tested in real time and the best ones selected and used again. Clearly, this is a new game with new rules. Are you playing yet?

Changing the rules means either finding a way around the legacy issues of the past or working with them. Recently, I spoke with Martin F. Parker, a vice president for the e-business product portfolio for the Enterprise Networks Group of Lucent Technologies, who had this to say:

> Lucent sees the legacy issue as a major problem. In telecommunications, for example, networks are so different today. There are web centers, data centers, call centers for multimedia, e-mail, and messaging for e-mail, voice, fax, and chat, as well as all the areas of business telephony. All of these have to be linked, but all have different access devices such as PDAs, computers, phones, and so on. So the new economy is not really the Internet but the Internet protocols that are growing, and the wireless economy (for example, the GSM in Europe) creates a virtual desktop as well as a data network that is Internet- and telephone-based. What does this mean? That in communications everything will converge—portals, applications, services, and network infrastructure—70 percent of your communication will be interrelated. That is why we at Lucent are working with many portal companies, like iPlanet at Sun, to plug our communications software into their portals.

Lucent has been changing its corporate personality. The monopoly approach ("We are big and you have to deal with us") has given way to a softer, kinder Lucent. The company now functions as two entities, one of which is a smaller business that focuses on helping enterprise customers solve their problems. The other emphasizes open technologies, meaning that customers have more choices (possibly even applying a competitor's component as part of their solution). Parker emphasized the change in the company: "The customers have forced this change. They will not buy products that limit them. Companies have to open their technologies."

The companies who "get it" have their focus firmly fixed on the transformation of the e-economy into e-services, information appliances, and an "always-on" infrastructure and mentality. One such company is Hewlett-Packard (HP), which is living with huge change. Carly Fiorina, HP's CEO, has made sure of that. When I spoke with Gina Cassinelli, executive director for marketing and responsible for e-service partnerships, she shared the following:

> The shining soul of HP will be even stronger at the end of this major change that is happening. We value and revere our culture at HP. Carly appreciates that, and while she respects the best, she wants to reinvent the rest. There are many inefficiencies at HP. We must take those out. In the past we have not put the customer at the center of our experience as well as we are doing now. We also must trust in our peers to do what they are expected to do. Carly's message has been very clear. We want to unleash the vast talent within HP to serve the customer better. There are some things that must be centralized—for example, marketing communications. This is something that gave so many messages that it was very confusing. Carly has centralized it. Everyone now is being aligned behind the electronic services that are delivered to the Net. People are saying *how*, not *no*. Yes, there are still some sacred cows—perhaps in the area of compensation systems. But that, too, will change since performance evaluations are being looked at right now. Some organizational groups are taking the lead, but all of the HP businesses are rethinking the road map. For example, the printer. Now it is a communication device, a device for receiving services at home—like stamps, or tickets for a concert, or news delivery. The way we think about the device has changed. So the rules change along with that.

An example of the changing rules is the rise of *exchanges*. In the automotive industry, Ford, GM, and DaimlerChrysler (along with Oracle) have teamed up to create an exchange for their suppliers. At a recent *Industry Week* conference where I was a speaker, an automotive supplier was incensed: "It's just a way to drum us down further on prices. Many suppliers will go out of business due to this. Besides, how will those gorillas ever learn to work together? Their cultures are so different and they are competitors in addition." The rules have changed. Suppliers will consolidate. Those who can create FastStrategy approaches will survive and the others will not. The trading exchange is here to stay. Some believe that there can be only one winner in each industry segment (e.g., in the plastics industry, PlasticsNet). It's too early to know definitively. Certainly, the exchanges that build to critical mass will win in the short term. However, incidents of poor integrity or other mistakes will spread like wildfire, and exchanges can lose volume as quickly as they build it. The jury is still out on the single-player idea, but there is no question that these new corporate entities could save costs for participants, earn profits, and even generate huge returns in initial public offerings (IPOs). The key challenges will be getting fierce competitors to offer up the tender insides of the actual workings of their businesses to each other, as well as expecting large companies that are already unwieldy to suddenly become speedy, sleek, and streamlined in their new partnering manifestation as an exchange.

Exchanges can take a number of forms. Sometimes, a site enables buyers and sellers to post their bids and buy prices in real time, with the exchange taking a fee. But how does the exchange collect if buyers and sellers are dishonest and call each other on the old technology (phone), thus bypassing the exchange altogether once they know the bid/buy range? The other issue now heard from participants in the exchange is, "What value does the exchange bring in order to justify its fee?" The answer is not clear.

Other exchanges use a more familiar method, limiting the seller to one party and allowing many buyers, thus mirroring the offline auction model. Christie's puts a piece of jewelry up for auction and many buyers bid for it. The highest bidder wins. The highest bidder could work through an agent to conceal his or her identity (similar to the techniques that can be used on the Net).

Some exchanges have continuous bidding and asking and move very fast—similar to the Chicago Mercantile Exchange, but online. There could be membership and transaction fees associated with this kind.

The rules-changing event in this arena is the disintermediation *reversal*. The past five years have seen the destruction of many intermediary businesses in their old forms. A good example is the travel agent business. Many agencies have failed as commissions have plummeted since consumers are able to make their reservations online. However, increased services for which customers are prepared to pay enabled the FastStrategy adapters to stay in business. Now, however, there is yet another change. New intermediaries have entered the b2b environment. They are the *aggregators*—the agents of buyers—who put groups of services and products together and sell them as systems or stand-alones. It is cost-effective to do this through the Internet. For travel, there is now a leisure services portal, through VerticalNet, which is the portal of portals for all subject categories (health, financial services, etc.), with 57 vertical portals and growing all the time. Leisure services are found at e-hospitality.com, accessible also through www.VerticalNet.com.

I have spent many hours with companies who are struggling with the decision of whether to join the aggregators or compete with them. One medical products company provided products to aggregators while simultaneously adding perks to those same products. By offering volume discounts to loyal direct customers, providing information and services (the chamber-of-commerce effect), and sometimes even adding a competitor's product to its bundled offering, this company retained and added value to its customer relationship.

Two of the strongest aggregators who act as agents in the b2b arena are Ariba and CommerceOne. Many companies see no option but to digitize their catalogs and provide them to these companies, while at the same time reserving some of the highly customized services for their own portals. The positive news is that the costs of an expensive direct sales force can be diminished. However, as aggregators become more sophisticated and customers become more accustomed to using them, those delicious services that add revenue streams and value (e.g., financing and bundling, data mining, and selling of information-based services to other companies) could become the value-added products of aggregators, cutting out the ultimate vendor. Again, a FastStrategy approach is needed to think through and create a proactive positioning and to respond with speed to these growing challenges.

Jeff Smith, vice president of business development and global alliances at CommerceOne,[2] shared his company's strategy for creating and providing the infrastructure for exchanges:

> We essentially have two products—one is the electronic procurement application, which runs over the Internet and automates the procurement of corporate spending for all kinds of products from pencils to manufactured goods. The other product is a b2b portal infrastructure product called Marketsite, which is being used to create exchanges. For example, Boeing, Raytheon, Lockheed Martin, and BAE Systems have joined together to create an exchange. We have created over 72 of them, with more in development, compared to Oracle, who at last report had created 3, and SAP, who had created 1. We are the world leader and are present on four continents.

I asked Smith to give me an idea of how CommerceOne has created the exchange. From our conversation I have synthesized the following process:

Creating the E-business Exchange (CommerceOne): FastAlliances Tool #4

1. Analyze an industry in which automating corporate spending would save costs.
2. Approach the leaders in that industry—separately.
3. Present the value proposition of saving costs by automating their own spending, and present the concept of doing it with others in the same industry.
4. In parallel, introduce the possibility of generating revenue streams by creating an industry exchange. Propose a profit-and-loss scenario for that and suggest the potential for a future IPO.
5. Then, having approached all the players individually, meet together as a group at the CEO, CFO, or COO level.
6. *Don't* bring in the lawyers until after the business agreement is reached and memorandum of understanding (MOU) is signed by the parties—also, many groups will do a press release before signing the actual agreement.

7. Make the agreement come together fast—become operational within two months.

Many of the early consortia were developed this way. Now the players are gathering themselves together as a group and approaching CommerceOne to be the technology provider. As mentioned earlier, there is general sentiment in this arena that there will only be one or two major exchanges per industry. In addition, the suppliers to many of the manufacturers have now formed their own consortia and have said to the purchasing consortia, "It would be really helpful if you created industry standards instead of each asking for your own peculiar stuff, so that even though we can each do business with you separately, we can work off the same standards of excellence, saving costs for us, too." Now the movement is into subverticals where, for example, a truck manufacturer may join the industry portal of DaimlerChrysler, Ford, and GM, but may also join a subvertical portal for trucks only.

How are these different from normal consortia? Says Smith:

> What's different is the fact that competitors are coming together and making this happen. It is critical that there are security and firewalls between the bidding and pricing activities of the individual players in the consortia in order to be within the federal antitrust guidelines. The participants are not aggregating their purchases, they are aggregating and combining a purchasing mechanism or automated supply chain that they invest in and take advantage of for their own benefit. What's different is the willingness of companies who had been fierce competitors to come together in the expectation of saving costs and refining their processes. And if none of them are successful externally in offering this service or opportunity to other players in the industry, there is still huge savings and benefit to be gained for their own companies.

Where will this all end up? Smith feels that once all the industries have their exchanges organized there is still a lot of value to bring to the table:

> All the Electronic Data Interchange (EDI) activities of the past need to be put onto the Net. GM is beginning to look at that—it's a huge undertaking. In addition, all the procurement processes such

> as indirect materials, many of which are still paper transactions or by fax, can be put on the Net. There is a lot of work yet to be done. These relationships are FastAlliances in their creation, but they are transitioning into long-term traditional alliances over time and must be managed with both perspectives in order to leverage all the value possible for all parties.

There is no question that the exchanges have changed the rules of the game, and CommerceOne is a major enabler of the activity, earning revenues in two ways. "We have the traditional software sales and licenses and upgrades. But the real growth in revenues comes from the revenue-sharing arrangements that take place on our portal or site—we get a percentage."

Until now (as this book goes to press), neither Dell nor Wal-Mart have participated in any exchanges. They don't want to share their best practices—because they believe they *are* the best. Jamie Freedman, an analyst in Global Investment Research for Goldman Sachs, told me recently,

> I believe that eventually the exchanges that can really penetrate their industries will start to move from their position as verticals and start to go diagonal and begin acquiring other exchanges. As analysts, we will start looking across industries to see the multiples, and when an opportunity comes up where the participants will play together against other groups within their same industry, we will become more interested. There are so many issues that have yet to be resolved: For example, are the exchanges going to repatriate their savings to the parent company? They need to save something for the public shareholders. At the moment, it's wait and see for the analysts regarding exchanges.

Certainly the phenomenon of exchange-to-exchange (e2e) trading looms as another form of e-commerce. Here buyers and sellers do transactions not only *within* exchanges but also *between* them. Since CommerceOne is the world leader in enabling exchanges, its e2e interoperability capabilities will be a competitive advantage. When e2e becomes commonplace, the speed of making transactions will increase even more, making winners out of those who can keep up.

Channel conflict is not an insignificant issue. Nor will it go away quietly. Electronic Data Services (EDS) has changed the channel relationship with the EDS professional service group. I recently spoke with Dr. Martin Hofmann, director of the digital supply chain practice for EDS, who had this to say: "Our FastStrategy is that we want to change our percentage of sales that come from our salespeople and alliances and increase the revenues from the alliances with other companies that face the customer. This way we can grow the market and not be so dependant on a particular person's relationship with a buyer even though we value the hard work by our salespeople involved in creating and maintaining relationships."

Barbara Babcock, corporate vice president and president of e-business services for Unisys corporation, adds her concerns. "There are a number of key issues that still lurk in the early stage of the e-world. They are the issues of privacy, antitrust, patent protection, and globalization. It will be a long time until these are resolved." Barbara's former life was with The Gartner Group, and her well-honed analytical skills are valuable in her position at Unisys as it pushes to take the lead in the arena of e-business services.

The summary of new players and our earlier imaginary web site conversation illustrate why strategy has to be fast, fluid, and flexible while the company maintains its vision (and focus). The web site provides something that, in the past, companies (b2b or b2c) would know about only at the street level (i.e., through their sales and service people who had actual contact with customers): That is, who are our customers, and what do they like, dislike, feel, and think (by the minute, the hour, or as often as we care to measure it)? Now pilot programs of new ideas, products, or services, the entrance of competitors, and a myriad of other issues are a click away from the collective knowledge of your company. You can do something about it only if you are willing to adapt internally to a FastStrategy approach, which takes continuous input, interprets it, and quickly adjusts our thinking. From that thinking, we can then create a series of actions by which we implement our focus and vision in a changed environment.

Brand Positioning Castle: FastAlliances Tool #5

One of the major differentiators in every FastStrategy winner will be the strength of the brand.

Brand has taken on a critical role in e-business. FastAlliances between companies where one has a strong brand and the other does not may not make any revenues in the short term, but could nevertheless be the right relationships if the value of the brand adds recognition, customer acquisition, and web real estate value—all of which will ultimately be translated into revenues. Brand, which has been the trusted asset of traditional companies, is now the leverage point for transitional companies as they evolve into e-businesses. Brand plays a critical negotiating role in many of the alliances they are developing with online, dot-com, and other companies. The most powerful new competitor is the brick-and-click combination—companies that take the best of both worlds and combine them.

Let me give you hypothetical description of such a company, and see if you shudder at the thought of such a competitor. If you do, then FastAlliances, which are preemptive in staking your role early in the game, may be your best choice. (See page 134ff for further discussion on preemptive FastAlliances.)

Competitor from Brick-and-Click Hell: Dominator of the Empire of E-business

1. Strong and well-proven brand
2. Takes existing large customer base and leverages it to reach new customer groups
3. Has the brick environment for those customers who need to touch and take
4. Facilitates the click environment with information, chamber of commerce, and links
5. Can get both the impulse buyer and the price/value shopper (b2b, b2c, or m2m)
6. Knows the customer deeply, continually, intimately, both online and offline behavior
7. Increases, tests, refines new/existing products and services as well as how, where, when, and with what they are offered (packaging and bundling of services, promotions, links)
8. Provides continuing link to customer with information and added services
9. Improves internal operations and customer activities for cost and efficiency

10. Combines physical competitive advantages (e.g., infrastructure, management expertise, intellectual property, and global competence) with speed of response and flexibility of the Internet world

Pretty impressive? Don't doubt for a moment that companies with all these characteristics and more will be your competitors very soon, which is why FastAlliances are happening across the dot-coms, transitional, and (as in the case of AOL and Time Warner) traditional companies. The most interesting partners are those with the biggest brands. The high cost of building an impressive brand is one of the most compelling market entry barriers for dot-coms and a good reason for a FastAlliances. But unless traditional and transitional companies are able to leverage their brands by understanding what it is that they do that can be translated to the Internet, the brand value will diminish as a leverage tool and market share will be lost to e-businesses. A classic and early example was the entrance of the formerly only brick-and-mortar Barnes & Noble into e-business. Its strong brand was fast losing market share and value to the rising Amazon.com, but its aggressive action has now begun to level the playing field.

Office Depot Online's Keith Butler talked to me about the elasticity of brand: "Starbucks have an extremely elastic brand. Coffee

FastAlli, by Larraine Segil

and related products, food, even books. A key issue for any company with an e-business strategy is the future positioning of their brand. Then, once that is decided, the e-business strategy should follow it, not the other way around."

The elasticity of Starbucks' brand was tested in its portal, designed to expand the brand into other products and services. The customer reaction was initially not thrilling. "Stick to what you do best" could have been the interpretation. The key question is, are you diluting or expanding your brand? How elastic is it? The FastStrategy approach must use this as a fulcrum around which to measure balance and swing.

FastStrategy means thinking strategically all the time—not just in an off-site session. When applied to branding, it also means that every action, alliance, and design of product or service must be measured against the projected position of the brand one to two years ahead. The e-business approach must derive from that point.

Brand Positioning

The following questions will help clarify the brand positioning area:

- *What are the services that enhance your brand regardless of its application, and what are the alliances that can help you achieve that?* For example, is selling fine gourmet pastries in a boutique pastry bar at a gas station an extension or a dilution of your brand? Put that in an e-business scenario: What about a convenience store portal that sells industrial goods at the same time as food products—does that work for your brand?
- *Does a strategy and the alliance that implements it add value in an economic sense (by reducing costs to the customer and/or increasing your margins/growth) or in a brand perception sense (by adding value to my brand)? In other words, does it add value to both sides of the transaction?* Brand growth and customer loyalty may be more important strategically than profit. This is the paradox of the Internet world. Many portals will tell you they can get it cheaper (having used buy.com often, I can vouch for that), whereas on many transactions they actually lose money but are building brand. Today's money will seem cheap as the price for brand becomes hugely costly within a few years, and few will be able to build a brand of any real value. The race is on for brand and market critical mass. Are you winning? The

best solution may be to develop an alliance (a Spider Network of your own) before your competitors do, or to acquire someone else's brand (which is more valuable) if you have the stock currency or resources to do so. One company I advise is developing a direct alliance with another e-business company in order to provide the overnight service that will differentiate it from its competitors. This company is trading valuable real estate on its web page to do this. The currency opportunities are web real estate instead of money, data interpretation instead of plain information, bundles of solutions instead of just services or just products.

• *Can your partner assist in increasing the value of your brand?* Use a collaborative method of brainstorming with your potential alliance partner to elicit brainpower, brand power, and Internet experience in adding value to your brand. One of the peculiar and rather pleasant aspects of the Internet world is that everyone is learning on the job. No one has all the answers. Creativity has been unleashed in the strangest of places—the young, the inexperienced, the revolutionaries. Put your ego aside and use your potential partners to find solutions you may not have thought of. Of course, a Spider Network of partners can leverage this opportunity. This is the reverse of the traditional approach, in which strategy is first and partners come after. In FastAlliances, it is all one swift continuum: The input is given, the strategy is developed, and the partner is requalified for that particular purpose—and may or may not at that time be the right partner after all!

• *What is your strategy to build your brand value in ways other than advertising?* Building brand value by advertising remains incredibly expensive. That is not to say you shouldn't do it if you can afford it. However, the value of building brand on the web through web advertising is exploding. According to e-stats (a research firm), the amount of money spent on web advertising as projected by a number of research organizations in 1998–1999 varied from $560 million to $2 billion. Regardless, web advertising is going to grow—no doubt about that. The e-stats report projects growth of to close to $9 billion in 2002. However, the cost per thousand of banner ads is dropping. Adknowledge, a research group, analyzed the drop in cost per thousand from June 1999 to September 1999 and found that building a brand with an advertising strategy alone will be insufficient. There is already too much noise (i.e., oversaturation). It is the positioning of alliance partners with your brand that will make the difference. Look at the cost of alliance development as an indirect advertising cost—and in addition you may be able to include cooperative advertising with your partners in their ad campaigns regardless of the method used.

Brand Valuation

A venerable company whose brand has been synonymous with security since its founding in 1817 is Chubb Electronic Security. Headquartered in the United Kingdom, it is a division of Williams PLC, a public company in the United Kingdom, with sales of over $1.6 billion worldwide, including significant market share in the United Kingdom, France, Australia, Asia, South Africa, and Canada. Chubb operates in b2b, b2c, and business-to-government modes.

Dr. Robert Farquhar, director of marketing and technology for Chubb, described Chubb's understanding of the value and application of its brand in such a graphic and visual way that it was but a short step for me to create the diagram shown in Figure 2.2. The challenge that is looming for many companies looking at FastAlliances is the valuation of their brand when in an alliance with another brand of equal, less, or greater value. This is not an easy issue to resolve. Nor is there only one answer. There are many ways to value brand, not the least of which is as a percentage of the market capitalization of an organization. Whatever the value, it is important to determine the brand impact *before* entering into the alliance. I used the brand valuation castle in Figure 2.2 as a base for creating fast-track answers to the brand value dilemma that is on the short list for business development in FastAlliances.

The rationale behind brand valuation analysis and brand valuation can be illustrated as follows: Many large, valuable, and world-class brand organizations—companies like ABB SATT AB in Malmö, Sweden, Psion PLC in the United Kingdom, Fujitsu Siemens Computer Company (for its advanced network server production), Ericsson's Visby Sweden Operations, and more—are outsourcing their entire manufacturing operations to Flextronics International (see my conversation with Michael Marks, chairman and CEO of Flextronics, on page 222ff). Flextronics has grown from $93 million in revenues in 1994 to close to $10 billion today.

Figure 2.2 Brand Positioning Castle (Chubb): FastAlliances Tool #5

Layers of protection must be created in order to protect the king and queen (the brand and organizational assets) and their family (the organization and its employees).

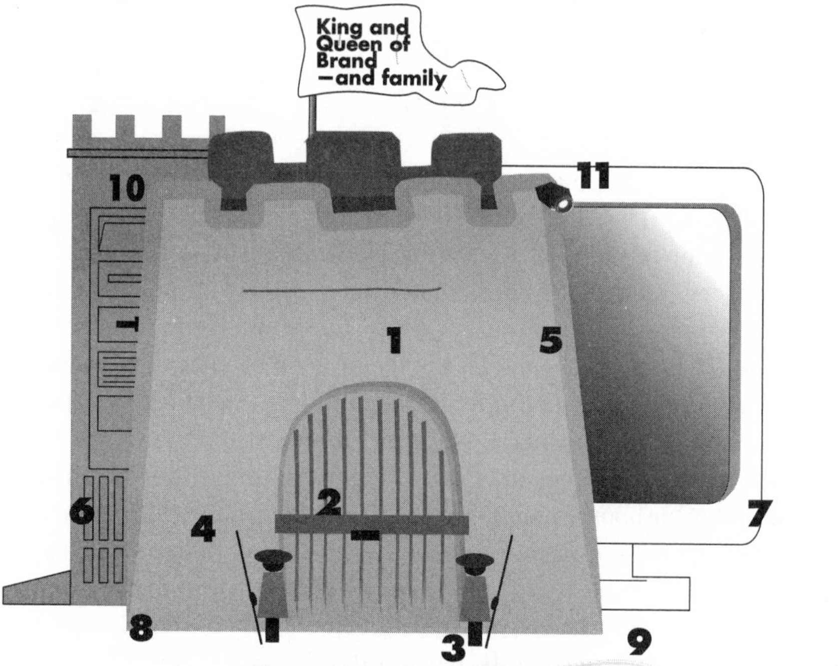

1. A safe to hide the jewels
2. Locks to bar the doors
3. Guards to maintain watch on the outside of the doors
4. Fire extinguishers to put out any internal fire
5. Fire systems for special vaults
6. Intrusion alarms to warn where and when guards aren't present
7. Monitoring stations to respond to alarms
8. Special response patrols to act on the monitoring stations
9. Physical security gates and walls around the castle
10. Access control systems that allow only accredited people entry (including biometric sensing, genetic identification, smart cards, and remote readers)
11. Closed circuit television (CCT) systems to provide remote view of threats

What I am suggesting is that the speed of information transfer on the web requires that brand be managed differently. It is not sufficient for brand management to be in the hands of marketing communications, or public relations, or even competitive intelligence. My recommendation is that the brand value issue be cross-functional, cross-divisional, and global, dipping into every corner of the company—at the corporate and business unit levels, online and offline—so that no FastAlliances (whether strategic or tactical) can take place without a brand value check. It doesn't have to be another meeting—it can happen with an awareness of the issue by the FastAlliances managers, who, in advance, should have their data points of reference within the organization ready for input from an electronic roundtable (and at the necessary speed, even by instant messaging).

Let's take an in-depth look at Figure 2.2. I've found that people learn and retain information best if it is described in everyday terms (hence *cookies* on your hard drive, *sticky eyeballs* if you work at your computer for hours on end, and so on). In that same vein, here are my metaphors (as shown in Figure 2.2) for the brand valuation approach:

1. *The safe.* What is your brand value? Do you have it well protected in a safe? In the Internet world, value is all about three major assets: brand, customer knowledge, and innovation. Are you diluting your brand by letting it be displayed by some unworthy jeweler who promises to protect it well? Are the alliances you are contemplating worthy of your brand? Disney will partner only with those who add brand value—the market leaders in both its traditional and Internet alliances (see comments by Larry Shapiro on page 93ff). Disney looks for brand extension value and balances the risk of a start-up against that. Do you have a series of metrics or criteria that every FastAlliances partner (tactical or strategic) must meet with respect to brand impact? What about the customer relationship? Who is nurturing that? Is yours a totally customer-focused organization (or still lagging in the old-technology-focused world)? What about innovation? This doesn't have to mean technology innovation. It could apply to every aspect of the organization, from the way employees are managed to information systems.

2. *The locks.* What protections do you have in place to protect your brand on the Net—and worldwide—when knockoffs abound?

Even the intellectual property trade laws are not enough to protect a valuable brand, since they rarely have the enforcement teeth that enable the brand owner to stop the infringement. Microsoft has its own army of "brand protectors" in China, but it's a constant effort. What about your customer-knowledge data bank? Could you unwittingly be transferring this knowledge without being remunerated? How secure is your customer information database from prying eyes?

3. *The guards.* The guards represent those in competitive intelligence, who should be continuously scanning the Net worldwide for competing brands and, more important, looking outside your industry for the invisible competitors who may pose a threat but are not yet in your industry. (Examples of this include the advent of cable into telecommunications and the emergence of Wal-Mart or Marks and Spencer into banking.) Who should be overseeing brand risks? Brand is everyone's issue in that it affects a major asset of the company. What about reporting accountability for the brand? One school of thought is that this should reside with the CFO or a corporate risk manager reporting to the finance chief.[3] Certainly, current events like a tire recall (affecting both vehicle and tire brands), a plane crash (airline brand), or product tampering (Tylenol) can impact brand valuation financially. Some companies develop multibranding strategies to insulate their major brand from risk. For example, Allstate has multiple brands, and a number of companies (e.g., Procter & Gamble) have created new brands to sell on the Internet in order to avoid channel conflict.

4. *Fire extinguishers for internal threats.* These are the brand valuation checkpoints within the organization that facilitate the transmission of brand-related information to the rest of the organization so that even small and apparently tactical FastAlliances don't dilute the brand.

5. *Fire systems for special vaults.* If the brand has been applied in a particular way, perhaps to a partner who has a nonexclusive relationship in keeping with the "spirit of the alliance," the owner of the brand should make sure that no one in the organization abrogates that spirit of specialness. In one supplier alliance situation, the term *exclusive* was not permitted by one of the partners in the contract. However in all the discussions the term *spirit of the alliance* was used by that partner's team members, with the understanding that they would not contract

with other suppliers in particular areas. In other words, the supplier had preferred status without the legal terminology. However, a middle manager merrily went about making arrangements with another supplier. Only the vigilance of the supplier's people (who called it to the attention of the alliance team at corporate) avoided the breakup of an extremely valuable relationship. Things move fast in e-business alliances. Sometimes human communication systems don't keep up. This is a brand communications issue—something the alliances group should be integrally involved with.

6. *Intrusion alarm systems when guards are not present.* This is covered by the information scanning and communication connections accessed by the cross-functional and divisional networks that the alliance manager or business development people must have within the organization.

7. *Monitoring stations to respond to alarms and special response patrols.* This could be the internal roundtable mentioned earlier—an intranet FastAlliances brand chat room in which alerts are posted and discussed will virally disseminate information faster than memo writing. Again all of this is related to the fact that the brand (along with customer knowledge and innovation) is *the* asset worth protecting in an organization, so the protection structure must be oriented to this idea.

8. *Special response patrols.* These could be representatives from the alliances group (if there is one) or the division or business unit whose job it is to find a solution to a brand overexposure problem. Their role is to discover a way to make the situation work, *not* to say no, which is the easiest (or most politically correct) way out.

9. *Physical security gates.* These barriers are great for the normal issues of security. Certainly, intellectual property can be stolen by observation, so keeping people from observing physical layouts and activities could be useful. In the e-business world, however, it's knowledge that really counts—data that has been communicated as information but has been made so much more valuable by its interpretation. *That* is what must be protected.

10. *Access control systems.* This is the best way to protect information related to the brand and other assets of the company, and all intranets have them. But are your partners leaking information you give them to their partners? If they are, your access control systems,

biometric or not, will not discover that. By asking some of the questions raised here you will reduce that possibility.

11. *The closed-circuit television.* This approach will spread the awareness of your brand throughout the organization, adding remote eyes to the issue of brand dilution. One of our consulting clients was a major consumer-products company that desired an alliance with an oil company. The effect of the alliance on brand image had been evaluated in the development stages. Even though the brand consultants gave the thumbs-up signal to the deal (i.e., they determined that brand would not be negatively impacted), field reps within the consumer-products company disagreed. Since many of them were owners (franchise holders), they sabotaged the alliance, which could not be properly implemented. For that and many other reasons, the alliance failed. At this point, we were called in, but there was no way to salvage the deal—too much bad blood, negative perceptions, and resistance from the field. A companywide brand valuation awareness would have revealed strong resistance to this alliance, portending the internal mutiny that was to evolve. The oil company would also have had some insights into the difficulty of implementing an alliance in an organization driven from the bottom up rather than the top down.

Before moving on, let's pause briefly to summarize:

1. Strategy cannot be done the careful, traditional, sequential way. FastStrategy requires lightning speed, continuous self-correction, and input from many places.
2. FastStrategy must be interlinked with brand positioning and brand-critical value propositions. Brand positioning, Chubb's brand valuation castle, and the brand evaluation approach are key success factors in securing and building the economic value of the brand in a fiercely competitive world where big winners will be few. Short-term economic loss may be acceptable for long-term brand value (as of the summer of 2000, giant brand Amazon.com has yet to make a profit), and shareholders have bought into this one—for the moment, at least.

Before leaving the subject of Chubb, a name synonymous with security, no book on any aspect of e-business would be complete without some mention of Internet security issues. For most of us, the

Internet is a tool for information. Those who provide information want to know about about us, and methods have permeated the web to find out everything there is to know about us, even interpretations about our behavior that we are not conscious of. I have provided a glossary of terms, extrapolated from a convenient list in *Business Week*, in the appendix at the back of this book. In addition, I have listed a number of companies who are supplying weapons and countermeasures in the escalating war for web customers. Over 20 states are now moving to protect Net privacy, and the federal government will no doubt soon follow.

Another aspect to the security issue is the unwitting transfer of knowledge. Often, one of the most valuable assets of FastAlliances is the *knowledge* that each organization has. In traditional alliances, the issue is the same, and in my first book I addressed it as *embedded knowledge transfer*. It is knowledge about how your organization does business, possibly including the processes you use, your corporate culture, even your unique compensation system. The best test for having unwittingly transferred knowledge that really matters to you is to look back after the implementation of the alliance and discover that you regret having transferred it! It is the knowledge that could not only make your partners better partners, but could actually turn them into competitors. It is critical to distinguish between the knowledge you intend to transfer and that which you do not. Sometimes the latter is more critical as a competitive advantage to your company. Unwitting knowledge transfer can happen from informal and social conversation, even from observation. Partner meetings, instruction, joint seminars on common issues, common integrated work environments, conflict resolution meetings—all of these could be opportunities for unwitting knowledge transfer. The key question is, *do you care?* Maybe the knowledge transfer is exactly the reason you (or they) are in the relationship. Maybe it is incidental to the main activity of the FastAlliances. Maybe it was part of the package for which you received remuneration. The issues are as follows:

1. Do you know what your own and your partners' embedded knowledge is?
2. Do you/they care if it is transferred?
3. Do you want to be paid for it? If so, negotiate that early in the relationship, because embedded knowledge diminishes in value

over time. (If you try to value it later, your partner might say, "Gee whiz, so sorry, we knew that already.")

4. Put parameters around knowledge you want to transfer (and then do it) and around knowledge you don't (and don't do it unless you get paid for it). If you want to get paid for it, it's best to negotiate up front and put it in the contract.
5. Identifying embedded knowledge is not easy, but it's worth the effort. Do it early.

Once the initial approach to FastAlliances and its continuum of change has been created, the next tool will add structure to the refinement of the initial strategy and its ultimate implementation as well as to the discussion of embedded knowledge and its transfer.

It is difficult for a large traditional or transitional company to gain access to the information needed to create external alliances with dot-coms or start-up organizations. There are two reasons for this:

1. Uncovering within a multidivisional company the technology, product, service, or innovation needs that that could be potential areas for alliances is a time-consuming and complicated process. Whom do you speak to? Who has this information? Who has the authority to make an alliance even if there is a need? Is the company going to be able to make the decisions fast in order to create a FastAlliances that will satisfy the needs of the external dot-com or start-up and its stakeholders (venture capitalists and others)?
2. Discovering the outside alliance partners who are start-ups or maybe even at the next level of funding means having a deal flow mechanism, which for many traditional and transitional companies is not a slick, efficient process.

In order to address this dilemma, I spoke with executives at Compaq,[4] a company that has effectively reinvented itself as an Internet leader. The process described is one that Compaq has perfected and that has enabled it to become a major corporate strategic partner for some of the most exciting emerging companies in e-business. The process pulls together the needs of internal groups who are well positioned to take advantage of partner opportunities but may not have had access to deal flow or may not have formerly articulated their needs clearly. In addition, it creates deal flow by interacting externally with the venture community at the center of the action in new e-business opportunities. The two groups are connected by the business development people at Compaq who make it all happen.

The FastStrategy Playbook (Compaq): FastAlliances Tool #6

This strategy-making process happens in an iterative way and is constantly changing. It occurs before implementation, which causes it to fall into the general definition of *strategy* (the art of arranging and conceptualizing prior to engagement). Those who are from traditional strategic planning have the skills to adapt to this method, even though initially they may be uncomfortable making recommendations without sufficient information and market analysis. That is the name of this game, however—never having enough information for a considered and well-thought-through decision.

The FastStrategy playbook works as follows: Compaq divisions that are providing products, services, and solutions to customers are listed on the left side of Figure 2.3. Technology and Corporate Development (T&CD) is seeking to find a strategic fit between Compaq's divisions and the start-up community. The way Corporate Development does this is to work through top-tier venture capital partners (@Ventures, Benchmark Capital, etc.) who act as a screen for thousands of start-up companies (BizBuyer, NorthPoint, etc.). The role of Corporate Business Development is to find the strategic fit, to continually review the portfolio, and to provide internal company reviews and investment support. Compaq leverages the due diligence of the top venture capital (VC) firms. (The VCs and the start-ups shown are examples only, not necessarily the ones Compaq is working with.) The VCs provide business guidance and support as well as the traditional role of incubation.

The chart shown in Figure 2.4 is the result of information gathered in a series of internal meetings and interviews with the key stakeholders in the various divisions of Compaq. (Names are fictional and for illustration purposes only.)

Business development representatives Brian Bonazzoli (senior business development manager) and Adrienne Higashi (business analyst in Corporate Development) created a series of internal rela-

Figure 2.3 The FastStrategy Playbook (Compaq): FastAlliances Tool #6–The Map

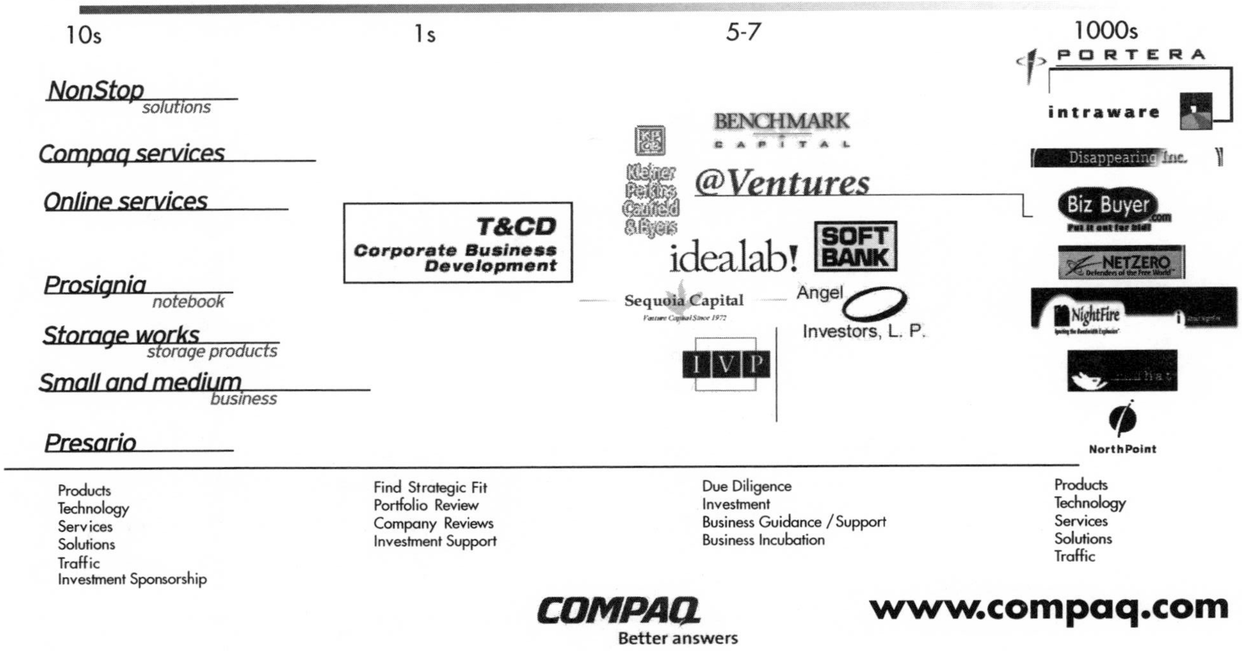

Figure 2.4 **Compaq Consumer Division: Stakeholder Interests**

- **Contacts:**
  - Sponsoring Executive: John
  - VP/Dir/Mgr Bus. Development/Mktg Ted
    - Futures — Fred
    - CPQ.Net /Operations — Eugene
    - Broadband — David
    - Destinations / Portals /Content — John
    - Service / Support — Monica
    - Access / ISPs — Heather
- **Focus Areas:**
  - Enhanced out of box experience (OOBE)
    - Automated and easy access (Compaq.net)
  - Generating and Directing Traffic
    - Internet Keys (Holding 1 button for retail central to point back to reseller), Email button, etc.
    - Consumer CRM
      - Phase I - Service and Support through XXXX
      - Phase II - TBD
  - Vertical OEM Markets
    - Mass Customization through direct and traditional distribution channels.
    - Customize the system to a Vertical affinity

COMPAQ
Better answers
www.compaq.com

Figure 2.4 Compaq Consumer Division: Stakeholder Interests (*Continued*)

- **Focus Areas continued:**
  - Banking / personal finance
  - Information
    - Search
  - Entertainment
    - Gaming
  - Personal productivity
    - Gaming

- **Existing Relationships:**
  - Company X - personal banking
  - Company Y - personal investing
  - Company Z - collecting and organizing web content

COMPAQ
Better answers

www.compaq.com

tionships with key stakeholders in the various Compaq divisions in order to understand their interests and needs. From phone calls, then meetings, relationships and trust grew until Bonazzoli and Higashi were able to tap into the issues and opportunities that internal stakeholders shared with them. For example, from the lead-in "I am working with a dot-com already—what do you know about them?" they would create a chart that showed all the evolving strategies around product or technology needs for each group.

They played an advisory role. As Bonazzoli put it, "Many of the internal customers within Compaq that we serve are on the line to deliver. Because of the speed of change, it is impossible to create all the technology in-house, so external alliances are accepted as part of the game. Our value is as an intermediary. When an internal group is already working with a company, we say go ahead and do it on your own, and we will provide the extra information that you may not be able to get as a support mechanism."[5]

One of the key success factors for business development in Compaq is the internal alliances that business development has been able to grow. Adds Bonazzoli,

> The head of business development, Bill Strecker, decided that we should be based in Silicon Valley, not in Houston, since all the action is here. That's why he started the Silicon Valley initiative, coupling market initiatives and business development. We work with venture capitalists and a number of angel investors who have an association here, and many times they will access companies at very early stages. These start-ups are very keen to have relationships with Compaq for marketing or distribution. So the added value we bring is to access companies for our colleagues in Houston that they have never heard of and would be unlikely to access at such an early stage.

Decision making also pulls from the concepts in the Cool Decision Process (see page 83 ff). Bonazzoli is emphatic about this:

> The key is finding the person within each product or service group at Compaq who has the responsibility—once you know that, the process speeds up. One of the services we provide to the venture capital and angel community is that we know who is empowered within Compaq and can accelerate decision making. And the Compaq people know that we are positioned for decision making here

> in the Valley. We can provide a service to both sides by knowing who is empowered. It is critical to know the people at Compaq who really understand and are passionate about the Internet and are really looking for dot-coms to help them. Our CEO Michael Capellas is seriously committed to the Internet—and that helps a lot. For example, in customer services at Compaq there are 27,000 employees [out of a total of 70,000]. They struggle with how to leverage the Internet to efficiently serve the customers. The customer service group realized that there are many companies who can help us do this. So once we [in business development] knew their needs, we looked at Voice Over IT, e-mail authorization, automatic FAQ, help agents, and numerous other technologies to add value.

This approach is also useful to others at Compaq. Phil Wood, Compaq's high-energy alliance manager for its Disney relationship, scans the whole of Compaq constantly for Disney-appropriate opportunities, working closely with the sales team, Leigh Morrison, Dave Fusco, Karen Kennedy, and Dave Epstein.

The FastStrategy playbook at Compaq also looks at a variety of legal structures for its FastAlliances. Bonazzoli explains: "Early-stage companies may want to trade—they want to promote their brands, and in return we want discounted service or product development. In addition, Compaq will bring the legal help and accounting support."

The deal flow is high. Only one out of every 20 deals actually is consummated. The reasons are numerous, but some key ones are as follows:

1. A more advanced competitor to the dot-com may be unknown to them.
2. The deal may be a good one, but not within the top-10 strategy focuses of Compaq (i.e., not among those derived from the development of the playbook). Because the mode of the FastStrategy approach is a moving target, strategy is reviewed/revised continuously.
3. Normally, there is a key individual within every company who is the initial champion. If that key person leaves, even though the team remains, the company may determine that the driving force or intelligence behind the concept has diminished and, if so, may forgo the deal.

A critical success factor for FastAlliances is the speed and ease of decision making. In many ways it is *the* critical success factor, since it will preempt competitive moves by others, streamline and extinguish bureaucracy, and empower and inspire greater levels of driven, high-energy, independent thinkers. Not having it will extinguish any e-business initiative, no matter the resources thrown at it.

Making clear decisions, whether for traditional businesses or FastAlliances, is a critical success factor. However, in the Fast-Alliances environment, making them with *speed* is the differentiator.

How to do it inside a traditional or transitional corporate culture is the challenge. A number of tools can help. The tools derive from the methods some successful companies have used. You can also adapt these tools to your existing methods to facilitate decision making in your organization. If you are a dot-com, a successful Fast-Alliances with a traditional or transitional company may very well depend on your ability to understand and manage your partner's decision processes, which may be less than cool!

The Cool Decision Process (Office Depot Online): FastAlliances Tool #7

The point of having a cool decision process is to speed up and facilitate action. In other words, the result of a cool decision process will be taking action—not deciding to make another decision. The following questions must be answered:

- Where lies the authority to make the final decision?
- Who is empowered to act (not just decide), and what is the relationship between the decider and the one who acts?
- Is it clear what the action will be? Who knows it? Who measures it? Who is accountable for it? Who is rewarded if it succeeds, and how?
- Do you have these answers for your company as well as your partners?

The four main categories for a Cool Decision Process are as follows:

1. Reporting structure
2. Resources committed
3. Risk to brand
4. Responsibility

Figure 2.5 shows a Cool Decision Process that was derived from the activities of Office Depot as the company created a transitional organization to address e-business.

Office Depot, a successful offline company selling office supplies, has expanded its existing markets and created additional ones. The transition to an online company has not been without its challenges. Nevertheless, Office Depot has an impressive interconnection with online customer relationships supported by offline activities, a situation that has evolved quickly and with some interesting success factors. Keith Butler, who, when we spoke, was the architect and senior executive for Office Depot Online (see www.officedepot.com), gave me the background:

> Three years ago the company realized the importance of the Internet, and the senior vice president, Paul Gaffney, did a business plan that resulted in internal resources being allocated to this initiative. Clearly, the web business was different from just having a web site. They created an internal team to build the e-commerce version of the web site and brought in people from outside of Office Depot who knew what they were doing in this space. They located the group in San Francisco, where web resources were located. This approach was followed by Wal-Mart and Toys 'R' Us, which validated the strategy.

The company had a private web site for a long time. The public site opened on January 16, 1998. It was a fully integrated web site, meaning that customers could make a purchase and see live inventory and credit card and address verification, as it was connected to Office Depot's inventory and delivery system. In this desktop-to-doorstep system, the customer knows if the item is available, when it will be delivered, whether it can be returned, and whether COD is permitted in lieu of using a credit card. There is, in addition, a dedicated customer service group for the public web page activity. Office Depot

Figure 2.5 The Cool Decision Process: FastAlliances Tool #7

Reporting

E-business group reports to president or CEO. Ultimate decision is a phone call away. Result is autonomy and facilitation of internal alliances due to political positioning (physical location helps).

Resources

Office Depot committed to creating an e-business, not just another channel for selling. Company has the ability to change the rules and value proposition since it controls the value chain from desk-top to doorstep.

Risk to Brand

Alliance partner criteria:

- Positive brand impact (adds elasticity and value)
- Financially viable
- Stable and scalable
- Add click - through revenues

Taking equity not mandated, requires working with non-web internal group.

Responsibility

Originator of alliance idea is responsible for alliance management - "you suggested it, you do it".

Online owns the infrastructure and the value chain back to front. It doesn't outsource any part of the transaction, and it utilizes its own massive warehouses and existing truck delivery system.

A number of important value propositions evolve from Office Depot Online's business model:

- Its products are needs-based.
- Office supplies are not fashion items. They are consumables, so easy and convenient access add value for the customer. Delivery is key.
- The concept of good service must be combined with fair pricing.

The web is the ultimate self-service tool. The combination of price plus service is an unbeatable combination. Value America had great price but no service. Office Depot Online has both.

The essence of the success of Office Depot Online is its decision processes. The e-business group, set up as a separate entity with its own profit and loss responsibility, reports to the president of the company. The unit has its own strategy and budget and is somewhat autonomous, a characteristic that I have found is a common success factor for many former brick-and-mortar organizations (e.g., E-GM). However, other organizations (e.g., Kodak) use the fully integrated approach, where each division has an integrated chief e-business officer, consistent with a decentralized management approach.

The Cool Decision Process is the result of an intimate team methodology that requires brainstorming and thinking out loud. Butler explained, "Rarely did we do something that we hadn't brainstormed or verbalized in discussions, and the one who created the idea was given the responsibility to carry it through—all the way through." This means that the originator of the idea, who could be a technical or marketing person, *never* hands the project off to someone else. The philosophy is, "You thought of it—you go and do it." This is possible because the strategy is clear: Although a FastStrategy is constantly open to change, whatever it is at a given moment must be clear to all players. Everyone on the team should be responsible for executing the strategy. This kind of environment was very familiar to the people on the Office Depot Online team—most of them came from a small business experience, the most active and intimate business environment. For this reason they hire only people who have web experience. In other words, retail experience is not essential—it's understanding web commerce that counts.

Another company that applied the FastStrategy and Cool Decision Process is Praxair, a leader in the industrial gases market. These concepts came together in a consortium (multipartner) alliance, one of the most difficult structures in the alliance portfolio. Developing the execution skills needed to do this well can create the beginnings of a Spider Network for your own company.

Dot-com companies may be irritated by the processes described next. However, if you are partnering with traditional or transitional companies, it will serve you well to read the Praxair example so that you will be aware of the mind-set of what could be a very important type of brand partner for you.

The E-business Consortium (Praxair): FastAlliances Tool #8

This tool, developed from the approach that Praxair used, is one of a number that I have used over the past three years in converting traditional organizational alliance approaches into e-business ones.

Here are the steps taken by traditional or transitional companies to create an e-business consortium:

1. It starts from a revolutionary group within a traditional company whose members know and understand the importance of e-business and are brainstorming about how to reinvent their company to play in the new economy.
2. Next they get senior management to buy in and create an e-business team.
3. They create a FastStrategy approach and realize that there is an opportunity for a consortium (multipartner) solution.
4. They address their company culture, the capital committed to the venture, the power and collateral of their brand, and domain knowledge: Is their company the best in class in its industry?
5. They choose partners who can match/equal/exceed the preceding four steps.

6. They set an artificial deadline to speed things along.
7. They create an understanding of knowledge to be transferred and intellectual property (IP) issues, then set up knowledge transfer sessions to ensure that the promise of value is kept.
8. Dedicated alliance managers from all partners are connected to the Cool Decision Processes, ensuring senior management buy-in, deliverables being met, and expectations being managed.

These steps will work for any industry. Consortia are complex by their very nature, because multiple partners are involved with different interests and expectations. Figure 2.6 shows an application of the approach by Praxair.

Background to the Application of the Tool

Praxair (formerly Union Carbide) is a world leader in industrial gases and other industrial arenas located in Danbury, Connecticut.[6] The story of its e-business achievements actually began in 1997.

Praxair's e-business consortium tool evolved from an approach used by Bal Agrawal, vice president of e-business at Praxair. He had the idea for an extranet and consortium-type alliance while he was general manager of a business unit at Praxair. The alliance is called SYNGAS. Its goal was to develop a technology and to share that technology to create value for the participants through an extranet. Agrawal called a number of contacts he knew in the technology groups at Amoco and BP. They had the inside track on the decision makers for a large project of this nature. Out of those calls came the first meeting of the prospective partners, on January 3, 1997. Remarkably, the consortium was fully formed and launched six weeks later (on February 17, 1997). The extreme time pressure was due to the fact that Praxair was putting the concept to public bid on February 24. Unless the consortium could come together before that time, the opportunity to do something with these particular participants would be lost. The main partners were Amoco, BP (separate companies at that time), and Praxair. They had different strengths in materials, design, and commercialization. Other partners had competencies in the gasification of coal and other delivery mechanisms. Some were competitors as well as partners. In fact, during the implementation of the consortium activities, BP and Amoco merged, causing a delicate situation that was

Figure 2.6 The E-business Consortium (Praxair): FastAlliances Tool #8

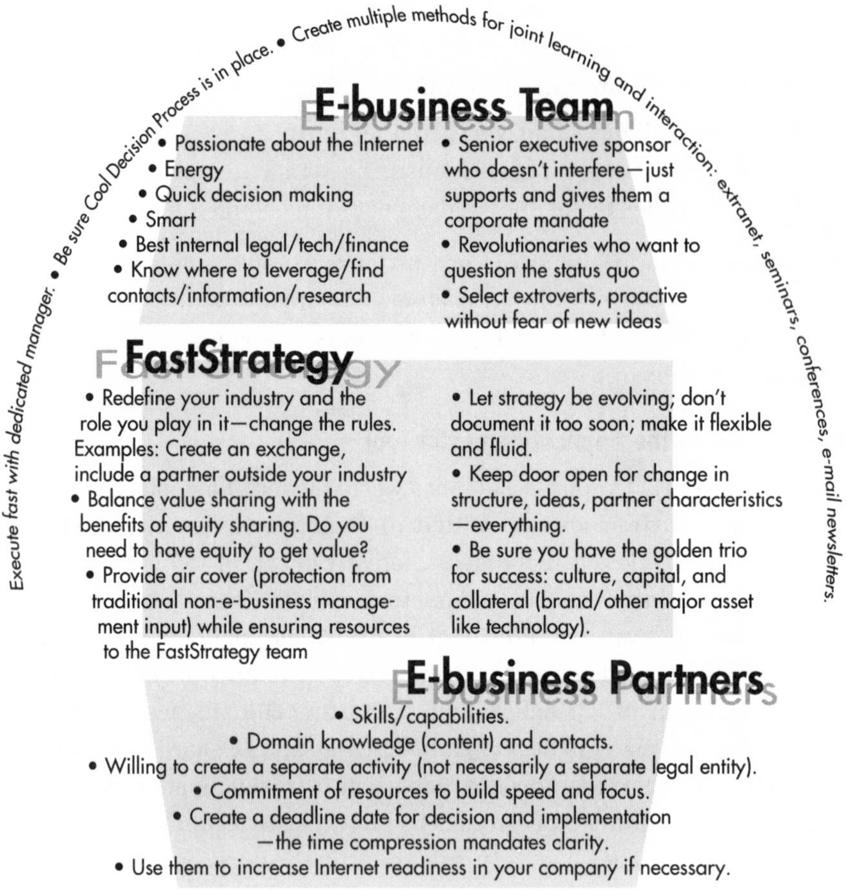
Execute fast with dedicated manager. • Be sure Cool Decision Process is in place. • Create multiple methods for joint learning and interaction: extranet, seminars, conferences, e-mail newsletters.
E-business Team
• Passionate about the Internet
• Energy
• Quick decision making
• Smart
• Best internal legal/tech/finance
• Know where to leverage/find contacts/information/research
• Senior executive sponsor who doesn't interfere—just supports and gives them a corporate mandate
• Revolutionaries who want to question the status quo
• Select extroverts, proactive without fear of new ideas
FastStrategy
• Redefine your industry and the role you play in it—change the rules. Examples: Create an exchange, include a partner outside your industry
• Balance value sharing with the benefits of equity sharing. Do you need to have equity to get value?
• Provide air cover (protection from traditional non-e-business management input) while ensuring resources to the FastStrategy team
• Let strategy be evolving; don't document it too soon; make it flexible and fluid.
• Keep door open for change in structure, ideas, partner characteristics—everything.
• Be sure you have the golden trio for success: culture, capital, and collateral (brand/other major asset like technology).
E-business Partners
• Skills/capabilities.
• Domain knowledge (content) and contacts.
• Willing to create a separate activity (not necessarily a separate legal entity).
• Commitment of resources to build speed and focus.
• Create a deadline date for decision and implementation—the time compression mandates clarity.
• Use them to increase Internet readiness in your company if necessary.

well managed by the consortium, with respect for certain confidential or awkward areas. They did not choose a separate legal structure (i.e., *no* joint venture). The reason was to keep the alliance with a *value-sharing* approach, not a profit-sharing focus. This way also preserved certain tax advantages. However, there was a board, of which Agrawal was chairman for two years, a dedicated manager to manage the alliance, an extranet for technology sharing, and multiple seminars and symposiums to accelerate the shared learning opportunities for the partners. The internal legal, technology, and finance representatives participated in every step of alliance development for each of the participants. The companies chose only their best representatives, those with a sense of urgency and high levels of competence. The value of the consortium has increased dramatically over time—the wishful dream of every alliance participant. A sixth partner who recently joined (would-be partners are lining up to participate) paid a significant premium over the first participants.

From his experience in creating the consortium, Agrawal developed an approach that proved critical when, in 1999, the CEO of Praxair appointed him vice president of e-business. Agrawal and a number of other key executives in the organization would meet on Mondays to discuss their mutual commitment to e-business and its potential application at Praxair. In these informal sessions, which became FastStrategy sessions, it was clear that Agrawal, with the SYNGAS consortium feather in his cap, wanted to challenge the organization to ratchet up its Internet activities.

The idea was that the pressure of the Internet revolution happening in every industry could create an environment in which an Internet revolution could succeed within Praxair. When the CEO called Agrawal and said, "I want you to create an e-business group; be a revolutionary with my mandate," he jumped at the opportunity. The company was lagging behind competitors in its Internet strategy. Bal wanted to be in stealth mode so that Praxair could develop its strategy without pressure from the outside. Agrawal told me, "It's difficult enough to do—but knowing we were behind and that the competition had a head start was overwhelming. On the other hand, not doing it first gave us a chance to see the mistakes that were being made—and to avoid making the same ones!"

To create the team, he chose people from within Praxair for their breadth of knowledge about and passion for the Internet as well as their speed in making decisions. "My job," he said, "was to provide the team with air cover. That meant I had to keep the traditional organization and management away from them so that they could evolve in their own cocoon. They had to make mistakes, brainstorm, create a strategy one day and throw it out the next. I gave them lots of room. It was key that they not have to worry about resources or nickel-and-dime for what they needed in terms of technology or be second-guessed on their good ideas as well as their silly ones."

The e-team, untouched by corporate bureaucracy, had the advantage of speed and quickly developed focus. Agrawal's role was to stimulate thought—not drive it in one direction or another. The

FastAlli, by Larraine Segil

e-business team developed a FastStrategy containing some of the characteristics found in the ideal business development person described on page 144ff. This essential collection of individuals who are freed from other activities to devote themselves to this project will set a foundation for those who follow.

Outsourcing: The "New" Hot Competency

No doubt that outsourcing has been around for the last two decades—so it is not new. What's different about outsourcing in e-business is that there are now end-to-end outsourcers that are integrating e-commerce needs with back-end systems, often with logistics, warehousing, and supplier services (Pandesic, Compaq Computer Services) as well as the manufacturing services traditionally required by original equipment manufacturers (Flextronics International). The usual risks of IT outsourcing (a common technique used in acquisitions where competing IT systems exist) increase dramatically. Once the buyer clicks to make a purchase on the web site of the seller, the entire operation is outsourced, and the next contact between buyer and seller is when the payment is received. The manufacture, shipping, customer service, and all the technology to support them are managed by other organizations, many of whom may actually be outsourcing portions of their own services. Time-to-market issues may be solved (a start-up company in e-commerce can launch very fast), but the real issue is, how robust are the partners of your partners? Is there a weak connection or player in their Spider Network on whom they (and you) are depending?

Although outsourcing is important, essential, and attractive, in e-business it requires deeper ongoing management than does a traditional outsourcing arrangement of the past—and high-level project management and quality-setting skills by you and your partners.

The many tools presented in this chapter will stand you in good stead as you speed forward with FastAlliances. Chapter 3 discusses the deliverables you should be looking for and how to make sure you have them.

CHAPTER 3

Step 3: Define the Deliverables for FastAlliances

This chapter gives you the answer to "tell me how to do it." It's not answered at the beginning of the book because first you need the mind-set to create a strategy and the ability to think about the context into which that strategy falls. We also discuss some of the new issues in the e-business world. What you now learn will be more effective because you have some basic tools (Spider Network, FastStrategy, Cool Decision Process, Brand Positioning, Strategy Playbook) and a clear understanding of the contexts to which they apply. This chapter gives you the details of the FastAlliances Capability Quiz—the essential criteria for success in FastAlliances.

Because of the need to be faster and more efficient, the deliverables for a FastAlliances are sometimes confusing. They will change throughout the alliance, which itself may last only a year or less. Keep your process light and available, for definition and measurement of deliverables is essential. Express it in simple language, and make sure all partners know what the essentials are. That way the process will act as a communication tool and lead to continuous change, hopefully creating better returns for each alliance partner.

One of the most fluid processes has been developed by the Walt Disney Internet group formerly known as the Go Network. Larry Shapiro, executive vice president of legal and business affairs, was enthusiastic when we spoke about the potential gains from the Internet group's existing and future alliances. Creating the deliverables and measuring them is a key method of keeping alliance relationships valid and legitimate over time as the industry changes.

Shapiro's background makes him a great respecter and protector of brand. He worked for Disney's e-business for over two years and was with Disney in other capacities for five years before that—an eon in Internet time. His solid network within Disney is a great asset in his position at the Walt Disney Internet group, since many of his decisions will have a direct impact on one or more of the members of the Disney family of companies.

The Disney combination of providing tools, applications, and content to make users' lives easier has been very successful. These have traditionally been the b2c deliverables. This way, the user can make choices in a fast, comprehensive way, and the medium can teach and entertain as well as sell.

What follows is Shapiro's approach to the deliverables that the Walt Disney Internet group must have for the ultimate customer experience—and how his company measures results over time. He gets more than five new qualified opportunities a day.

He first evaluates whether the opportunity has value for an equity investment alliance—namely, equity in addition to added value through the alliance relationship.

Equity Alliance Deliverables

1. What is the impact on our brand? Disney is the number one kids and family site, ESPN is the number one sports site, ABC is the number one news site in the United States. That's power and that's value, which must be protected at all costs. Every alliance must be evaluated according to its impact (positive or negative) on the company's brand.

2. Does the technology or content have a broad application across Disney's existing businesses? That would include groups that cover media networks, studio entertainment, parks and resorts, and con-

sumer products. Company names that also may be familiar to you include ABC, ESPN, Disney, and the other members of its corporate family (40+ companies). In deciding to partner, the company that cuts across the most family members in application will have the advantage.

3. Does the company have a valid business model that would enable the growth of the business, one to which the Disney family of companies could add value and facilitate further growth? Even though the candidate company may be doing something valid and worthwhile, the Walt Disney Internet group does not act as a venture capitalist, investing only where there is value. It wants the deliverable of the value to have specific application to its family of companies, with the result that the alliance will differentiate them in the market in some way. For example, a buying cooperative is not a company in which the Walt Disney Internet group would create an equity alliance. It might look at another kind of relationship, but not equity.

4. The company must have the ability to put the deal together within four to five days (yes, *days*). How is that possible? All decision making is centralized regarding business development. The CFO is integrally involved, as is Larry Shapiro (as executive VP of legal and business affairs). All deal flow goes through them and has to fit within the context of points 1 and 2 while taking into account the driving concerns of the general managers of each business unit (see internal alliances later in this chapter). Their goal is the cross-property growth of the whole business family, not just one business unit. For example, if they were to look at instant messaging, it would be across all the business units, not just one. One of the ways to do this is to create proactive buy-in at the division level. If the opportunity is concerning technology, the general managers of the business units are brought into the process early on and give substantial input. If a general manager is not happy, it sometimes could mean that unit would opt out. It does not happen often. Everyone knows each other well enough, and since four or five general managers have to interact, it is not difficult to build relationships.

Distribution Alliance without Equity

In a distribution alliance, for example, with an Internet service provider, Shapiro and his team would want to know the customer numbers and demographics and psychographics of the customer base. In addition, they would need a clear understanding of the value for the Walt Disney Internet group and would measure that continually. One example is the product called Eye-opener (a *netpliance*, or Internet appliance). This is how the reasoning was done:

1. There will be a number of players in this space and the products will be relatively ubiquitous.
2. Here is a situation in which the judgment call has to do with whether this company will be the leader.
3. If it will be, then this should qualify as an equity alliance. If not, then it may be better to have simply a nonexclusive distribution relationship.
4. This is an example of a situation where no one knows the answer and it is difficult to establish the economic models for either partner. The result is a need to be flexible.
5. Some concerns: An alliance with a netpliance maker will scale up (incurring high expenses and capital investment) in the first year to enable the companies to start making money in about 18 months to two years. This may be different than their projections, but it is a conservative estimate.
6. The solution is to create a nonexclusive arrangement—but *don't* make it short term because you will lose the upside potential that could kick in after three years.
7. If a distribution relationship is based on content reaching everywhere, then the resources must be placed with the largest partners who bring the most traffic or number of devices or whatever the measure is for that platform. For example, when the Walt Disney Internet group looks at the Internet service providers (ISPs), it will examine who comprises its Spider Network of partners, when those relationships will expire, where they do and do not have services, and where they can add value to the Walt Disney Internet group as partners.
8. There is an inherent dichotomy in choosing partners. If they will have broad-based application, the Walt Disney Internet group definitely wants to partner with them. The dilemma arises because, on the one hand, the Walt Disney Internet group wants their ser-

vices exclusively, while on the other, it wants them to be ubiquitous. There is no single right answer. Each situation requires its own evaluation and risk analysis.

Internal Alliances

Shapiro explained how the internal alliances work at the Disney family and how he can sometimes find external partners to fill internal needs:

> There is another tier of alliances, no less important than those just mentioned. These internal alliances will be directed by those people actually managing the product or business unit. For example, I need to be close to the internal needs of the general manager of each business unit, such as the general manager of ESPN. He will tell me of a need, for example, to improve the quality of his service to customers. My mandate then is to go out and find a way to satisfy that need. Many companies want a relationship with ESPN. When I find one that meets his needs, I pass it on. It is essential that I stay close to my internal partners so that as opportunities come to me I can do a triage [fast analysis of needs and directing solutions to meet them] and send them on to him. Because of the huge deal flow and the speed with which they happen, it is necessary to focus my energies and decide on which areas to spend time. Many people come in to give a presentation. They have venture capital money but don't even have a web site yet, so its difficult to say, "Okay, we'll send our engineer over to do due diligence." Focus is key, and of course, that comes from knowing your strategy, which we do.

Deliverables

The deliverables cannot be itemized in a formula because they are specific to each FastAlliances. However, what follows is a list of the *areas* in which deliverables can be found. You need to decide which ones apply to your FastAlliances.

1. *Cross-selling.* This entails selling your products and services with your partners on their portal or yours.
2. *Upselling.* This means selling a more expensive product but adding value.

3. *Click-through selling.* This includes revenue sharing, commissioned sales, and passing through your portal to your partner (when the transaction takes place you get a percentage).

4. *Sponsorship.* This means selling your real estate—selling a place on your portal or web site for up-front money as well as the click-through selling. Companies like Amazon.com can charge a hefty fee for prime anchor space on their web pages since it gets so many viewers. (This is similar to the huge premiums that companies will pay to partner with Disney for the opportunity to be seen by the tens of millions of visitors who pass through a Disney property every day.)

5. *Bundling.* This entails selling products with services bundled as solutions for higher value. Sometimes you can charge more if you combine services. (This works especially well if you offer three options; psychological analyses show that people are more likely to choose the middle option if offered three, whereas they will choose the lower one if offered two.) A partner's contribution may add higher value to the bundle and should be measured by testing with and without value added in order to find the right combination. For example, hosting companies offer dial-up services and ISPs offer hosting and domain registration.

6. *Selling analytical data.* Here you take a partner's data or your own and repackage it along with analysis as a more valuable product or service. This could be another deliverable from an alliance, especially if your partner increases the amount of data you can analyze or mine (click-through rates, buy rates, traffic flow, location of click buttons). Other patterns that have come under close scrutiny are purchase behaviors on other sites through e-wallets, which follow customers wherever they go—not only on your site. This could raise privacy issues. Other metrics include growth in numbers of users or page views, revenues per page view, conversion of users to buyers, and a whole series of other metrics that are evolving even as this book is going to print.

7. *Miscellaneous services.* These include consulting, data-mining, reselling of analyzed information, scenario planning with projected analyses of what could happen based on present performance, financial services, and delivery services. All of these are potential partner contributions and need to be measured vis-à-vis customer perception and satisfaction as well as for the revenues that they generate.

8. *Anything that produces customer satisfaction.* This is the ultimate name of the game—whether your company is b2b, b2c, or m2m. The customer has many options, the web being the democratizer of information and price comparison. The customer must perceive value in his or her relationship with your company, and anything a partner can do to improve that relationship is a metric that will add to the value of the partnership. Keep alert and flexible in adding to the metrics over time.

9. *Create it as you go.* Since the medium is in its infancy, there are almost endless opportunities for the development of revenue streams. Be open to new ideas. Be creative. Don't be limited by the past.

Now that you have the essential tools in mind, let's apply them in an analytical exercise to Chubb, the venerable company mentioned in Chapter 2.

Chubb: FastAlliances Analysis

Chubb has created an organization that matches well when measured by our FastAlliances tools:

- FastStrategy, the consortium-based open architecture tool (Praxair)
- Spider Networks
- The Cool Decision Process (officedepot.com)
- FastStrategy playbook (Compaq)

This application of these tools to Chubb exemplifies the essential elements for success in the Internet world.

FastStrategy

From concept to launch time was three months. For a 200-year-old company, that is remarkable. The strategy was to extend the brand and make it more elastic. The method Chubb used to extend its brand is itself a valuable lesson (see Chapter 2). The strategy implementation was left open. The group that was created to make it happen was given the leeway to make the strategy as flexible as needed. Substrategies could be made and discarded as Chubb became more experienced in this area.

Cool Decision Process (officedepot.com)

The group was set up differently than the normal structure of Chubb. Team members were removed from the geographic structure of the rest of the company, in which regional geographic groupings were run by regional sector heads (general managers) who had responsibility for local application and operations (selling especially) for the six to seven business units. These sector heads were an integral part of the Cool Decision Process since they were the internal stakeholders who could accelerate or sabotage the project. They were kept very well informed (through constant updates, meetings, and communications) to ensure their input and, more important, their buy-in. These same sector heads would be responsible for selling the concepts to Chubb's 2 million customers worldwide. In no way could implementation occur smoothly without their cooperation.

The managing director of the new group created an unusual structure for the e-business organization. First, he reported directly to the managing director of the whole company, which meant speedy decisions and top-executive sponsorship. Next, he took the unusual step of outsourcing much of the development and technology to small consulting firms and start-up companies that could add services or expertise and make Chubb Internet-ready. Working with entrepreneurs was not something that Chubb had done in the past. Although the company had used technologists as product developers in the past, most of the focus had been on licensing or buying a product or technology and absorbing it into Chubb itself. The current approach was entirely different. No longer did Chubb wish to *acquire* the smaller companies, but rather to work with them. This meant overcoming the understandable reluctance of the entrepreneur partners to reveal their secrets to Chubb. However, Chubb's advantage in this arena is its integrity. A Chubb promise not to steal a smaller company's secrets carried more weight than the word of most large companies. As mentioned in Chapter 2, Spider Networks have the habit of spreading bad news as quickly as (or even quicker than) good news. Dr. Robert Farquhar, director of marketing and technology for Chubb, described the relationship to me: "We [the large Internet-ready company] provide the shovels needed to dig the ground in the rush to mine Internet gold to those who do the digging [the dot-coms]."

Part of the Cool Decision Process is the compensation structure. The bonus system for the e-business group was redesigned to include *team bonuses*—allocated to team members according to the recommendation of the managing director of the group. (Not all team members got identical bonuses, but everyone on the team was rewarded.) The rewards were based on very short milestones—no more than a month. As the team reached or exceeded the milestones, bonuses were paid. Although the project itself was inherently rewarding and exciting, frequent bonuses provided additional incentives to speed up activities dramatically.

Chubb's holding company, Williams PLC, was also included in the Cool Decision Process and was kept well informed and enthusiastic about the activities in the e-business group.

Another challenge was to create a group culture that would entice the necessary talent. It is clear that Internet security is a hot issue. Associating the golden brand of Chubb with that concept (and its concomitant resources to finance development and application) offers great appeal. Also attractive is the fact that employees on the team are rewarded in short time spans. In light of all this, even though Chubb isn't a dot-com, the value proposition to new hires is exciting. The activities of its e-business group are nontraditional. Instead of working in multiple layers of decision making and bureaucracy, the team is lean, outsourcing and working hand in hand with small entrepreneurial companies. It's the combination of *culture, capital,* and *collateral* that makes the large-company option appealing to those who are willing to incur some risk—but not the bottomless kind.

The principles mentioned in this chapter regarding FastStrategy and the deliverables are the essence of creating a healthy FastAlliances. Implementation is the key to making the deliverables happen. The following is a fictional example.

LookMaNoHands.com: FastAlliances Start-Up

The goal is to sell high-risk adventure travel on the web through a portal. The idea for the company was conceived by two 19-year-olds while white-water rafting down the Salmon River in Idaho. They created the web site, raised some initial seed money from friends and family, and were off and running. The company would be based on the concept of strategic alliances. But without business connections in the travel industry and a structure to help them execute and follow through, they didn't have a sustainable competitive advantage (if they actually had one at all!). Creating FastAlliances was key. They had a business plan and the beginning of a Spider Network. They identified potential partners—package travel groups that specialized in the kind of adventures they promoted. They created a revenue-sharing program with these vendors, adding links to their sites. Our two entrepreneurs also built a service to put up web sites for all the adventure travel operations worldwide that didn't have one already, connecting them to LookMaNoHands.com and creating an online adventure travel community. Many of these organizations were mom-and-pop businesses, seasonal, poorly managed, but hugely interested in this method of reaching customers. Revenues started to dribble in. The young men hired online salespeople to pitch to these small businesses and sign them up. They outsourced the web hosting to another company and revenues began to slowly increase. They had to find a way to make the revenues come in faster. In order to change the rules in the industry in which they were playing, they needed to bring in a partner with a huge brand. After doing some research, they chose American Platinum Travel (APT, also fictional), a global brand associated with expensive customized travel services. It seemed like a perfect fit, because both companies target the newly rich who have money to burn and are often looking for adventure and excitement.

LookMaNoHands.com has just entered the real world—trying to create a partnership with a very large but not traditionally entrepreneurial company. They go through their checklist (from a book about FastAlliances) and discover the following:

Tool	For Themselves	For Proposed Partner
FastStrategy tool	Check	A problem if they don't have it
Cool Decision Process	Check	A problem if they don't have it
Brand positioning	None	*Yes*
Strategy playbook	N/A	A problem if they don't have it

It's the classic dilemma of a start-up: needing to raise capital while simultaneously growing the company. For both reasons, LookMaNoHands.com is considering entering into a partnership. Here's what start-up entrepreneurs spend nights and days brainstorming:

1. They need a big name strategic partner in order to raise capital from venture capitalists (VCs). The VCs are looking for revenue growth: Will this partner act quickly enough to grow the company's sales immediately?

2. Even if the partner does apply FastStrategy and a Cool Decision Process, can the little dot-com scale quickly enough to meet the new customer demand this relationship will yield? Will the partner's referrals all come at once, overload the company, then stop for six months or altogether? Imagine that APT puts out the word by sending a marketing brochure about LookMaNoHands.com to the appropriate, demographically selected segment of the population. In response, say that 20,000 adventure-hungry people deluge the site and expect fulfillment of their reservation/delivery orders. (Stephen King's book, offered for sale online, nearly brought Amazon.com to a standstill due to high demand.)

3. It becomes clear that some deals make immediate growth happen and other deals make long-term growth happen. Both are necessary. The first kind can come from the business development kind of FastAlliances. They can also be simple sales deals. The second are the true business development deals, and the problem with them is that they may take months to happen. These, however, may be the very ones that you need to raise VC money. Alliances with big-name brands (like the American Platinum in this example) will prove valuable for luring institutional investors. Yet the time (and effort) needed to make that business development deal bear fruit could destroy the start-up company.[1]

It is the dilemma of many dot-coms to balance these issues. Larger companies who partner with e-business companies face the dilemma from the other side—how to partner with a company that is in the space you want to be in, has a great idea, but could be trampled by too much too soon.

The solution follows.

Capability Quiz: FastAlliances Tool #9

It's all in the timing. The requirements and deliverables for a FastAlliances must be viewed through the lens of what I call the FastAlliances Tool #9, Capability Quiz.

1. What are your partners' capabilities in terms of projected referrals/demands/resource requirements? How much business can they send you? What will be the processes you have to go through in order to do business with them (government rules, contractor approvals, technology or scientific requirements, etc.)?
2. What are your capabilities in being able to scale up to meet the these demands?
3. What infrastructure, capital, human resources, and internal (in a large partner) approvals are needed in order to make the promise of a huge business development deal a reality?
4. Can you afford to do this partnership? Can you afford *not* to do this partnership? (See Chapter 5 on preemptive FastAlliances.) What are the opportunity costs? What is your cash on hand? What is the net present value of the new revenues from the deal? Does this equal a positive number?
5. Can you stage this FastAlliances so that some things fall into the FastAlliances characteristics and some into the slower, more traditional methodologies/processes? (See Chapter 9 for more on this.)
6. Which teams will work on each facet if you use both FastAlliances and traditional processes? When will you phase them in? (They require different skills—see page 144ff regarding business development and dot-com self-esteem.)

FastAlli, by Larraine Segil

7. Are you paying attention to the capability differential between your management team and your partner's management team? And are you taking into account the fact that the alliance will require different kinds of human capabilities at different stages of its evolution?
8. Do you have the technology to make all these wonderful ideas happen (provided you get the money/financing).

By using the tools laid out in Chapters 1 and 2, you will be able to diagnose all these issues.

The *Capability Gap* is a common problem. I spoke with a brilliant young man, Josh Benegal Marks, who has some interesting experiences and insights on these matters. Though only 22, he has already built two companies, one of which, a value-added reseller (VAR) for Compaq products, he sold at the age of 16. After receiving undergraduate and graduate degrees from Harvard, Marks was asked to become CEO of an e-business start-up (for which he raised $10 million in venture capital) and is now CEO of Silicon Planet.

Our conversation took place at a monthly salon evening I hold at my home in Los Angeles, California, where I invite about 25 people for dinner. The mix includes young Gen Xers and not-so-young yuppies and baby boomers. The young are brilliant businesspeople who may be CEOs of e-business companies, entrepreneurs, investment bankers, lawyers, institutional investor representatives, venture capitalists, or those employed in e-business divisions of large organizations. The not-so-young people are colleagues of mine from traditional businesses, former or present CEOs of Fortune 500 companies, a smattering of those from the entertainment world (since I live in Los Angeles), and the occasional politician, athlete, lawyer, accountant, or physician. The conversation is always mind-bending, challenging, full of laughter, and laced with new ideas. Generally, the guests never leave before midnight—satiated mentally, often musically, and certainly gastronomically.

On the particular evening in question, Josh Marks and my good friend Monty Hall (a very astute businessman in addition to being known for *Let's Make a Deal*) entered into a typical conversation. In other words, everything they said was challenged by the other with a story, a concept, or an analysis. These kinds of stimulating yet friendly exchanges happen often at our salons.

Marks's new company, Silicon Planet, has as its market the nonprofit sector. The company has discovered a way to assist fund-raisers to understand their donors better and to access them more appropriately by using data management technology. Marks has enticed former executive director of strategic alliances from DoubleClick, Scott Dorman, to become COO of the company. Silicon Planet is a for-profit company offering services in the not-for-profit sector. Its services include a template-based rental web site that includes all the essential tools for fund-raisers—online donations, loyalty-based shopping, e-mail tools, and a community site. Fund-raisers can aggregate their donors online and use Silicon Planet's tools to target them with personalized donor-centric campaigns. The idea is to reduce the $25 billion that is spent annually on fund-raising campaigns so that more of the dollars raised can go directly to the actual work of the charity/nonprofit.

Monty Hall, performer, comedian, and philanthropist, has donated time and talent to more nonprofit organizations than anyone on the planet. It was fascinating to see them sparring with each other about various concepts regarding this sector. Whereas Marks's experience comes from research, Internet knowledge, and understanding e-business, Hall's experience is from the school of hard knocks. He has what is called in the e-business space *domain knowledge* (which means he knows his way around the not-for-profit industry like few others). Their conversation ended with a high level of mutual respect, the exchanging of cards, and the expansion of their respective Spider Networks.

Marks is currently in the middle of the capability dilemma with his new company, a dilemma he has faced before with the other companies he has started:

> The toughest of situations is where you have a terrific management team going for a brand-new market. Even though the VCs tell you that they are interested in the market opportunity that will change the rules, remake the industry, or make a new industry, the fact is that they don't want to take such a risk. The term *venture capital* has lost its meaning—most of the money is going after the things that appear to be partially proven. Raising money for something that is brand-new is much more difficult. And I have seen the capability dilemma many times. It's a chicken-and-egg dilemma. First, you need the alliance partner's brand name to raise the money, but you can't increase revenues right away from that partner, because often they are big and bureaucratic. However, they take up so much of your management bandwidth that you don't have time/resources to go out and make short-term revenues happen. The VCs want both the revenues and the partners, so you are caught in the dilemma of making business development deals, increasing sales, and raising money, all at the same time. If it is technology-related, the VCs don't want the technology to be developed since, if it is, the valuation for their investment will be too high. Yet they don't want to invest in a technology that is unproven, since the risks are too high. It certainly is an interesting time!

Interesting is an understatement. *Breathtaking* is more appropriate. The short Capability Quiz offered earlier in this chapter will raise your awareness for the challenge so that you can plan your resources to manage it.

Managing variables is always difficult, especially when they occur at different times and with increasing or decreasing levels of importance. In aerospace manufacture (I once ran an advanced materials distribution company in that industry), certain processes require a vast number of details to be intricately interconnected and timed so that the sequencing happens when it is supposed to and no one task prevents the completion of any other task. One of these processes is called a *Gantt chart.*[2] I have adapted the Gantt for our use in FastAlliances. (See Figure 3.1.) This is a very flexible tool. I have taken some liberties in my adaptation. I will refer to this again in Chapter 9 when we wrap up the tool applications.

The tasks are clearly adaptable. You can insert whatever is relevant to your application as long as you make sure that you insert the predecessors correctly. This means you must examine which activities have to come before or in tandem with others and prioritize them. This is a wonderful way for all team members to be on the same page. Depending on how fast your alliance is, the weeks at the top of each column could be days. The FastAlliances Gantt chart can be used for any aspect of the FastAlliances or for the whole relationship.

A number of stakeholders who are also partners play an important part—except that participants don't often manage these stakeholders as well as they should. The next chapter addresses the particular needs of a number of different stakeholders.

Figure 3.1 Gantt Chart: FastAlliances Tool #10

ID	TASK	PREDECESSORS	WK 1	WK 2	WK 3	WK 4	WK 5	WK 6	WK 7	WK 8	TO END
1	FastAlliance idea and Cool Decision Process		X								
2	FastStrategy and Spider Network analysis	1	X								
3	FastAlliance contact meeting	1,2		XX							
4	Competitive/E-mindshift analysis	1,2,3		XXX	X						
5	Develop deal and resources (people/finance)	1,2,3,4		X	XXX	X					
6	Agreement	1,2,3,4,5,6				XX	XX				
7	Test or launch	6,7,8					X	XX	X		
8	Baseline and tracking metrics implemented	5,6,7,8,9				X	XX	XX	XX	XXX	XXXXX
9	Spider Network expansion	2,4,5,6			X	XX	XX	XX	XX	XXX	XXXXXX
10	Mutuality tracking	7,8,9,10,11					XX	XX	XX	XXX	XXXX
11	Transition into traditional alliance	8,9,10,11,12					XX	XX	XX	XXX	XXXXX
12	Team adjustment for parallel fast/traditional alliances	1,4,5,8,10,12,13					XX	XX	XX	XXX	XXXXX
13	Managing capability differential between partners	4,5,8,12,14					X	XX	XX	XXX	XXXX
14	Technology/infrastructure suitability	2,9					X	XX			
15	Brand positioning and integrity	2,3,4,8	X	XX	XX	XX	XX	XX	XX	XXX	XXXX
16	Tiering Process	2,4,5,11,12		X	X		XX	XX	X		
17	Other related FastAlliance partners identified	1,2,4,9		XX	XXX						
18	Integration of new/existing FastAlliance partners	5,6,7,12,13,14,15,17		X	XX	XX	XX	XX			

CHAPTER 4

Step 4: Managing Stakeholder Expectations

You must leverage the stakeholders of your FastAlliances for every ounce of value—whether internal or external to your alliance. This means their contacts and their Spider Networks, their titles, influence, power, knowledge, insights. You must leverage these relationships in order to get in front of the right people at the right time with the right positioning. Leveraging these stakeholders will ultimately derive the benefits for them that they collectively want—your (and their) success. Is it easy? Of course not. One of the biggest challenges in creating FastAlliances is this layer of relationships that are outside of the external company-to-company alliances related to business-to-business transactions. They are also partners, but are rarely managed as if they are since they fall into nontraditional partner categories. These partners can be clearly identified only by doing a stakeholder analysis and managing the expectations of those identified. They are the angel investors, the venture capitalists, the lawyers, accountants, board members, consultants, executive search consultants, and investment bankers. Government may sometimes fall into this group. Also included are those within your company who may be doubtful about the whole e-business thing and whom you need to educate and co-opt in the short term or bypass in the long term.

Huge successes in the e-business environment have led all those whose lives and livings are vested in them to have goals that just five years ago would have been laughable. Now they seem almost reasonable. After all, once you have seen a 1,000 percent increase in your investment over 12 months, it raises the bar to a level that makes anything else seem lackluster.

The Internal Stakeholders

For traditional and transitional companies, these internal stakeholders can be the biggest challenge. They may be non-e-business employees or executives who are fearful of losing their power base or even their jobs. The jealousy, disparagement, concern, and anxiety that has been part of the e-business revolution is the dark underside that is rarely spoken about in the excitement of the high-adrenaline dot-com environment. As the stock market corrections have taken their toll, the naysayers have gone from told-you-so relief to concern about the future.

As an internal e-business visionary, your role will be a controversial one. Since your company may be either traditional or transitioning, your role is that of advocate, educator, and, in many respects, revolutionary (see Chapter 7). Begin with this approach:

1. Map out the stakeholders who are both decision makers and decision breakers.
2. Develop a strategy to inform them and manage their expectations. This will be essential so that they don't pop up at unexpected times to sabotage your activities. They may do that, but you will be ready for them.
3. Be sure you have your own internal advocates (preferably senior management) who have the power to endorse your actions or assist you in bypassing the negative inputs and influences.

Garnering internal support may be a fairly laborious process—and a continuous one. It is essential for FastStrategy and FastAlliances implementation that you address this early in your activities and keep it in mind until it becomes less of an issue over time.

Angel Investors and Incubators

On the one hand, angel investors can be as their description suggests—angels that save the day by giving start-ups what they need to prove their concepts in order to raise the next level of money from a venture capital firm, corporate investor, or even further angel financing. On the other hand, angels can come from the netherworld, looking like angels but behaving like devils. (Okay, maybe that's pushing the analogy a little too far, but speak to those entrepreneurs who have experienced the latter kind and they will endorse this view.)

Generally, these people have built a sizable net worth and created funds for investing in start-ups. They can afford to lose their money. It's a game. However, they can also be sore losers. Some angels have a committed belief in the target industry or arena of investment and a desire to see others succeed in that area. Others are looking for grand-scale toys or intellectual stimulation. Vast personal wealth may create a game in which the scorecard for angel investors becomes "mine is bigger than yours." Angel investors may join groups like Ron Conway's Silicon Valley Angel Association, which includes a number of major players who have made their fortunes in the Valley over the past decade. There are angel groups all over the United States, and they have access to substantial deal flow. Potential corporate partners like Compaq and others stay connected to them to benefit from that access.[1]

One of the earliest angel groups was developed by George Kozmetsky, cofounder of Teledyne and the visionary founder of IC2 Institute in Austin, Texas. With his wife Ronya, George, through his institute, foundations, teaching at the University of Texas Business School in Austin, innumerable angel funds, incubators for new companies, and numerous other projects, has been responsible for spreading knowledge about entrepreneurship and venture funding worldwide.[2] His early angel investments in Dell Computers and other hugely successful companies have paid off enormously. He organized angel groups in Texas, then took the idea nationwide, and eventually worldwide to the United Kingdom, China, and other countries.

"It's the way to spread the knowledge wealth as well as to create continuous, viral innovation connecting the old and new economies," Kozmetsky commented to me at our annual IC2 Fellows get-together.

"But the angel investors are only the beginning. They must be followed by the incubator system, which gives an early home to these companies and the supporting infrastructure to take this concept to its logical conclusion—the betterment of all people and the spreading of knowledge and wealth throughout the economic system." The legacy of the Kozmetsky family (Ronya Kozmetsky is a visionary philanthropist in her own right) will last many years.

The Technology Alliance of Southern California (formerly known as LARTA)[3] is a non profit that provides services and community to over 8,000 start-up and e-business companies in the region. LARTA's CEO, Rohit Shukla, who has in-depth experience in this arena, shares his strong feelings: "There is nothing more important than an intelligent and experienced venture capitalist. We see all kinds invested in our member companies. And there is a definite difference in the potential for conflict resolution when a VC has been there and done that many times before—even in the new areas of e-business."

Guy Kawasaki, CEO and founder of Garage.com (a public company that prepares the entrepreneur for the grueling task of raising money, among other things), told me in a recent interview that his success came from "looking for values, not valuation." His business model screens thousands of business opportunities through a web-based application process, which generates a qualified deal flow for his group of about 50 deals a year. Then Garage.com packages them right. That means that the company arranges rigorous schooling for all start-ups—informal but rigorous nevertheless. Each start-up team goes through instruction from the Garage.com team on presentation skills, writing a business plan, financials, management, investor frequently asked questions, and so on. Garage.com arranges for counseling by competent, hand-picked lawyers, accountants, and other consultants. Garage.com then presents its neatly packaged clients to venture capitalists and investors—and will later position them for IPOs and acquisition if appropriate.

Operating from an overcrowded but charming building in the heart of Palo Alto, Garage.com's informality is misleading. The evaluation of candidates is rigorous, and Kawasaki's biting wit and short, at times flippant, comments leave little space for squirrelly vacillation. I heard one associate muttering as she ran up and down the stairs (reception is upstairs, Kawasaki is downstairs), "Who on earth would spend $900 to come and spend ten minutes with Guy Kawasaki?" The answer is, *many would*. He has succeeded where others have failed and has learned to cut to the basics in the start-up area. Truisms pop out in his conversation: "Build from strength not to cover weakness" drives home the point that joining two partners who are weak will not make either of them strong. "Find a lawyer who wants to do, not prevent, business" speaks for itself. Of course, within his Spider Network he has more good lawyers than most will meet in a lifetime, but he has little time for those who don't subscribe to his way of thinking.

Kawasaki is not foolish in his expectations. He told me that he doesn't go into deals unless he can create an "out" clause. There is a problem in being "too smart," he said. Namely, don't be greedy, sneaky, or sly. And above all be brief. Ah yes—the speed thing, the way the e-business world moves: If you can't be brief around Guy Kawasaki, don't show up at all. His golden rules? No more than a 1-page e-mail, a 20-page business plan, a 12-slide presentation, and a 1-hour meeting. "Any more than that is too much." He's right. If you can't raise money or convince investors or investment bankers within that time, you probably never will. Their mind-set is that every moment they spend with you could be used to evaluate another candidate and make more money. Don't waste their time.

This may sound rough. There is no doubt that Kawasaki has the dot-com self-esteem discussed later in this chapter. More than once he started a sentence with, "Now this may seem arrogant, but . . ." (then went on to say it anyway). However, along with that go the nuts and bolts of plain old good business sense: "Keep burn rates low and cash balances high." His philosophy and methods account for his success and the success of those who invest with him. His record is better than most (which, in venture capital talk, means that the losers are more than made up by the winners), and the company does very, very well.

However, not all incubators are the same.[4] More than 100 new incubators have been launched in the past nine months, bringing the total in the United States to 800 according to the National Business Incubation Association. The new incubators offer not only T1 access lines and guidance, but some have, like Garage.com, intricate blueprints that are meant to accelerate the market entry of start-ups. In 1996, William (Bill) Gross started idealab!, said to be the first Internet incubator, which resulted in Etoys, CarsDirect.com, and others. Then two quasi-incubators started in CMGI and Internet Capital Group. These have been the gold standard. One novel idea is already proving its worth: Village Ventures has a new twist on the incubator, venture capital, angel, and start-up mélange. The goal of founders Bo Peabody (age 29) and his former college roommate Matt Harris (age 27) is to provide venture capital seed money in small college towns across the United States. They will fund businesses that fall underneath the radar of the major VCs (mainly because they are not in one of the major so-called start-up cities in Silicon Valley, Southern California, and New England). Their plan is to find a local VC or team of VCs in each of their small-town target markets willing to raise $10 million from local banks and other sources in order to create an entirely local source of funding for about 15 local companies. For every dollar this group puts in, Village Ventures will add 50 cents, making the total pot worth $15 million.

Peabody is no novice in this area. He started and ran a successful company called Tripod, which he sold to Lycos for $58 million (which was in turn acquired by Terra, making that equity worth more than $600 million), and he is determined to spread similar opportunities to those who have little access to cash but great innovative talent.

My conversations with and observations of Peabody on a number of occasions have convinced me that if anyone can do it, he can. I also have no doubt that this model will be equally applicable worldwide—which means that Village Ventures will have to move smartly to align itself with others of like mind in Asia, Europe, and Latin America. This approach will not only facilitate the democratization of information, but also the democratization of access to capital. Couple this with the global expansions of Nasdaq and small-cap exchanges that will make that capital liquid again, and it becomes clear that major global and local social and economic evolutions are at hand.

Probably the best description I have heard of the start-up process is from Bal Agrawal, Praxair's VP of e-business, at a Global Leaders Conference where I was a speaker. He said, "Conceiving an idea is like conceiving life—its lots of fun. Executing and implementing is the real challenge."

Regardless of whether the start-up process is within a large company or as an entrepreneurial activity, the fun of idea creation eventually must be accompanied by the hard work and 24-hour-a-day, 7-day-a-week (24-7) implementation.

Government

Government is not a preferred partner for any start-up in general due to the perception of bureaucracy and heel dragging. However, there are instances in which government intervention or assistance, and indeed the size and access of government, can be exactly what is needed.

Stamps.com is a highly successful company that was started by three former UCLA MBA graduates. Two of them gave a blow-by-blow description to me and a group of colleagues with whom I sit on the Price Center Board of Entrepreneurs for the Anderson School of Management at UCLA. There is no doubt that this enterprise could not have started if not for the U.S. Postal Service. Miraculously, this group of high-energy entrepreneurs not only located the key decision makers in the USPS, but arranged a meeting and wowed them into buying into their concept: to offer stamps over the Internet. The USPS licensed its stamp verification to Stamps.com, which is now public with a market capitalization of over $1.5 billion.

Jim McDermott and his two colleagues, Ari Engleberg and Jeff Green, have since left the company and started another called Archive.com. Of course, they are now old hands at raising money (and in keeping a bigger chunk for themselves). The lessons they learned in launching Stamps.com were extremely valuable, not the least of which was the potential role of government. McDermott shared some of what he learned:

> True alliances are hard to make with the government. The reason is that they are interested in fairness rather than a strategic advantage, and when dealing with the government that means that they want to align but not exclusively. The idea is that the general public will benefit. The other issue is that the government fears failure. So you have to be very clear as to why you absolutely will not fail and why you will succeed. Also don't stereotype—we found the USPS to be very efficient. William Henderson [postmaster general at the time] had done a great turnaround—after all, the USPS would be the sixth largest corporation in the United States if they were in the private sector. And they have been increasingly exposed to market forces with FedEx and UPS and are aware of competition.

McDermott and his colleagues did their homework. They actually started the process with a series of cold calls to find the right person.

They were steered to a program called the Information-Based Indicium Program (IBIP),[5] which helped them put together a cogent proposal and prepare for their first meetings with the USPS. Of course, they also had the learning that came from presentations to venture capitalists. As most entrepreneurs do, they learned on the job.

Their approach is an excellent baseline from which to begin any presentation, whether to angels, VCs, or the government. The preparation meant that the trio would not show up at USPS and have a bad meeting. Once they got deeper into the discussions, they learned to send drafts accompanied by phone calls to the stakeholders before they showed up for meetings in order to smooth out the issues beforehand. Stamps.com received licensing (nonexclusive, true, but nevertheless a window of opportunity that beat the competition) that was the foundation of the business. Once they had that, the partners were off and running.

At times the government can be the entrance into the Internet. That is what happened in the United Kingdom for the venerable 200-year-old Chubb, part of the Williams PLC family and a name that is synonymous with security worldwide. (See Figure 2.3.)

However, not being an Internet-ready company (see Chapter 1), Chubb was concerned about finding the right resources to bring them quickly into the new economy. The U.K. government had created a consortium of experts to evaluate Internet trading and the infrastructure needed to support an Internet-ready economy.[6] This forum is made up of lawyers, legislators, consultants, and technology experts who look at many different aspects of the Internet (e.g., the framework for contracts that would be enforceable over the Net, legislative issues, privacy issues). Using that Spider Network, conveniently organized by the U.K. government, Chubb was able to easily and quickly interface with and create the beginnings of its own garage.com-type groupings of experts who would make the company Internet-ready.

Another challenge could result in the United States should the government decide to tax transactions on the Internet. Some members of Congress feel that taxing e-sales would be tantamount to destroying the greatest job-creating engine the United States has ever known. Representative John R. Kasich (R-Ohio) has said, "E-Commerce presents nothing less than a second Industrial Revolution."[7] He would ban all state and local taxes on Internet sales. The resolution of this debate could profoundly affect the ways in which Americans shop and retailers and e-tailers do business. It could also affect the relationship between Washington and the states, since some states have sales taxes and others don't. The discrepancy between retailers who pay taxes and e-tailers who don't will mean that more merchants will go to the Net to increase margins and profits in a relatively tax-free environment. If sales taxes diminish appreciably, state governments will be left with serious shortfalls. At this time, for example, Dell Computer has refused to collect sales taxes. Gateway, however, has been collecting taxes for online and catalog sales in states where its remote sales operations are located.

This issue remains unresolved. I raise it here because the government is your strategic partner. You cannot afford to wait for others to sort out these issues for you. Activist lobbying, proactive political influence, and good friends in high places at both the state and federal level are integral to your success. These stakeholders will play a role in your future. You should become active in industry associations and political groups at every level of government. We are in the early stages of the development of a whole new economy. Never again in your lifetime will you have a better opportunity to contribute to the rules by which we live. If you consider the government as a strategic partner, possibly even as a competitor with whom you are forced to collaborate, your FastStrategy and implementation plans should include some activity and resources for managing this relationship in as proactive a mode as feasible. Could Microsoft have better managed its relationship with the federal government? Intel, when faced with federal government action, took matters very seriously and handled them with careful attention and minimal arrogance. The matter dissolved quite rapidly. There is definitely something to be gained in regarding the government as a potential partner—albeit maybe not the most desirable one!

Governments in countries other than the United States may be involved in your e-business activities from the inception. Certainly the Singaporean government has taken a proactive role in proclaiming a commitment to a wireless economy by putting its money where its mouth is and dedicating funds and resources to make this happen. (See Chapter 6 for more on the global picture.)

The Lawyers' Checklist: FastAlliances Tool #11

The legal and consulting communities have seen a windfall of opportunity in the new economy. Many have created venture funds to participate in their clients' good fortune; others take equity in addition to fees. Everyone in these professions is developing some sort of specialty in the Internet space. Ask your counsel the following questions:

- How many of these have you done?
- How short can you make the contract? Make it as boilerplate as possible so that you won't have to wordsmith ad nauseam.
- Who is the expert in your firm on intellectual property rights? (This is the major issue in most alliances.)
- What is the decision-making process in your firm, and who will be working on this project?
- References? Whom else do you represent and how will you be sure to avoid conflicts of interest?

If possible, have legal counsel attend all the in-house executive briefing sessions to ensure that they are up to speed regarding all the issues before the deal comes in the door. Same for accounting firms. My preference when hiring consultants for my own companies was to stay with the boutique firms. They have lower overhead, you get what you pay for (instead of high fees and junior associates, you get lower fees with more senior people and you have their full attention). Although it may take a while for the boards of large companies to catch on to this (since a certain cachet often accompanies the appointment of huge mainline consulting firms), they can generally get better advice at lower fees from small, highly specialized firms.

Jim McDermott says, "The lawyers are the most important. They are also the most expensive. But if the legal stuff is not done right you can really get into trouble. There is parity in accounting firms—not much to differentiate them—but not with the lawyers. You need them early."

Gary Trujillo, an attorney with an MBA who practices law in Silicon Valley, agrees. Gary works on the front lines in the corporate department of Morrison & Foerster LLP's Palo Alto office. He also represents Archive.com, whose founders are Trujillo's friends from business and law school. Many of his opinions of the critical success factors for FastAlliances mesh with this quote from Jeff Yang, a partner of the Menlo Park office of venture capitalist IBP/Red Point Ventures: "It used to be that the big ate the small; now the fast eat the slow." Trujillo summarized the situation:

> One of the biggest challenges is operating on Internet time. Change happens regularly and it happens quickly. Because of the success of many Internet companies and Internet entrepreneurs, people and money have been attracted to almost anything that is Internet-related. The result is that for any given Internet market, there is likely to be fierce and well-funded competition. Recently, the vital importance of first-mover advantage in the Internet space has become painfully apparent. It is almost always the case that the entrepreneur believes so strongly in the idea that he or she cannot believe that such a great idea did not occur to others as well. Whether real or imagined, for most Internet entrepreneurs the sensation of a competitor breathing down their neck is unavoidable. That sensation, combined with the enthusiasm of the founders, increases the level of stress. While we place a lot of value on the enthusiasm of the founders, we invariably try to temper that enthusiasm with caution. That said, a sense of urgency still seems to surround most everything an Internet entrepreneur does. The result is that deals (for example, a round of venture financing) that used to take a month to complete are now expected to be completed in half that. For some types of deals—again, a round of venture financing is a good example—the terms are increasingly standardized. The established Silicon Valley firms have been dealing with one another for so long, there just aren't that many new things that come up in a classic VC deal. In addition, when you know you will face the same attorneys regularly, sometimes as company counsel, sometimes as investors' counsel, you quickly learn that it doesn't pay to grind the other side on minor deal points. Transactions that are less contentious benefit the client, because less time and less money are spent arriving at a reasonable compromise. Now that many of the firms that traditionally did not have offices in the area are setting up here, there is a noticeable difference in the time it takes to get a deal done.

There are some differences in the way a lawyer will advise a client in a FastAlliances. Trujillo explains: "What's different now is that the speed of change and transaction flow has increased the risks, so exceptional foresight and planning is necessary. The other significant change is that in the past, entrepreneurs had some level of business knowledge. Now many of them don't, especially early-stage companies who haven't brought in professional management."

Most lawyers work long hours. Trujillo's clients are on such a fast track that it's sometimes overwhelming. Nevertheless, he loves it:

> Of course, there is also new ground broken daily as the technology driving the Internet evolves. The lines of competition are not as clearly defined as in the past. The technology allows for greater benefits to be gained from forming strategic alliances. While the basic premise may still apply, achieving a greater value from the combination of assets that can be achieved by both entities operating individually, the ways in which assets can be combined, have changed. Content sharing, co-branded web sites, hyperlinks between sites, and so forth all present unique challenges to an attorney trying to protect the interests of his or her client by memorializing the intent of the parties in a document. In the past, when similar challenges have arisen, it was easy to rely on the historical database of knowledge that exists in any office of a major law firm. Because the depth of knowledge may not be sufficient, it has become critical to look instead to the breadth of knowledge. For example, as of the writing of this book, Morrison & Foerster LLP is comprised of over 850 lawyers practicing in 16 different offices worldwide. While it is possible that an issue could arise that has not been addressed by anybody here in Palo Alto, it is unlikely that that holds true across the firm. To facilitate the exchange of information among offices, we have instituted something call *e-Lawyers,* which is an e-mail forum that attorneys can turn to when difficult questions arise. Participants tend to be those whose practice revolves around electronic technology, so they not only have experience that they can bring to bear, but they also tend to keep current on new issues as they effect e-business. On a regular basis, participants receive information regarding recent developments and updates on significant developments. Participants also use the forum to ask questions, with the responses being shared among all participants, making for an efficient distribution of knowledge.

In addition to discussing general issues the lawyers face when negotiating FastAlliances in e-business, Trujillo also shared with me a number of deal points that he and his colleagues at Morrison & Foerster have negotiated for clients. I have summarized the key elements that seem to be critical negotiating factors. Of course, this list cannot replace sound legal advice from your lawyer, who will have access to facts that might affect the application of each of these points. However, the list will provide a helpful starting point.

The Lawyers' Checklist (Morrison and Foerster): FastAlliances Tool #11

1. **Will a distinct entity be formed as a vehicle through which the relationship will be conducted? If so, what is the appropriate legal form—partnership, corporation, limited liability company (LLC), or limited liability partnership (LLP)—for the entity?**
2. **Does the nature of the relationship result in its being subject to any specific regulatory issues, particularly antitrust or Hart-Scott-Rodino issues?[8]**
3. **Are the entities based in the same jurisdiction? If not, has adequate consideration been given to issues of foreign law? For example, assuming intellectual property is involved, is there any risk from it being developed or used offshore?**
4. **In terms of the goals of the relationship, what is the nature and value of each party's contribution to the effort, and is that value accurately reflected in the proposed terms of the relationship?**
5. **What is the potential for conflict as the relationship develops? Is there something about the culture of the entities or the personalities of the people involved that makes conflict likely?[9]**
6. **Have the parties carefully considered any contingencies that may arise and prepared for them?**
7. **What is the planned duration of the relationship? Is an exit strategy in place for the termination of the relationship?**
8. **How will the parties address disputes that arise between them? Have the parties planned any form of alternative dispute resolution such as arbitration or mediation?**
9. **Does either party have existing or planned affiliations or relationships that could potentially be a source of conflict for the other party?**

(continued)

The Lawyers' Checklist (Morrison and Foerster): FastAlliances Tool #11

10. Has a representative from each entity been selected to be the primary point of contact during the term of the relationship?

Since technology is the basis for e-business, it's no surprise that most of the relationships proposed in that context revolve to some extent around intellectual property. Since many of these companies will live or die based on the success of the technology and the company's ability to protect it, it stands to reason that particular attention is paid to IP issues.

11. Do the parties in fact own, or have a license to use, the intellectual property they propose to contribute to the relationship?
12. Are both parties licensing the same technology? After the strategic relationship is formed, will one license be sufficient? If so, is there any reason why one party rather than the other should be responsible?
13. If a party's right to intellectual property is in question, have adequate provisions been made, in the form of representations and warranties, to allocate the risk between the parties?
14. Assuming that each party's intellectual property rights are certain, have adequate provisions been made to protect those rights with respect to both the other party and possible third parties?
15. Are there any significant licensing issues between the parties themselves? If licenses will be granted, what will be the scope (in terms of geography and exclusivity) and duration of those licenses?
16. Are there any Internet-specific legal issues present, such as privacy or potential infiltration by hackers?
17. Will anything of value be produced (software for example) as a result of the relationship? If so, have the issues of ownership been resolved?
18. Will data or user information be collected? If so, will it be limited? Who will own the data or information?

The Lawyers' Checklist (Morrison and Foerster): FastAlliances Tool #11

19. **Will content be shared among the parties, and is access exclusive or will it be available to third parties?**
20. **Will links be established between the parties' respective web sites, and which party will be responsible for developing and maintaining those links?**
21. **Which party will determine the functionality and the look and feel of the links?**
22. **If advertising space is available, for example on a co-branded web site, how will that space be allocated and how will revenue be split?**
23. **Will a press release announce the relationship? Who will be responsible for its content? How much will be disclosed?**

Morrison and Foerster's e-business lawyers clearly know what they are doing in this space. Other firms also have expertise and experience. In fact, most national and international law firms have groups that focus on the e-business environment. The question is, how many deals have they done and with what results? Corporations may use these firms as outside counsel to help their in-house lawyers become more knowledgeable or they may outsource jobs to them. With all the smoke and mirrors out there, it pays to do some research rather than relying on the fancy brochures. In addition, even settling for a junior associate in a firm with a good reputation in this arena could be unwise. An inexperienced lawyer with poor supervision may be no better than hiring a firm with little knowledge about e-business.

The Venture Capitalists

Venture capitalists are not a one-dimensional group. They come in various sizes and preferences. The traditional Venture Capital group consists of representatives of institutional investors. And then there's Bill Hambrecht.

Bill Hambrecht is a legend in the venture capital community, having participated as an early investor in Apple, Adobe, Genentech, and Netscape. He also founded the first technology-centric investment bank, Hambrecht & Quist. Brian Frank, director of venture capital at Hambrecht's new investment firm, describes how Hambrecht is innovating again:

> When Bill left Hambrecht & Quist to form W.R. Hambrecht, he wanted to build a new investment bank from scratch, based on technology enabled by the Internet. For example, he invented a new method to price and allocate IPOs, OpenIPO, through a dutch auction. The method has gotten support from both retail investors and institutions such as American Century, American Express, Fidelity Investments, and Instinet, a division of Reuters. The dutch auction is substantially different than the legacy pricing method. In the old process, a traditional investment banker builds a book of interest from their favorite institutional clients and then prices the deal at a substantial discount to reward those clients. These investors are often short-term investors who flip the stock, and the process invariably leaves a lot of the money on the table for the issuing company. The game is that the investment bankers make money, but the company doesn't—and ends up with a lot of volatility in their stock, going up maybe 100 percent the first day and trickling down thereafter. So Bill said, "Why don't we allow more people to indicate their interest, real interest, both smaller and larger institutions, and they can bid whatever the market will bear?" A baseline clearance price can be set, those who bid under that price will not get any equity, and everyone above it will share and get in on the deal. So Bill has created a technology-centered, emerging-growth-focused, principal-and-agent investment bank.

On the venture side, W.R. Hambrecht has also tried to do things differently. The firm does not have a venture capital fund. Instead, it invests off its own balance sheet and syndicates a portion of each investment to high-net-worth electronic brokerage clients. The majority of the deals Hambrecht invests in are in b2b, Internet infrastructure, and telecommunications firms. As Frank explained:

> We are very opportunistic and will also consider alternative investments such as incubating companies or purchasing the orphan divisions of large corporations. Overall, we have built a portfolio of 45 companies, with seven liquidity events to date. As part of our

> goal of attracting high-net-worth investors, we are building a [Spider] network of angel investors. The difference between our firm and others is that we invest our own firm's capital and the remainder comes from a syndicate that we put together. Our whole approach is targeted at eliminating the closed-room allocation of deals, which was the way it was always done.

The company's web site features the OpenIPO, traditional IPO offerings, private equity offerings, private equity finance offerings (which are password-protected), research reports, and complete online brokerage capability. Hambrecht also has a number of alliances that create e-business competency in the company. One is with Fidelity, one of the largest online brokerages. Another is with Instinet, the leading off-exchange trading network and a subsidiary of Reuters, and through it, OpenIPO reaches more than 95 percent of all institutional trading desks. Other partners include companies like Novell for technology and ePartners (part of News Corp., a global media company).

Bill Hambrecht and his firm have created multiple Spider Networks with a Cool Decision Process that has leveraged his sterling reputation and connections to create a new way of raising money and of managing, analyzing, and creating a portfolio of investments. W.R. Hambrecht is a cutting-edge, flexible, state-of-the-art organization. I spoke with Bill Hambrecht about how he has started a revolution in his industry.

> The dutch auction is appropriate since the Internet has enabled us to communicate with lots of people and gave us a tool to reach out to people who have not been included in the process before. In the current distribution channels of brokerage firms, they tend to give the deals to their best clients. So even if you could communicate with large numbers of the company's customers or affinity groups who would be interested in the company's stock, they still didn't get any stock since the deal was deliberately underpriced and the guaranteed profit was given to investment firms' best customers. The only way was to give an allocation system based only on someone's interest in paying a certain price, as opposed to the old way, which was preference based on the amount of commission business they did with a firm.

Hambrecht's Spider Network came in handy in starting the ball of credibility rolling in his direction. He explained how, in spite of stakeholder reluctance, he found the right FastAlliances partners:

> Fidelity and Instinet were the two very important opinion influencers. Large institutions received very favorable treatment in the old type of funding syndicates. So we needed to find someone who had a broader vision and could see things strategically. The president and principal owner are two people at Fidelity who are always thinking ahead, and they could see the potential. We have changed the rules of distribution. The old way gave investment bankers lots of leverage since they could offer their clients underpriced deals. We have allowed people to have equal access to the shares on an auction basis rather than on a preferential commission basis. Many firms have not wanted to participate in this since they can make so much money the old way. Many Internet companies philosophically agree with what we are doing, but it is hard for them to turn down a financial services company who would then make a market in their stock. We are trying to sell a logical way of pricing an offering.

With volatility in the stock market, unpredictable stock pricing has given Hambrecht's ideas even more validity. He explained:

> The volatility in the market is healthy for us. The point we try to make is best illustrated by looking at the example of Palm. They went public at $38. The stock traded as high as $130. Today they are at $30. In the first few days that their stock traded publicly, many of the original shareholders sold and made good money. Even if they held their stock, $38 to $30 isn't bad. But now Palm is probably left with a group of shareholders who paid from $170 on down. So most of their shareholders have lost a lot of money and start judging the company as a dog or loser. Our system could be a driving force of rationalizing the market. We are trying to take out a lot of the emotion where people jump in—its what I call a *sucker play.* It's destructive in the long term. It's not bad to give a slight advantage to the first time buyer, but not 130 points.

Time will tell whether W.R. Hambrecht's approach will prevail.

There are many aspects to the venture capital relationship. One is selecting the investment banking firm that will make the IPO happen or sell the company. But even though that may be the goalpost, there are a lot of hurdles to overcome before that moment. From the very first second of money raising, the VC/investee relationship needs attention. When things go well, everyone is happy. When they don't, the problem must be managed with a strategy rather than permitted to deteriorate into personality slashing. The first step is raising the venture capital. Jim McDermott, cofounder of Stamps.com, gives solid advice in choosing the venture capital investors:

1. Pick a group or individuals who have had management experience. Don't have someone who has never managed a business or been in operations. It's like asking someone to coach football who has never played the game—insanity!
2. Ask for coaching and management teaching from your VCs who have had management experience. Bounce ideas off them and learn from their experience.
3. Choose VCs with a strong network and a willingness to tap into that network. Ask them about their Spider Network before you make a decision. Confirm their commitment to connect you into that.
4. Be sure they are a source of long-term funding. You can't spend all your time raising money or you will not be able to run and grow the business.
5. Manage expectations. Be careful of what you promise. Underpromise and overperform.
6. Prevention is more effective than cure. Keep the VCs informed and choose them well. It is difficult (nearly impossible) to implement damage control when things go wrong. The first time, be candid (especially if the VC is a businessperson, he or she will understand that in business things happen that were not planned) and have a plan to fix it. The second time, VCs who have not run businesses will run for the hills and look to dump the company (sell it or cease funding).

Another interesting phenomenon occurs when a traditional company joins with venture capitalists to raise money for the development of its e-business. A case in point is Toys 'R' Us, whose CEO Robert Nakasone decided to create *the* online retail store for the toy business by the end of 1999. Toys 'R' Us approached Benchmark Capital, a VC firm that has had spectacular success with companies such as eBay and Ariba. Benchmark committed to bring in the dot-com self-esteem group of employees and to partially fund the venture. The deal was announced—and then fell apart. The reason? Good old-fashioned tribal control and territoriality. Benchmark wanted enough control to get what it was used to—unlimited potential returns. The company was not interested in playing the role of consultant to the corporation. In addition, the online business had not resolved the issue of channel conflict and was unwilling to compete with its own bricks-and-mortar stores. VC Benchmark and traditional Toys 'R' Us were too far apart in culture and personality. (See Chapter 5 for more on this subject.)

Three leading venture capitalists in Los Angeles are Brad Jones of Redpoint Venture Capital, Bill Woodward of Avalon Investments, and Todd Springer of Trident Capital. All feel that alliances are among the top three critical success factors in e-business—with some qualifications. Here are some of the methodologies they used with their portfolio firms. I have extrapolated from their interviews with me, added some hypothetical chatter, and put it into the form of a panel discussion. (Trying to get these fellows together is similar to herding cats, so I have taken literary license and created a "virtual" meeting! This is done in good humor and with great respect for each of these high-energy leaders.)

BRAD JONES OF REDPOINT VENTURES: I have been around a while, guys. Our firm is made up of people from Brentwood Capital. You could call us the graybeards of the LA VC community, and that would sum up our experience well. We have been in the trenches a while, and there isn't much we haven't seen. If you ask me what we like to invest in, it's pretty simple. We don't want to make a little money—we are in for the winners. And that means the company must represent a platform change in the new economy, not just a rerun.

TODD SPRINGER OF TRIDENT CAPITAL: What's new about that? We all want the winners. Let's get to the point quickly: The market we invest in has to be growing aggressively, the management must be top quality, with domain expertise, not just Internet knowledge. Most important, our target company has a structural advantage—even an unfair advantage. We get over 5,000 business plans annually, and there are many competitive players in each arena. We want the one company that stands out. Maybe it's the management team that has had great success before; or it could be in their product or service differentiation or better technology. We want to know the company will have at least a 6- to 12-month lead. Frankly, for structural advantage we look closely at the alliances. Are they vertical alliances? If so, can they be exclusive? Or are the relationships part of a combination channel strategy with an alliance approach that gives ubiquity to the company? For example, we have an investee company called I-Benefits. They are in a vertical market—smaller companies who could outsource their human resources function. Instead of disintermediating the benefits broker, I-Benefits is working with a national network of brokers and is offering its service to employers with the benefit brokers by their sides. This is the kind of structural advantage that makes the difference to us. The company either gets it and can create these deliverables or we are not interested.

BILL WOODWARD OF AVALON VENTURES: LA's the place for the new dot-coms. There is incredible growth happening here. Fortunately, we have the deal flow and the network. [I am sure he meant to say *Spider Network*, just didn't get it out in time.] I am essentially a technology person, so I am looking for new spins on business models. There is no doubt that there is some consolidation happening. Our focus now is more on software infrastructure than on building brands. We have 25 investee companies—I guess we are quite different from your group, Brad.

BRAD: Well, we have a network, and we, too, are looking for new spin on an idea. We commonly coinvest with others. Generally, however, we don't have permanent alliances for ourselves. The reason is that if we did we might preclude ourselves from working with the alliance competitors. We have to be able to work with everyone. But we sure do have contacts—banks, lawyers, investment bankers.

BILL: When we look at an opportunity, we have to look at it against the returns that we have been receiving. But our perspective is different. With respect to my colleagues here, I was an operator. I have been an entrepreneur, too. I consider this my competitive advantage. I make sure that the companies we invest in get my expertise and my time. I spend a lot of energy in doing business development for our investee companies and helping to hire the right people. Plus, I understand the fanaticism that is required to succeed in a start-up. You have to be obsessed. I've been there. Besides, I invest my own money—and that gets the mind focused, if you know what I mean!

BRAD: There is no doubt about that! You may have been an entrepreneur, but believe me, I (and my network) have been around a while in this business, too. Things are really different in venture capital now compared to the 1980s. Then, it was on a much smaller scale. The size of the market is larger now. In the 1980s, building $50 to $100 million in annual revenues was good enough. Now that's multiplied by a factor of 10. And we can get that only from companies that have either unique technology or some competitive advantage protected by patent or trade secret. Alliances alone won't do that.

BILL: Okay, but alliances can leverage it into the market and grab the share needed to be in the front of the pack. We are no longer saying to portfolio companies, "You need to raise more money." Now we are saying, "You have to *make* money."

BRAD: Sure . . .

TODD: Can I ever get a word in? The real issue here (since the purpose of this panel is to give the readers of this book some concrete methodologies) is this: What are the deliverables that every VC looks for? I mentioned our three deliverables: market, structural advantage, and management. Management is of particular concern since other problems arise after the companies start growing. They are equally important if you want to have the big win. What is the maturity and expertise of the management team as the company changes? CEOs have different skill sets. Some are more suited to start-ups than to companies growing from $10 to $100 million, and then again from $100 million to over $1 billion.[10] So management has to change. And that causes lots of problems. Also, success breeds complacency. If the company is growing too fast in the open capital market and valuations soar, it tends to become overconfident. We encourage our companies to be continually paranoid and assume the competition is nipping at their heels. Of course, not all companies will reach this level. But if they meet our initial three criteria, the possibility is there. So I would advise wanna-be's to come to the VC only when they have our deliverables all worked out.

If they do, we want them. If they don't, go see Bill. . . .

BILL: Very funny. Remind me the next time you want us to join one of your deals. . . .

TODD: Just kidding . . . sort of. . . .

BRAD: Will you guys cut it out? Lets get to the crux of the question. What kinds of alliances would we like to see our companies doing? I can tell you from our point of view—we think the Internet is into much more than a three- to five-year cycle. Big companies are being created here, and if you understand the power of the Internet in lowering costs and increasing productivity, you can see that it has affected every area of the economy. It is still at a very early stage, and I feel that it will be impacting us for the next 30 to 50 years. Many alliances are created fast, but they better transition into the longer, more stable ones if they are to remain valuable.

BILL: I agree. In addition, we believe that the time of the money grab is over. Companies have to have a strong business model *now,* not five years from now. Alliances are critical if you have to build brand or add onto your technology base.

TODD: In fact, we consider a key position in our portfolio companies to be the vice president of business development because this person can create competitive advantage for a company if he or she is good.

BRAD: And the big opportunity, which is presenting itself as a major problem at the moment, is to find the professional managers who will run these large companies that are being created. It's already happening—just look around at some of the larger companies. They are being run by professionals; the founders have moved on. It's just very difficult to find these managers—everyone wants them. We are investors in Stamps.com, and the original founders have gone on to start other companies.

BRAD: That's my cell phone ringing. . . . Gotta go.

BILL: That's my cell phone ringing, my pager, too. . . . Gotta go.

TODD: That's both my cell phones ringing, my palm pilot signaling, and my pager vibrating. . . . Gotta go.

The need for professional managers means that as the click world has realized the value of the brick world, the integration and management skills of both have started to overlap.[11] Managing creative people, technogeeks, entrepreneurs, and those who fall into the personality categories discussed in Chapter 5 is no easy undertaking. I know—I did it. And many of my clients (Compaq, Sun, and others) have learned how to improve the way they do it as the challenges change. But managing them well takes experience, and many dot-com entrepreneurs don't have that. (Pages 144ff discuss dot-com self-esteem and the need to understand and manage it.) *Adult supervision* is a term that I have heard used in some dot-coms. Young managers and entrepreneurs who are going to be winners eagerly inhale whatever wisdom they can get—from any source and (of course) in fast time. But that may not be enough. Often, the only solution is for the fraternity/sorority-type atmosphere to be adapted to include some fairly clear metrics that define expectations for performance, follow-through, and delivery. Many gray-haired managers start as consultants to a company, then slide into operating positions (if that is their preference) as they are accepted, respected, and valued. As the executive labor shortage increases, this will become the standard, not the exception.

The Corporate Strategic Venture Partner

Another kind of venture capitalist is the corporate venture investor. Although many of these operate like an internal venture group within a company, there is a difference. Their underlying interest in a company may be in the technology or business activities rather than as a straight venture investment.

James Goldfarb, who works in strategic ventures for MP3.com[12] and was formerly with Bain Capital and Knowledge Universe, explained in a recent interview:

> We are interested in strategic investments. This is a combination of venture capital and classic business development. At MP3, my focus is helping to structure and negotiate acquisitions and direct investments in other companies who are major strategic relationships. Then there is the partner-marketing group that works closely with partners to be sure they are happy. It does feel as though we are making it up as we go along, however. In my former

> positions in investment banking, when doing a buyout or classic equity investment, there were lots of standard parameters. Now there are so many new services and products with uncertainty about exactly how they are going to work and be accepted. When you try to value that with another organization, it gets complicated. Most often, you have to leave parts of the deals undefined. Companies' business plans are changing so often and so radically that it benefits both sides to have flexibility and openness. If you are dealing with partners who don't trust each other or with deal makers from the old school of bureaucratic processes, you get much more defined terms and tighter implementation procedures, which slows down the deal making and decreases flexibility. We call it the *tiptoe deal*. We often start off with low-risk, low-reward relationships (see Chapter 9) to see how well we work together. Many of our deals are still in the initial stages since, although we are a public company with a huge market capitalization, we had only eight employees as of January 1, 1999. These were really the early days of our corporate life. (As of early 2000, we had 300 and growing!)

Many corporate deals include equity stakes in their partners. Goldfarb had some thoughts on this, too:

> Possibly, equity stakes cause companies to overdeliver. But it is more often the personal relationship between the parties. In many deals, the CEOs have a great relationship; the deal gets done without defining it clearly; and it can be very successful. My attitude is that life is too short to be dealing with people who are difficult. Could that be considered arrogant? Not really—it's more that I feel there is so much to be done that I want to focus on projects that have the potential for success with likable people and not waste effort with those who are difficult.

The FastStrategy may be no more than a few sentences. Goldfarb described it this way: "These are the strategic principles: Focus on viral marketing and no-touch (we want our business to grow while we sleep and on holidays); don't spend too much money; and be sure the partner is compatible and trustworthy. That's it—ultimate viral leverageability!"

Stakeholders may also include those who actually hold equity in another company to accelerate the FastAlliances commitment level.

Many large organizations are taking equity in the b2b sector. IBM now owns a piece of Ariba and i2Technologies (companies that create Internet marketplaces for businesses). IBM's marketing savvy will enhance the relationship in excess of the monetary value it adds, and it's also contributing intellectual property to both ventures, as well as competency in both FastAlliances and traditional ones. Microsoft has put $100 million into VerticalNet[13] in order to link business-oriented web portals to Microsoft's network of web sites. The marketing partnership and web page/storefront promotions sponsored by Microsoft will generate good revenues for VerticalNet—and Microsoft now has a seat on its board. This is typical of what I call the *Preemptive FastAlliances.*

The Preemptive FastAlliances

What is it? Although there may be a positive result for both companies, the real motivation behind a preemptive alliance is for one or more of the partners to preempt a competitor. That is to say, the grabber (company X) is grabbing a grabbee (company Y) in such a way that company X will preempt any competitor from partnering with company Y in that particular application or market space.

This effectively takes company Y out of the competitive play and inserts it into the company X network of partners. The result is a different strategic positioning for the connected companies and possibly a new set of market dynamics for all players to contemplate. In the e-business world, the Spider Network creation is often implemented through a series of preemptive FastAlliances. It's important to recognize the distinguishing factors of these kinds of relationships.

For example, Microsoft has made an art of preemptive alliances, such as the one with VerticalNet. By ensuring that VerticalNet will use Windows 2000 software and other Microsoft technology on its business portals, Microsoft has effectively preempted any other competitor from coming into that very important market niche. In addition, the board seat gives Microsoft a window (pardon the pun) on whatever is going on in that space. It is clearly a winning, preemptive stroke for Microsoft in its duel for Internet dominance.

How are preemptive alliances different from other alliances? The main difference is that preemptive partners are generally not good partners. A purely preemptive play will bring a partner to the table who delivers access, size, and market share—sort of the Godzilla approach. What preemptive partners often *don't* deliver, however, are some of the capabilities and resources that are essential to the management of effective partnerships, including the following:

- Willingness to increase mutuality after the deal is done (actively building the other partner's benefits so that value increases for both partners)
- Compromise in resolving differences
- Commitment of time and resources in the management of the relationship
- Internal champion with increasing interest in the relationship over time

Preemptive alliances have been used for decades, generally in the form of acquisitions with the intent to control and/or remove the grabbee from the market or to control its activities therein. Now, the market grab for share, presence, and brand is propelling this approach into a familiar one for all e-business players.

What are the downsides of a preemptive alliance for the grabbee? The grabbee companies in preemptive alliances run the risk that their market-heavy partner may decide to become a competitor. The question they must consider is this: How will the grabber manage the alliance? The answer depends on the level of priority the grabber places on this alliance. This is what I call the *project personality*.[14]

Project personality is the priority placed on the alliance by the partners. It does not have to be the same for each partner, although some companies prefer that it be of similar priority to all partners or they will not enter the relationship. Corning is one such company that prefers a level of commitment similar to its own, especially in joint ventures. Other companies (e.g., USAA, a U.S.-based insurance company primarily for U.S. veterans and their families) are perfectly willing to partner with companies that have a much higher project priority than they do. USAA has many suppliers that consider USAA their most important customer (i.e., the project personality is higher for the supplier than it is for USAA). USAA helps its supplier alliance partners become more professional at partnering[15] by setting high-quality standards, metrics, and monitoring processes.

For VerticalNet, the preemptive FastAlliances with Microsoft was of great importance. It could be said to be at least a midlevel project priority, which is called *market-extending,* or could even be of significant importance, a *bet-the-farm* alliance, because the partnership could be said to be integral to the future survival and strategic positioning of the company. As such, I would expect that the grabbee will devote excellent resources (time, human, and financial capital) to making sure the alliance is positioned for success.

Preemptive alliances typically do not carry the same priority for the grabber. In most cases, the alliances are likely to be considered experimental—or perhaps even less than experimental (extremely low priority)—in terms of importance within the organization. By their very nature, experimental alliances may create interest in the initial stages of alliance development, but, should conflict arise, the grabber will be unlikely to resolve it and will withdraw or lose interest in the alliance. This being the case, grabbers are apt to devote very limited resources to its implementation and will expect to see concrete results in a short amount of time. If its relationship with VerticalNet falls into hard times, it will be interesting to see whether Microsoft commits extra resources to manage through the problems or loses interest.

What can smaller companies do to enhance the likelihood of success of preemptive FastAlliances? Smaller, start-up companies should take steps to protect themselves when partnering with well-established companies. One way is by using *speed.* Not only must the relationship come together quickly, but implementation and metrics of short-term milestones must be achieved quickly as well. The attention span of grabbers is extremely short. Grabbees have to get their attention when it is focused, in the early stages, and there is still some bargaining power to get what they need. In addition,

FastAlli, by Larraine Segil

approach the FastAlliances as a stepping-stone. Take immediate and aggressive action to integrate the grabber's Spider Network: Get the contact people, meet them, and start to increase the connectivity for your company. A lot can be achieved within the first month, so plan the allocation of resources in the weeks/days before deal closure and apply this leverage to the relationship in the short term. Move into the alliance with a clear understanding that the pressure to perform will be acute until the concept has been proven. This means maintaining high levels of communication with the partner company, observing its action or lack of it, and filling the gaps where necessary, finding shortcuts to approval cycles so you are not overwhelmed by the amount of paperwork that may be required until the project grows and proves its worth. Even then, the grabber partner may have little interest in being a working partner, preferring instead to provide a brand and market presence.

Many corporate venture partners may talk of partnering but, in reality, have the preemptive FastAlliances in mind. Aligning expecta-

tions for their contributions with their behaviors will be one of the challenges for the grabbee.

The Executive Search Consultant

Another stakeholder in the FastAlliances group is the executive search consultant, or headhunter. One of the best in e-business is cFour (Houston and Los Angeles). Founding partners Paul Kors and Bob Bellano, along with their associate Christine Ramstein, combine experience from the VC explosion of the 1980s with specialties in digital media, Internet companies, telecommunications, and Internet-related software. Kors looks with experienced eyes at the e-space:

> Probably the most difficult to find and the most valuable resource is an executive who understands the workings of a large company, knows how to grow a business and understands the e-business environment. A good question to ask is whether a candidate minds doing his or her own copying. In other words, if staff and support are necessary for this person to be effective, he or she is the wrong person for the job. If you are used to people reviewing your decisions, and if others are doing part of your job or your job function is duplicated somewhere else in the company, it will be tough. In e-business you must be willing to fail, to have the people who work for you observe and learn from your failures and make their own.

Compensation levels have moved to positions that would have seemed fanciful just a few years ago. Kors goes on:

> Salary levels of $225,000 to $250,000 are normal for the CEO of a dot-com, in addition to equity of 3 to 7 percent. With this package you can attract people who are making $300,000 to $400,000. The most important VP positions are marketing, sales, engineering, and business development. Each earns about $175,000, with stock varying from 1 to 3 percent. People under 30 without a college education can get to this level. The value added by the executive search team is in digging beneath the references for the subtleties. How does this person really work with others? People who give references talk in code. You have to understand the code. For example, "He really works his people" may mean "He is tough on the guys who work for him." So you follow up and ask, "How do they

> feel about him?" Then play those subtleties into the next reference, saying you understand that he works his people really hard and that people who work for him say he is way too tough—and see how the second reference responds. They may say no, his people love and respect him. Another device is to listen carefully when the person talks about his job. Is he tooting his own horn too much and taking credit for everything? Did they really do this, or were they just there when it happened? Ask who else was involved in it. Candidates who say they did it all themselves are generally stretching the truth. Check it out. Be a good and astute listener.

The executive search consultant can be a tremendous resource as an alliance partner. Kors also had some wisdom to share on managing boards:

> Dot-com boards are not like traditional boards since many of them are there as friends of the CEO or investors and are not truly unbiased. If they are VCs, they are looking for a liquidity event in the near future to benefit the class of investor they represent, sometimes to the detriment of other classes of investors. When you see a divided board, the company cannot succeed. When you see a board where there is not a single member who has a record of success, same problem. If there is no deep belief in the company's technology or in what the board is doing, your job in finding executives will fail. You are no smarter than the executives you will bring, and they will walk away from it.

Once you have hired the talent, the next challenge is to retain it. The approach has to be different. You want to manage the flow of talent into and out of the organization, not stem the flow altogether. Since it is accepted that executives will not stay with one company for life, companies must plan for attrition and manage it. Different employees and job functions will have different attrition rates and therefore different approaches to retaining them. For example, try looking at jobs as processes. Repetitive processes should be segmented so that high-skilled and costly personnel don't do them, because turnover of these employees will be expensive. In the Internet world, as with everything, no single size fits all. Managing employee attrition must be seen as segmented, specific, and different for various jobs and employee groups depending on retraining costs and relative value to the company.

With such a team—the lawyer (with real experience and a track record), the angels or VCs (with line experience and long-term commitment), the executive search consultant (with insight and piercing investigative skills), the corporate partners (who understand dot-coms and can move quickly), and the accountants and other consultants who may be on a short fuse (necessary, but don't keep them hanging around too long as their fees will drain your resources)—your e-business is poised to leverage the Spider Network of your advisors. Remember, however, to find out whether the consultants you use who have their own venture funds have created firewalls around these investments to prevent your competitive information from leaking.

All that remains (and it is *the* issue) is the viability of the business model and the people who execute it.

The Investment Bankers

The ultimate aspiration will be to associate with the golden triangle team: the *investment bankers*, the *key investors* who have stayed with you in the past and reinvested over and over as you have evolved your concept, and the *star management team*, whose members have proven their worth. When it comes to investment bankers, one of the most active in this area is J.P. Morgan.

J.P. Morgan has raised more IPO Internet capital than anyone in the world—over $5 billion as of March 2000. The company also commits its own capital to start-ups and to growing small companies in addition to making markets in and trading these companies and others in this space. I spoke with Robert Woolway, managing director of J.P. Morgan's Los Angeles office, after I watched him and his colleagues in action with a mutual client of ours: J.P. Morgan was raising money for an Internet start-up client that was partnering with a large company in a related space (my client). The irony of "large investment banker consulting with small start-up company" juxtaposed with "small boutique consulting firm (me and my partners) consulting with large corporate client" was not lost on me. I was curious about Woolway's perspective. In his opinion, "The Los Angeles community is fast becoming the hotbed for new Internet start-ups and capital raising, whereas the San Francisco office has traditionally been the place. Our approach is traditional investment banking and capital raising, and we are recognized for our history and credibility."

Maybe so. But there are new players in this space, and none more exciting than Wit Capital, an online investment bank. In order to make itself even more competitive in the fights for the big deals, Wit has bought a bricks-and-mortar investment bank (not unlike AOL buying Time Warner). Wit Capital Group bought SoundView Technology Group at the end of 1999 for its combination of institutional abilities, sales, and trading desk. Wit was known as a stock distribution outlet for individual investors. Wit Soundview is another example of the democratization of deal making (like Bill Hambrecht's vision, the auction exchanges, and other vehicles that give power to the consumer). If there is no value to be had, those who have carefully guarded access to knowledge and opportunity will be squeezed out of the system.

However, a peculiar phenomenon in this time where nothing seems to surprise us anymore is the investment banker who underprices the IPO so that the stock price goes up dramatically on the first day of trading. Traditional logic would indicate that the company suffered—since it could have raised more money if it had priced its stock higher. According to Mark L. Walsh, CEO of VerticalNet, when asked why start-ups seem to ignore pricing in an IPO, "These days an IPO is a branding event."[16] In other words, can you grab media attention? Using an underwriter with its own powerful brand will create the buzz that a start-up with a short track record will not have on its own. These firms can afford large marketing staffs and research groups who will track and promote the company's stock, especially on the first day. Some argue that the companies who "left money on the table" can make it up later with a secondary stock offering, and that it is better to oversell a stock at a low price than to undersell at a high price. However, when the inevitable corrections come (and there will be more than one in this volatile market), many of these companies may wish they had raised more money when the going was good.

As you can see, the investment banking world is a tight little club, as is the world of venture capital. Whether you are a large corporate investor or an entrepreneur, hanging out in the right company is an essential success factor. Keep in mind, however, that the web will have its way with these players as well as with those who are now creating auctions for commoditized supplies for their industries. As the WitSoundviews and Bill Hambrechts of this world democratize the IPO process, cracks will appear in the armor of the white-shoe firms. Stay tuned.

The Accountants

It would be remiss to leave out the accountants. Why? Because their time has come. Yes, the truth is upon us. The words can be heard loud and clear: *The SEC is coming!*[17] The following missiles are being loaded for launch:

1. *Recognizing revenues too soon.* Money from software upgrades should not be booked when the sale is made but before the contract is completed. Microstrategy was burned at the stake for this transgression.

2. *Using gross versus net revenues.* Now this is something my grandfather knew—and he had no schooling beyond high school: "Sell for more than you bought it for, keep your expenses low, and don't be a pig. Have integrity; do things right. You can never lose by making a profit." With this philosophy my grandfather became one of the major industrialists who built the furniture industry in South Africa in the early 1930s. This advice seems to have bypassed Priceline.com, however, which resold a $100 airline ticket for $150 and happily booked $150 in revenue (gross) instead of $50 (net).

3. *Boosting marketing expenses.* The SEC is going after Amazon.com for calling its warehousing "customer service" and some shipping costs "marketing expenses," thus inflating gross margins. My grandfather would have had a good belly laugh at that one.

The SEC has directed the Financial Accounting Standards Board (FASB) to review a range of Internet company accounting practices that could boost revenues or reduce costs unfairly. This could lead to a whole list of companies reissuing financial statements with decreased revenue figures. As revenue growth falls from its galactic highs, watch the market correct. *The accountants are coming!*

The Financial Advisors and Analysts

In a recent conversation I had with Alan McFarland of McFarland Dewey, a financial advisory firm, he discussed the FastAlliances concept as it applies to his perspective:

> Frankly, the announcement of an alliance to both ourselves and the analyst community is merely an invitation to us to investigate

further. Without the details, the announcement is next to meaningless. Yes, certainly there are those who will run up the stock price based on a large company name, such as Microsoft, associated with any company, but that was more the mode in the earlier days of the dot-com revolution. Now analysts and advisors are looking at more prudent standards of judgment and want to investigate more closely what the actual terms of the agreement are and how that will affect the cost savings, or the fulfillment issues, or the joint marketing budget, or the research investment requirements. The press release type of alliance is not as compelling as before, since various corrections have brought a level of sanity to the marketplace.[18]

Managing the expectations of all the stakeholders discussed in this chapter takes a certain kind of personality. In addition, creating the internal alliances necessary for traditional and transitional companies to develop external FastAlliances requires a set of capabilities that can be learned, but are rarely immediately visible in larger organizations. From observation and interaction with multiple groups and individuals over the past five years, I have created certain profiles. Chapter 4 lays them out for you to consider.

CHAPTER 5

Step 5: The Essential Characteristics for Business Development

Although I refer to the business development personality, in reality *every member of the executive team* must evidence these characteristics. Business development is *everyone's* job. The speed of FastStrategy execution requires every member of the team to pull in the business development direction. In order to grow the business and gain market share, creating and launching alliances may be the responsibility of the business development person but it is not a job for that person alone. Only a combined effort will achieve the result in the time parameters appropriate for e-business.

The Business Development Personality for E-space: Dot-Com Self-Esteem

Dot-com self-esteem is not only the concern of independent entrepreneurial companies, it is the foundation of the change in corporate culture that is sweeping through the brick-and-mortar world globally. Creating and adding to the business development team as well as the business development capabilities of all the management team members requires an understanding of this trait.

What do I mean by *dot-com self-esteem?* For convenience, I have assembled the most common characteristics here which should be part of the business development personality (everyone who has external contact within the top management team should evidence these characteristics):

1. Dot-com self-esteem requires leadership capabilities. "You suggested it, you go do it." The Cool Decision Process needs someone who will take charge and control and push an opportunity to completion.
2. Integrity is important in the Spider Network. In business development there are ways to work the system so you are doing not what is best for the company but rather what is best for the individual. Working with start-ups, the new currency is friends and family stock. This kind of stock is not made public knowledge, and it is essential that those working on the deal on behalf of a company not take this stock without company permission. To do so would violate your company's trust that you represent its interests in the deal—not your own.
3. Dot-com self-esteem requires not only an understanding of technology but also business knowledge. Both are necessary.
4. You must have the courage of your convictions. If you really believe in something, go to bat for it within the company and push hard (Cool Decision Process).
5. If you are the big company face (especially from the old economy), don't be arrogant—it will put dot-coms off. Be humble and win more often. (Remember the giant and the gazelle from Chapter 1.)
6. Arrogance in general is a characteristic seen a lot in e-businesses, especially in companies whose entire life has been e-business. There is no point moralizing about it. That's just the way it is. The best way to deal with it is to ignore it. As soon as you create value (e.g., doing something concrete and substantive), the attitude often changes into excitement, enthusiasm, and willingness to learn. Humility is rare. However, as failures increase in this space, it will start to appear.
7. If you deal with VCs, respect their time. The time they spend with you is time they could be cutting a deal. Don't waste it.

8. Be very prepared when dealing with outside partners or intermediaries. Have an agenda. Show the partnering opportunity and challenges, whether internal or external.

9. You'll need a traditional analytical background, but you cannot be wed to it (see Chapter 3 and the Walt Disney Internet group). You must be fast on your feet and make things happen quickly.

10. Be a good negotiator. Protect the downside from disaster (could be financial or length or shortness of term), but make the necessary trade-offs and compromises.

11. If you are already in a company with some e-business activity, make sure you develop an apprenticeship program for business development—that is, everyone who comes in is trained on the job. (Yahoo! now has MBA students making deals!) It doesn't hurt to have two to three years of background in finance (suggest people get it in a distance learning program on the web, which will let you leverage their time). After a short period of time, those hires will not only be the number two person in the deal, but will know where to ferret out good potential opportunities. If you are with a large company whose brand has position power, you could find yourself in front of the CEO of a major company (Chapter 3 and the Walt Disney Internet group).

12. Comfort with ambiguity and an ability to manage contradictions are critical capabilities. When operating at the speed of e-business, making decisions from in-depth research and access to all the facts will just about never happen. Decisions are more likely to be made on the fly, with few facts, lots of conversation, sketchy information, and a gut feeling (often from people with short-lived experiences and little to base them on). This has worked in many cases. As the experience base deepens, knowledge and wisdom will grow so that professional managers will have places to research and experts to call on if necessary. However, the new economy is too young to be able to garner much of that now.

13. Dot-com self-esteem requires the ability to take risks and make judgments while making it up as you go along. New hires may have a few moments with a senior executive (possibly the CEO in smaller companies) and then they are on their own. Often, there is no business case scenario, although there may be some principles stated regarding what the FastStrategy is. Then the dot-com self-esteem has to kick in.

14. Many e-business executives need a constant challenge. They get used to the adrenaline rush of the extreme highs (and lows) of this business: raising capital, securing huge strategic alliances, launching IPOs, attracting high-powered executives from competitors, dealing with sky-high valuations, and garnering press attention. It's tough to live without that level of excitement once you've had it. That's why these adrenaline junkies move often. Even if they make a lot of money in the first IPO as employees of the company, many will move elsewhere in order to do it again. Now the scorecard element applies—how many, how often, what industry segments have you scored in. The drudgery of day-to-day operations may not appeal, with its repetitive elements and group-diluted rewards. Meanwhile, hundreds of dot-coms are looking for high-energy managers. In this early stage of the e-business cycle, adrenaline junkies will be constantly on the move. This characteristic can be positive in that these people have experience (rare at this point), a high level of energy, and a Spider Network of contacts in the right places. Just keep their needs in mind and don't be crushed if they leave soon.

I have spoken about these issues in depth with Dr. Steven Berglas,[1] a clinical psychologist on the staff of Harvard Medical School and an instructor at UCLA's Anderson School of Management (where I sit on the advisory board of the Price Center for Entrepreneurship). His clinical perspective is interesting:

> There is a xenophobia [fear of strangers] between the professional managers of this world, MBAs pre-1995, who are generally not as sophisticated in technology systems as entrepreneurs. When they are brought into a company, there is a bifurcation in experience. Then there are the VCs who come in and fund but have little understanding of the characteristics of the management team—so the new generation gap is based on experience, not age. When you look at the skills that are needed to run and grow a business, they are orthogonal to the skills needed to attract capital. The management skills are monotony, subjugation of the ego to the ego of the organization. People are attracted to the glamour, but it is extremely unglamorous when you are trying to make a profit. So the victors will be those who will be able to combine and integrate the principles of good management into the plethora of opportunity. There is a need to communicate with empathy for the other

side's lack of understanding, whether it's brick companies or alliance partners.

One of the more interesting questions is the typology of the entrepreneur. Is there such a thing as a typical entrepreneur? Berglas interprets the conflicts that occur within a VC-funded organization this way:

> There is no single typology for an entrepreneur. They are control-seeking individuals. So when they are raising money, they attract the VC with their enthusiasm and drive that energized the start-up and the money-raising process. The VC is delighted, gives them the money, and then promptly puts constraints on the very characteristics that enticed them in the first place. They are buying a certain skill and talent and then putting it into a context where it cannot perform.

The solution may be this. Between initial funding and the IPO or sale of the company—give the entrepreneurs back their control environment, their freedom. I call it the *sandbox effect.* Put them back in the sandbox where they can create and play constructively, even provide them with seed capital to do it—and bring in professional management to run the company.

Dell Corporation has made a habit of doing this. When project managers succeed, they are "fired." That is, they are freed to do it again in a skunk works rather than being "promoted" to business manager of what they have just done. Not doing this builds the Peter principle into the organization (i.e., people rise to the level of their incompetence).

It all has to do with the definition of *success.* The implication is that once you reach the top you either sit there or get off. The irony is that neither of these actions constitutes achievement. Nor do they bring satisfaction. Berglas addresses this issue as pathological narcissism:

> People who suffer when they succeed have what I call the four A's—arrogance, a sense of aloneness, the need to seek adventure and adultery. The ones who hit all four are the televangelists. Part of what drives people who have any combination of these characteristics is realizing that the promise of the Horatio Alger story is a myth. They didn't know that money would be so dissatisfying

> when it arrived. So instead of turning inward and saying "I need a midcourse correction here" they look for more of the same. "If $1 million didn't make me happy, then maybe $2 million will." And the public humiliation of getting caught is turned around by the narcissist who says "Look at my impact on the world." Look at Dennis Levine who plotted to dupe SEC regulators with overseas bank accounts. Now he is consulting, giving lectures at business schools. He had the audacity to stand in front of students and talk ethics. You or I might have been shamed into suicide. I mean, I would die if, like Levine, I was arrested and my parents saw me dragged to jail. Something, maybe an ego deficit or an open psychological wound, makes these people obsessed with proving competence. At a certain level, success exacerbates it, making you more alone, arrogant, adventure-seeking or adulterous. You strive and strive to get more and then you wonder "How would I ever know if I am loved independent of my success? If everything was gone?" They almost have to dive off a cliff to test it.[2]

Extrapolating from these sentiments, dot-com self-esteem could be seen as the pride before the fall. However, there are those who are neither pathological nor psychologically unhealthy in their ambition. And their drive is directed not only into building the e-business opportunity, but also into community and philanthropy (fortunately supported by the right tax structure to facilitate charitable giving). They can redirect their energies into supporting the causes that make them passionate. The Gates Foundation is one example. Another is Michael Dell's Foundation and its many contributions to the Austin community.

For those who are in the dot-com space, whether as an independent company or a large organization, the real question is, "What is my passion *after* I succeed? How can I fulfill it?"

Possibly one of the most overt signs of a dot-com self-esteem is the speed with which one talks. At a recent alliance meeting between a large traditional company and a large e-business company, the distinguishing characteristics were many. However, the most obvious was the speed of presentations. Not the length, since both companies took up the same amount of time. But the speed with which the e-business executives' words reached Mach 4. Were they more erudite? Not necessarily. A major indication of maturing dot-com self-esteem is the inverse proportionality of *e-slang* (my word for spewing acronyms, unfinished sentences, buzzwords) to regular language. Namely, the less e-slang you use, the more inexperienced and non-dot-com you will appear. At this early stage in the new economy, a tribal territoriality exists. You are judged to be part of the "in crowd" if you sound, look, and speak like those who really "rock" in this space. Part of exhibiting dot-com self-esteem is knowing the lingo. Perhaps this is part of the newness and will diminish over time.

Another cycle of evolution will arise within the next 12 to 18 months. By the end of 2001, many mergers (i.e., takeovers) will take place in the dot-com environment. That is, dot-coms will acquire other dot-coms. It may be that the acquiree cannot succeed with its own brand or resources (i.e., natural consolidation of the e-business market). Or it could be that market entry points (e.g., providing portals for companies that don't want to create their own) have now been generally accepted and have fallen in value, causing companies to either ramp up or sell out. As these mergers occur, look out for another face of dot-com self-esteem. This will be the increasing tendency toward self-interest by those who are acquired and their potential difficulty in accepting the controlling regime. Many executives who are part of the acquiring entity will leave—some to retire young, some to join other e-businesses, maybe even some to join large traditional companies with their newfound skills. No matter where they go, they will spread their dot-com self-esteem culture into many avenues: government, politics, education, nonprofits, and social causes. (It's already beginning to happen.) They will change country cultures in ways that will last well into this century. Understanding dot-com self-esteem is a window into the future, not just an irritant necessary to do business in the present.

Can you learn it? Absolutely. The following example tells of an individual and a company who deliberately set out to create this self-esteem and learn from it over time. The names are fictional for confidentiality purposes, although the example is factual.

Case Study: Industrycity.com

Michael, a 24-year employee of Parentco (a large industrial conglomerate), was finishing off the laborious task of packing his bags.

He had given a commitment to the president of the European division of his company that he would join him as a troubleshooter for an eight-month period. He was going to commute for the first four months, and his family would join him for the second four. The phone rang.

"Hey, Mike, it's Tom." The chairman of Parentco, a $14 billion concern, had known him since he joined the firm while he was still in college. "I have an opportunity for you. I'd like you to develop the e-business initiative for our company."

"Wow! That sounds incredible. The problem is that I have given Jean-Pierre my commitment to help him in the Spanish project, and he has been waiting until I finished the southern deal to come over there. I gave him my word. I am going to have to turn this down."

"What if we guaranteed Jean-Pierre another person—would that help?" the chairman said.

"Well, I still feel bad. He's been waiting a while for me to get there. What about if we start the e-business project in six months?"

"Too late. We are already late in starting. It has to be now. Look, I'll call him myself. We'll get someone over there and find a way to give him the support he needs within the week. Would that do it?"

"I'm sure it would. I can call and explain, too. Is the company really committed to this? What kind of resources are you going to put behind it?"

"We are as committed as we have been to anything. You will have a serious corporate mandate. Start with a blank sheet and decide what you want, when, and where."

Mike spent the next 45 days on planes. Not only did he not have dot-com or e-business self-esteem or knowledge, he wasn't sure who did. So he started visiting companies, venture capitalists, anyone who might be able to educate him fast. He went to Dell, to Compaq, to Lucent. He met general managers of e-businesses, peers, chief procurement officers, vice presidents of business development, marketing, and especially marketing communications. He started building his Spider Network.

Mike realized that he would need internal as well as external resources. That meant getting good people from other divisions of his company. Mike had to negotiate for these people, and sometimes the chairman and CEO had to intervene to make the barriers fall away and the internal transfer happen. That was when Mike became even more confident, since the mandate from the office of the chairman of the company was weighty.

Mike learned a couple of quick lessons in his one-minute course in dot-com self-esteem.

1. He needed to interact *immediately* with customers. The entire e-business thrust is customer-centric, and his thinking had to be grounded in that perspective.

2. He needed a FastStrategy that could be flexible and responsive as well as visionary and creative.

3. *Think big, start small, and scale quickly* became the e-business motto. All of these things were done simultaneously. The company did some pilots with customers to learn about itself: What did its brand mean? What were the perceptions (right or wrong) of the company? Where were the gaps in credibility? Where were the strengths? The first e-commerce pilot programs were with customers to whom Par-

FastAlli, by Larraine Segil

entco traditionally delivered truckloads of products. The programs enabled these customers to get online to learn not only the status of their orders (commonplace), but also the historical data of their use patterns and consumptions (which added value and analysis to the data). This enabled customers to use the information in order to look backward and forward and see inventory projections for the future. Mike's e-business team created a click self-service component to add to the brick-and-telephone customer-service activities of supplier relationships.

4. The e-business team used five specific business concepts in its FastStrategy:

- Deep integration between Parentco and the customer would reduce total ownership costs by making products more convenient and buying more efficient. This was customer-specific. For example, *your* company logo is on the web page to welcome you personally and address how you and your company will do business with Parentco (similar to Dell's Premiere Page). This was called the *extranet*.
- Industrycity.com would be a new vertical industry portal. Mike's research indicated the need for a strong portal. No one was really doing it yet, and Mike felt that his team really understood the customers and the industry. His conversations with the Gartner Group and others (e.g., Forrester Research) led him to believe that although there are over 1,000 b2b vertical sites today, there would be 25,000 by 2001. His company's investment bankers predicted that b2b portals would generate over 20 percent in cost savings for industry. Figure 5.1 shows the requirements for an industry to be ripe for a vertical portal and for the portal to succeed. The potential for success in terms of the value of the brand and portal real estate is huge. Some vertical portals, like iVillage, get huge numbers of members/visitors per month (over 2.7 million), whereas portals like Yahoo! have an estimated 43 million visitors per month.
- Mike's team created a public web site as a lead management tool. This was to satisfy unplanned demand. New customers who looked up their product categories could find them on the web and make a one-time order. The sales group could then

Figure 5.1 Vertical Portal Quicktest: FastAlliances Tool #12

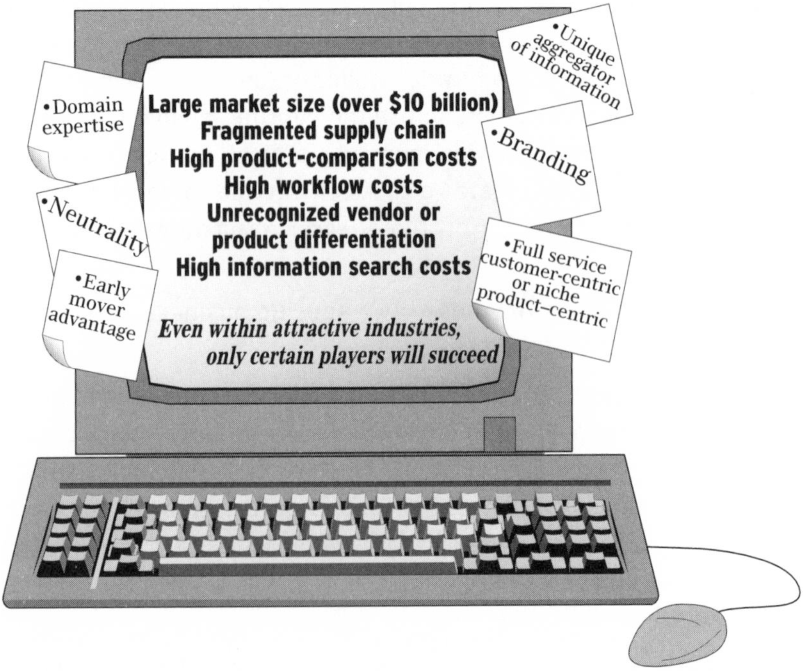

work on converting this customer to a long-term loyal user of Parentco's products and services. This would move this customer to a deeper level of integration.

- All company catalogs would be digitized so that when customers go to aggregators like Ariba or CommerceOne, Parentco would be able to source its products and services there.
- Each of the six industry segments served by Parentco was considered a vertical market. Mike felt that it was the job of his group to determine the endgame in each segment, examine each value proposition, and create an e-business approach. The evaluation was also to determine the relative importance of each industry segment and the willingness of each division president to give resources to this effort. Those who showed passion about the initiative and the Internet became key players.

Now the time came for implementation and execution. Failure was not an option. It was Mike's first test. If he could create the public web site and extranet fast and do it well, he knew that he would be given the green light for development of Industrycity.com, which was by far the most ambitious of the five FastStrategies. He put all his effort into building the group's credibility and delivering on time and within budget. It worked. The board and CEO gave him the seed money to start Industrycity.com, and team members threw themselves into the project in order to build the business case for final approval.

Mike was scheduled to get approval from the office of the chairman for the creation of Industrycity.com at the next board meeting. He realized that he was not quite ready. Issues were still unresolved concerning who would own the portal and who would run it. He agonized over what to do. Then he decided. It was better to ask for two more weeks than to make a presentation with holes in it.

"It took a lot of courage," he told me. "I wasn't sure whether I would lose credibility by not being ready, but I had to take that chance." Two weeks later, he made his presentation. Team members included the president of the industry segment from Parentco, the general manager of the e-business initiative, an interim CEO of the new Industrycity.com portal, a domain expert who had years of experience in the industry plus a customer perspective, and the treasurer of Parentco. They had been negotiating ownership and management issues for the past few weeks and had finally come into alignment. Mike knew if they were not in alignment, the board would shoot them down.

They were met with huge enthusiasm. The excitement of the group and the level of dot-com self-esteem that had evolved in the two-month process had everyone's adrenaline pumping! In fact, after the board meeting, the COO of Parentco became so enthusiastic about the dot-com possibilities that he said to the chairman, "I want to lead this new dot-com and spin it into a separate company. I have the entrepreneurial spirit, and this is a real opportunity. The money is no longer the issue for me—it's the challenge."

That set the stage for the next phase. Mike continued to hire new people from outside the company as well as from inside. He worked through the line organization to maintain his existing relationships within the whole company and to act as a responsible corporate citizen. He and the new management team went to the board on a number of occasions, laying out the risk and business model for the portal, explaining how they would make money, and relating what they heard from the customers. It was decided that Industrycity.com would be a separate entity, raising private equity and offering a stake in the new entity to all of its employees.

The team also created a partner strategy, which includes the following criteria:

- Partners must be industry leaders with national and global capabilities.
- Partners must have the same mind-set and passion—not be worried about cannibalizing their businesses.
- They need to have the capabilities to partner (i.e., they must already have digitized their own businesses).
- They need to have a strong brand in the marketplace.

The partnering methodology they will use is as follows:

- *Fast.* The six deals pending have moved fast.
- *Right level of buy-in.* This must include the CEO or top management team.
- *Marriage.* Think through lots of issues to avoid public divorces.
- *Differentiating factors regarding strategies and endgame.* Manage those.
- *Need for familiarity in the art of relationship.* Do you share the same objectives? If so and you have alignment, you will find a way to work it out.

Mike has used the Spider Network to access all the e-deals he is working on, and thus he has created a Connectivity Velocity (see Chapter 1):

> We have to have real clarity in what our value proposition is—what we bring to partners. My goal is that when we walk out of every potential partnering meeting with new candidates, I want them to say, "*Wow!* These guys really have the money, the network, and the intent. They are serious, and they are clearly going to do this. Do we

want them on our side or against us?" I make sure that our group does our homework and that we are able to negotiate from a position of strength.

Mike is building an organization. He is responsible for strategy and business development and will hire someone who will be the FastStrategy thinker, who will look over the horizon at the endgame for the customer—without day-to-day responsibilities. Industrycity.com will be looking for content providers, at least 50, and the people who do the deals will be accountable for execution (FastStrategy precepts) and will be measured by the value creation of the deal.

Mike will also have a FastAlliances competency center. This part of the organization will ensure that the deals are done right, according to metrics and ensuring value derivation. The center will offer best practices and benchmarks. It is Mike's greatest pleasure to build the organization and to see others being successful, building a sense of trust and camaraderie. Although he felt some sadness at leaving Parentco, he loves to learn and has really caught onto the dot-com self-esteem idea. Mike is always looking for challenges. He is the prototype of *intraorganization* dot-com self-esteem that will succeed. Says Mike, "I have been offered major CEO positions in the past six months. But to me, the most exciting challenge is being a dot-com CEO within (or closely attached to) a large organization. I know how to maneuver in that inherently paradoxical role. All my prior work in troubleshooting and reengineering and building businesses has taught me well and prepared me for this. I have never been happier!"

The preceding case study is good evidence that not every large company executive is heading for the garage in Silicon Valley. Some of them value the large organizational environment with brand and customer respect, and they can overlay the dot-com self-esteem on that set of experiences.

There are, however, a whole set of challenges that many headquarter-centric e-businesses have not yet faced. Chapter 6 addresses some of them.

CHAPTER 6

Step 6: Leveraging the Global E-Space

The Internet has connected the global community and accelerated entrepreneurship internationally as a result. Becoming global-savvy is an essential success factor for e-business because competition is global. The rush for customers will transcend language, culture, and geography. Only those who can flexibly adapt to all three of these variables will survive after the initial rush to the Internet is over (within the next two years). Interestingly, the traditional and transitional companies will quickly catch up once they learn how to operate in the e-business market, because they already have battle experience in the trenches of global competition.

My goal in this chapter is to give you insights about why it is necessary to think globally from the outset of your involvement in e-business, to give you the tools to adapt to the local mandates in different cultures and geographies, and to provide examples of companies who are both enabling and implementing global strategies and actions successfully.

Cross-Border FastAlliances

There is a perception that business and consumer needs will rationalize and overlap from country to country. In some instances that may be true—trends, fads, awareness of product or service availability, and price are all accelerated in a market and exchange mechanism like the Internet, which accesses information instantaneously.

Nevertheless, those global players who truly understand the differences and cultural preferences of local citizens and businesses will ultimately win in their cross-border FastAlliances and activities.

Carrefour SA, the French retailing multinational and world's second largest retailer, is not only *not* quaking at the advent of arch-rival Wal-Mart into its markets, it is actually winning. In Latin America, Carrefour's obsessive attention to the finer cultural details, such as how Argentine housewives like their meat cut, has decimated Wal-Mart's entrance into that market.[1] And Carrefour is moving aggressively into the e-business world in a b2b venture, creating the world's largest supply exchange (GlobalNetXchange) with Sears and Oracle. Wal-Mart has invested significantly in Electronic Data Interchange (EDI) processes with its vendors and might be reluctant to enter such a relationship because of sharing a percentage of equity with its partners. However, the company will have to play this game some way, somewhere. As we learned earlier from Jeff Smith of CommerceOne, many companies are translating their EDI investments into Internet activity (GM is an example). Carrefour has started to change the rules of the game.

There is another major issue that should be stated up front. Many companies that are going global with their e-business strategies would be well served to understand the following threshold issue:

It is often not possible to make incremental changes to infrastructure when globalizing. Your FastStrategy and infrastructure must be integrated in the beginning of your globalization process.

For example, issues of language, culture, dates, currencies, formats, tax, gestures, and technology architecture must all be integrated in the creation and implementation of the web globalization FastStrategy.

Many companies are well aware of this issue—the e-business ones and the dot-coms or infrastructure providers to the e-economy. Dealtime.com, a company started in Israel, set up operations in the

United States, did an IPO on the Nasdaq first, then offered shares on a succession of European and Asian exchanges. This type of scenario is becoming more frequent (see Commtouch mentioned later in this chapter)—particularly with companies from India and Israel, but I have been involved with those from Australia and France as well. These companies leverage the knowledge gained in each country, adding to their global skills as they go.

There are now Nasdaq-type exchanges in almost every financial center in the world (e.g., Frankfurt's Neuer Markt, and Easdaq, a pan-European exchange mentioned later in this chapter).

Nasdaq itself is globalizing—Nasdaq Japan launched operations in mid-2000 and Nasdaq Europe by the first quarter of 2001. They are partnering with other exchanges, making them co-owners of the exchanges and offering reciprocity by showing their companies on the Nasdaq screens. This would be for companies that want to be globally traded. Those companies that prefer to be traded domestically would continue to operate on domestic stock exchanges. The goal of Nasdaq is to be able to provide a forum for companies to go public simultaneously worldwide, which means that employees and investors worldwide can share at the equity trough. The social and economic implication of this wealth creation is mind-boggling. It could, in fact, create a new social order of haves and have-nots. The haves will be joined in communication and investment groups; the have-nots will remain separate. This is not a political book, but it would be remiss of me not to comment on the fact that this issue has social consequences—good and bad.

Companies that are in effect borderless, with technologies that can be exploited worldwide, can now continually replicate themselves in worldwide markets. A global Nasdaq will speed the globalization process in financial markets, too.

The World of Softbank

In a conversation I had with Ron Fisher, CEO of Softbank's global ventures group, he talked about this global phenomenon of IPOs moving from country to country:

> The model worked extremely well for Yahoo! in Japan and has good applicability worldwide. Softbank has just raised $1.4 billion

> to invest in at least 1,000 Japanese Internet start-ups, and we have created a joint fund with the World Bank of $500 million to bring the Internet to developing nations. Our global access is our greatest differentiator as an equity funding source and partner. Anywhere to everywhere. We are putting in place the global infrastructure to help companies wherever they start in the world.

Can the same model for company start-up, introduction, growth, and partnering to IPO work in every jurisdiction? The variations in business methods and processes (e.g., credit card issues, infrastructure problems, Internet access costs) will complicate duplication, and there will be added costs from concurrent financial reporting and regulatory and labor concerns (discussed later in this chapter). If you are thinking of taking your company global from the starting gate, make sure you have covered all the bases mentioned in this chapter. It will serve to protect you against nasty surprises. If you are considering multiple IPOs in a number of jurisdictions, remember this: We are far more forgiving of failure in the United States than are non-U.S. cultures, where memories of failures run long. Are the rewards of a multicountry IPO (more liquidity, brand and investor awareness, more incentives for international employees) worth the risks to which they expose a start-up (global market adjustment, overwhelming regulatory requirements, track record issues as in Singapore, which requires a five-year operating history)? Transitional companies or established e-businesses will have less concern about these issues since their experience and management depth will give them some level of confidence in managing many of the risks.

This is where Softbank's Spider Network has given the company a major competitive advantage. This is the strategy:

1. Find the leading player in the region (e.g., Vivendi in Europe, NewsCorp in the United Kingdom, Australia, and New Zealand).
2. Be sure that the local partners are indigenous or have local credibility.
3. Choose the leading player with a shared vision.
   - Choose one with a long-term approach of building Internet companies on a global scale to create long-term sustainable value.

- Choose one with a shared vision about how to build a company. The portfolio investors who are part of the Softbank family are young companies without organizational experience or history, and the regional leading players who constitute the large-company partners of Softbank have to be able to work with these small companies quickly and without bureaucracy. That means responding rapidly—with a Cool Decision Process and flat organizations. Softbank's own structure is lean and flat—an executive committee of six and regular contact and interchange.

4. Create a joint venture (with similar stakes for each partner), and be sure that the key figures and opinion influencers are on the board (e.g., Rupert Murdoch sits on Softbank's joint venture board with Newscorp).
5. Focus on local companies using these local market incubators to raise local capital for infrastructure and services. Access local markets so that there is a strong reinforcement between the local and the financial markets.
6. Start to move the portfolio companies out of the local market (using the Spider Network) and into the global market. Companies that Softbank helped to start in India or China are now moving into the United States (e.g., Ali Baba from China, which links tens of thousands of Asian suppliers). The Softbank joint venture with the World Bank is doing this in 100 developing countries in the world, which adds value both technologically and socioeconomically.
7. Obtain liquidity and provide access to capital for further expansion and investment.

Ron Fisher shared with me his favorite story, which gives an indication of Softbank founder and CEO Masa Son's perspective and 300-year vision:

> Just because Masa Son thinks of Softbank as a company with a 300-year vision does not mean that there is a plan set in stone. On the contrary, our plans and implementation of the vision change daily—it's the commitment to the long term and adding sustainable value globally that make the difference. Masa is an icon of

> sorts in Japan and elsewhere and has inspired thousands of Japanese entrepreneurs to create their own dreams and move forward. He never stops. I have known Masa for over 15 years. When I was running a company in Los Angeles [Interactive Systems, a Unix-based company] he became our partner—and then again when I was turning around another company called Phoenix Technologies. He asked me to join him just after he went public with Softbank in Japan and had these dreams of building the Softbank of today. I agreed and one Sunday not too long after that, he called me. "Ron," he said. "Today we have to fly to New York. We have a meeting with Teddy Forstmann of Ziff-Davis tonight." We did, and by the next morning we had a handshake deal to buy Ziff-Davis for billions of dollars. As we left the meeting to fly home, Masa turned to me and said, "Well, Ron, maybe someday we will get a chance to do something really big!" And he wasn't joking.

Fisher feels strongly, as does Masa Son, that the acquisition of Ziff-Davis was the entry point that put Softbank on the map in the media and IT community, as was its acquisition of Comdex. Ziff-Davis introduced them to Yahoo! and . . . well, the rest is history. Last June, Softbank launched a joint venture with Nasdaq in Japan to enable small companies to access the capital market and tie into the Nasdaq European platform, basically with its Asian and Latin American activities—thus putting in place Masa Son's dream of doing something "really big."

The World of ABB

Recently I met with Göran Lindahl, CEO of ABB, the company that is the global giant of the engineering and industrial world. Its customers are in power transmission and distribution, automation, oil, gas, petrochemicals, building technologies, and financial services. An energetic, enthusiastic Swede (headquartered in Switzerland but essentially a global citizen), Lindahl travels constantly, finding ways to create touch points with his 160,000 employees.

"I sit on the board of Ericsson, and connect with many different industries and people—always learning, observing, understanding," he told me. "It's not enough now to have an idea or to think about it, you have to execute and do it fast." Lindahl has the advantage of being close (culturally and with information access) to Sweden's

"Wireless Valley" and its huge strength in wireless communications. In addition, he has his own worldwide Spider Network of CEOs from many industries and countries.

ABB has been voted one of *Industry Week*'s Top 100 companies, and Göran Lindahl has been voted best global CEO. And although ABB is not seen as an e-business, Lindahl is on a mission to infuse the e-business sense of timing and energy into his huge company: "You know, at ABB we adopted e-business thinking a long time ago—in the seventies we were already communicating with our global transformer factories on an e-mail system, as well as a common design system that worked through the telephone between eight of our factories. It was slow but it worked and was the embryo of the e-business strategy we have today."

Lindahl radiates intensity. When he talks about his company's e-business strategy, his energy is contagious:

> Now we have a three-pillar e-business strategy. The technology pillar involves minority investment in a number of IT start-ups, which gives an overview of the technologies that are available and of use to ABB or our customers. Note that we only want to observe here, not control. The second pillar is where we will form majority-owned joint ventures to take new application technologies to market. For example, industrial processes in the design and manufacture of iron ore and steel. The third pillar is where we will develop and promote additional e-commerce channels to market, such as the trading portals and exchanges. Our e-business portal is part of a customer-focused e-business platform for key businesses, third-party web portals, and online marketplaces. We're putting over $1 billion into these initiatives this year and next. We plan to put over 30 percent of our standard products online in 2000–2001. In addition, we are adding to the efficiency of our computer environment through the $250 million supply and service arrangement we have created with IBM, which will cover our new equipment needs over a three-year period. ABB will order over the web in over 80 countries. This will support our move into knowledge- and service-based markets, giving us a solid worldwide IT infrastructure to support the flow of information. For example, one of the ventures that falls into the third category is a new company called b-business partners where we have joined with partners Investor and the Internet banking specialist SEB as well as AstraZeneca,

> Electrolux, Saab (aerospace), and others to invest over $1 billion euros to boost European e-business commerce.

Lindahl spends at least a third of his time looking at the structural changes necessary to make ABB a borderless company. Another third is spent walking around, meeting and speaking with employees on the factory floor and in the engineering office—those working in the trenches, not in the ivory tower of senior management. The final third of his time is doing the same with the customers, research leaders, and opinion creators in government and business worldwide. Lindahl knows GE's Jack Welch. "He has been breathing down our necks, and that is good for us—we will miss him when he retires!"

What about the old economy that has been the past strength of ABB? Lindahl has strong feelings about the terminology:

> I resist the idea of old and new. I would rather think of it as *classic* and *new*. We are part of both. We use the means of the new economy as a tool to become better with the product and user in terms of functionality and service. Many make the mistake of saying this is a new product or service. Warren Buffett, whom I talk to from time to time, says, "This creates a redistribution of value, but doesn't create value in itself." On the other hand, exchanges change the rules of the game since the choices are more. In fact, there is too much choice. One needs support to make the right one. Exchanges have also created more commodities and great fluctuation in pricing. Our goal is to have a stake in all of these areas, not to necessarily move from the classic to the new.

Many CEOs have the right e-business talk. What I wanted from my conversations with Lindahl was the e-business *walk*. I got it.

> We have to cut out administrative layers that block creativity. I have cut out the regional layer of responsibility in ABB. Each business deals with individual countries, and since they are global businesses, they are the ones who make the decisions about their futures. The global IT network is making this possible. The deal with IBM for IT supply and service is one example of a global process that supports global access and support. "Thinking globally and acting locally" has to do with responsibility. There must be the same technology and support worldwide. Twenty years ago there were two standards—one for industrial countries and the other for developing countries. Now it is one standard everywhere.

> However, one must promote local actions. The customers are owned by the local people who have the local culture, language, and value. These are the people who should be responsible for collecting the business and winning the customer. This is in contradiction with what many CEOs say about the Internet replacing local representation. I believe that the marketing must still be done by meeting someone and socializing, with all the information gathered from body language. Certainly you can sell games and commodities on the Net. But many other kinds of business cannot be done only that way.

ABB has 24 business areas, and more than half of them are truly global in scope (e.g., transformers). Each business has the mandate to develop its own e-business as fast as possible. Lindahl considers it critical to create a networking structure in which the whole organization deals with a certain category or customer. ABB's challenge is to increase the capabilities of the whole organization in interfacing with the customer. Although the Internet can provide the components to interface with the customer, the organization must be equally effective. This means that the networked organization has to evolve at ABB to the point where there is continuous sharing of responsibility. The combination of IT that works worldwide, with increased customer management skills, will lead to the realization of value in both classic and new economies. Adds Lindahl, "Destroying the classic is not our goal. There is much more to be gained from doing both classic and new effectively. You cannot alienate the channels that distribute your products."

The approach by General Electric in 1999–2000, which called for all GE businesses to "destroy" their normal business approaches to access the net, would not be ABB's style. In the white-goods arena, the destroy-your-business mandate meant that the distributor was cut out. This caused some pushback from certain GE divisions. Lindahl felt that this was a bold step by GE, maybe too bold: "We believe in collaborative partnering—with the channels as well as outside partners. For example, outsourcing is something we are embracing, but as a true partnership, where responsibility is shared to create transparency in the flow of information."

The FastAlliances of ABB will always take into account the local issues and adaptation while drawing on the resources of the global business. Göran Lindahl sits at the apex of world business. His vision of the world is multicurrency, multipolitical, and multieconomic. When asked to contribute his insights, he speaks not only from the single perspective of his heritage, his culture, or even his experience, but as a citizen of the world with a vision of world business that is unique. As a member of a number of boards, including Ericsson, Smith Barney, and DuPont, his global insights contribute to his value. He also has a spectacular personal network to call on when he has an interest in a topic of value to ABB. As for dot-com self-esteem, Lindahl has it—although it is tempered by years in the traditional (as he calls it, "classic") environment. He is indeed a man with a mandate, a corporate revolutionary—with the position, power, and resources to make massive organizational change happen. Look out—ABB is coming!

Partner with Attention to Cultural Issues

Culture has an influence on the levels of Internet usage. A study by International Data Corporation[2] in the last few months of 1999 found that within the 12 largest European markets (United Kingdom, France, Germany, Italy, Spain, Netherlands, Sweden, Denmark, Norway, Finland, Switzerland, and Austria) there are three distinct regions: Northern, Central, and Southern. The Northern group of countries, (Norway, Sweden, Denmark, and Finland) have the deepest penetration of Internet use, but the United Kingdom, Germany, Switzerland, and Austria have the highest percentage of actual buyers on the Internet. France, Italy, and Spain have the lowest rates of Internet penetration as well as Internet buyers (excluding the videotext system of Minitel of France, in existence since 1979).

This leads to a conclusion that has consistently held true: No matter the global communication of the Internet, local tastes, cultures, and adoption rates will dramatically affect the marketing and technology approaches around the world. It would be a mistake, however, to underestimate countries where Internet adoption rates are lower than those in the United States and dismiss them as "not getting it."

For example, wireless technology in Europe is much more sophisticated and user-friendly than in the United States—checking e-mail and news bulletins on Wireless Application Protocol (WAP)-enabled cell phones is old hat in both Europe and parts of Asia. Surfing the

Net and Internet shopping are a small step further. Smart-card technology has been widely adopted in Europe, and most people have a credit card with a memory chip that can hold a cash balance or access their bank account,[3] includes personal information to reduce credit-card fraud, and in France may include a medical history. All of these businesses may be based on smart-card technology, but their implementation has come about through effectively created and managed FastAlliances in addition to the traditional kind.

Nokia is *making* the market—not following it—in wireless technology. Its activities are enabling the further and deeper adoption of the Internet. Why? Because the web is now accessible not only through a PC, but literally anywhere, anyhow, especially wherever the consumer goes with his or her wireless (WAP) phone. In Europe and Japan, e-commerce is much more mobile than in the United States. The sim cards (smart cards) identify the phone user for billing purposes, encrypt the consumer's credit details and send them to merchants over the Net, and even debit the amount directly from the consumer's bank account. All of this can be done securely, with no fraud. American Express in the United States has seen the light and is issuing smart cards as fast as it can. Three French companies (Gemplus, Schlumberger, and Bull) hold 70 percent of the smart-card market. Motorola is now out of the smart-card business. As long as European politicians show restraint regarding taxes and labor laws, thus enabling a continuation of the expansion of their economies, Europe will be sitting at the table of the Internet winners.[4]

Having been around a while, I have lived through the venture capital boom (and bust) of the 1980s. Many of the venture and incubator-like parks created then are now coming into their own in the 2000s. In 1988, I held a conference of the World Technology Executives' Network (WorldTEN), of which I was chairman, in Nice in the south of France because it was a beginning technology center. Now the area is exploding with software and electronics start-ups. The Netherlands were well represented in that conference by software companies. Now the Netherlands has become a birthplace for many Internet start-ups. Some of our sponsors for the conference came from Munich. They were newcomers in the venture capital world and were having a tough time finding German (indeed European) start-ups to fund. Now Munich is *the* hot spot in Europe for venture capital, with

$10 billion of funds under management. Denmark, the location of another of our annual CEO WorldTEN forums, had remarkable entrepreneurial technology companies as members in 1989. Now Denmark is the world leader in hearing aids and audio technology, which are key elements in the huge wireless telephone market.

In China in the southern city of Shenzhen (where many of the risk takers and entrepreneurs have clustered in China), a new venture capital community is spawning. In my numerous business visits to lecture all over China, I find this city breathtaking in its inability to keep up with the exploding population of people looking to find their fortunes, evidenced by vast new construction and mind-boggling traffic. The city has created its own $120 million venture capital fund, one of a number of Chinese cities to do so, in order to stimulate high-tech development there. However, the influence of government (and large monopolistic Chinese corporations) tends to dampen the independence of such groups. Nevertheless, the change and intent is there and evolving.

I met my partner in China, Wang Xuezong, 10 years ago when he was my technical assistant during my working visits there. He was at that time a brilliant young aeronautical engineer with great interpersonal and political savvy who was part of the Science and Technology Commission of Beijing (my hosts). Even then, Xuezong was the living embodiment of a well-oiled Spider Network. Wherever we went in China, while I spoke to groups of business and government leaders, he connected with his network of contacts, developed during school and university days. Now he is the CEO of the main high-tech industrial park, near Chengdu in the Mianyang city of Sichwan province (population 250 million). He's a sophisticated businessman with two cell phones, a car and driver, and a varied international experience. His perception of e-business in China is very focused:

> This is a new economy that is affecting every country in the world. The same way that cellular technology has become part of every businessperson's life in China, so the Internet is becoming that way. It means that complicated joint technology programs are more easily and quickly implemented across many borders, not only from outside China, but also within the country. Joint research and manufacturing within China will be facilitated over time by the Internet, and especially with the advent of WAP technology.

China has scores of highly proficient researchers and engineers, but still the demand for skills and experience will remain unmet because of the huge potential within that market.

The talent drought for skilled professional managers is global. It is pushing development of technology centers to the locations of first-class universities, such as Catalonia in Spain, which is fed by nine local universities. Highly successful European companies are acting as starter kits for entrepreneurship—such as Oulu in Finland, an Arctic city that is a major manufacturing center for Nokia and a research hub, activities stimulated by a technical university and a government-backed science park.[5] The seeds were sown in the 1980s; the fruit is ready to be picked now.

What will evolve within the next four years, however, is an increasing dependence on engineering and technology talent from India and China. Neither Europe nor North America can satisfy their needs for highly skilled technology talent. India turns out over 122,000 engineers annually compared to a paltry 63,000 in the United States.[6] And engineers comprise 40 percent of China's university graduates annually. Only political collaboration between the private sector and government will facilitate the expansion of immigration policy and visa number allocations beyond the present limits. This is a continuing challenge. Between 1985 and 1996, two-thirds of all doctorates in science and engineering at U.S. universities were earned by foreign students. Although many stay in the United States, the statistics at Caltech, where I teach executive programs on traditional alliances and FastAlliances, reveal that about 40 percent return to their own countries. From my perspective, they are perfect alliance managers for the creation of traditional and FastAlliances since they understand the U.S. culture as well as their own.

Korea, with an Internet penetration rate of about 25 percent of the population, is another country that is creating a venture capital community.[7] However, here it is with a real difference: It is controlled and financed by the Chaebol (the name for Korea's conglomerates), such as Hyundai, Samsung, and the LG and SK groups. They have earmarked $1.2 billion to buy stakes in high-tech start-ups. Moon Young Woo, head of Golden Gate, Samsung's $35 million venture capital fund, notes, "You simply can't survive without adapting to the fast-changing Internet era, and one solution is linking with start-ups." There are quite a number of those—increasing at a rate of about 10 new start-ups a day. Could this be the driver that forces the old-line companies of Korea to become more nimble? Or more controlling if they pick the winners? It depends on whether the Chaebol invest without meddling in the start-ups. If they do, they will become the nonpreferred investor, since start-ups can now gain access to capital worldwide. The real competitive advantage for the Chaebol VCs will be their Spider Networks (and global expertise) and how speedily they can bring that knowledge to the table of the start-ups they invest in. The move is on for market share, however, which can be seen in the unusual business model that Samsung fell into when it created a mall portal for its employees in the late 1990s to help it weather the economic crisis of the time. Shopping as a group online on the mall, Samsung employees could get discounts of up to 15 percent on just about everything. But the real outcome was that Samsung realized that Koreans like gathering into cybergroups and buying that way. So most of the traditional social groups and networks are going online. Samsung[8] now manages the shopping web sites for many companies who want to cut costs and have, as a consequence, closed many of their brick-and-mortar stores in favor of the online ones. Freechal.com is a start-up that specializes in creating cybercommunities out of social and professional groups so that they can create home pages, bulletin boards, and so on. Freechal has a FastAlliances with Samsung (as do over 20 other start-ups) and directs its visitors to Samsung's mall, too.

An area that has brought the international community together is the concern about taxes on e-commerce. At the end of 2000, the Organization for Economic Cooperation and Development (OECD) Technical Advisory Groups submitted their recommended approaches to income characterization, business profits, and consumption taxes—the goal being to reach consensus on these issues. These decisions could either bring the explosion of innovation, global commerce, jobs, and wealth creation to a screeching halt or facilitate its growth. The world will be watching the politicians as they struggle to make the right decisions. And the world will vote—with its clicks—as it moves to countries who permit rather than deny.

Since my philosophy on life is to assume that the glass will always be on the full side, let's presume that most of the politicians will do the intelligent thing (a laughable thought, I agree) and make e-business possible in their respective countries. Then all web sites will have to consider themselves global. Internationalizing a web site is something that has become the core competency of a company called GlobalSight, which makes web sites culture-friendly and language-appropriate, enabling companies to use the integrated global web development approach mentioned at the beginning of this chapter. I spoke with Jorden Woods, cofounder and former CEO of GlobalSight, recently: "Integrated global web development must have centralized control with localized content and execution abilities. Customers want to maintain their brands with a centralized message and look and feel of the web site. But each local and country office has to have the ability to add localized content and cultural nuances. We have a process that starts at the highest level from headquarters and then empowers the local offices."

Working with Woods, Mike Grote (senior director of product marketing), and Meg Taylor (corporate communications), I have adapted his company's process and called it Web Culture Integration (GlobalSight Inc.): FastAlliances Tool #13. (For ease of description, the United States has been used as the headquarters. However, the tools in this book are not U.S.-centric but applicable wherever your headquarters may be!)

Web Culture Integration: FastAlliances Tool #13

The first step is diagnosis.

Corporate brand. The message to customers, includes look and feel—typically managed by headquarters.

Regional issues. Continent or regionally based strategies and programs—typically managed by area managers.

Local needs. Country-specific special events, customer profiles, select products and services typically managed by country managers.

Alternatives generally used by companies include the following:

1. *Central control and execution.* Companies that are operating with the mind-set of an exporter tend to prefer this arrangement. (See Figure 6.1.) Headquarters controls strategic decisions, so it is logical that it also controls the look, feel, and message of consistency

Figure 6.1 Central Control and Execution: FastAlliances Tool #13

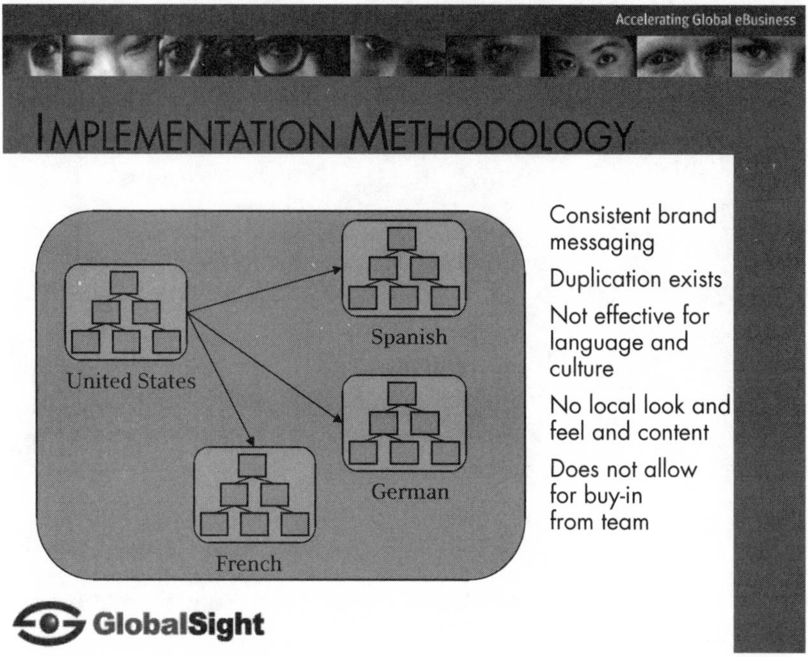

worldwide. The result is a loss of localization and buy-in, although the brand is presented consistently.

2. *Local control and execution.* Here the problem is that one country's e-business face may be excellent, whereas another's is unacceptable. (See Figure 6.2.) The brand runs the risk of dilution, and there is inconsistency in the message or the execution. Although local interests are well served, the company as a whole is not.

3. *Central control and local execution.* Figure 6.3 shows the best solution. The top box in each square is shaded, signifying central control, a consistent brand message, and no duplication. The headquarters square contains elements of all the other squares, but a single code for all seen in the square. The best of all worlds is the result—local tastes and customs are incorporated with the tailoring of a consistent brand message.

Two examples of web pages that show the globalization approaches of their organizations are those of Hewlett-Packard (HP) and General Electric (GE). HP's approach allows for localization as well as the stan-

Figure 6.2 Local Control and Execution: FastAlliances Tool #13

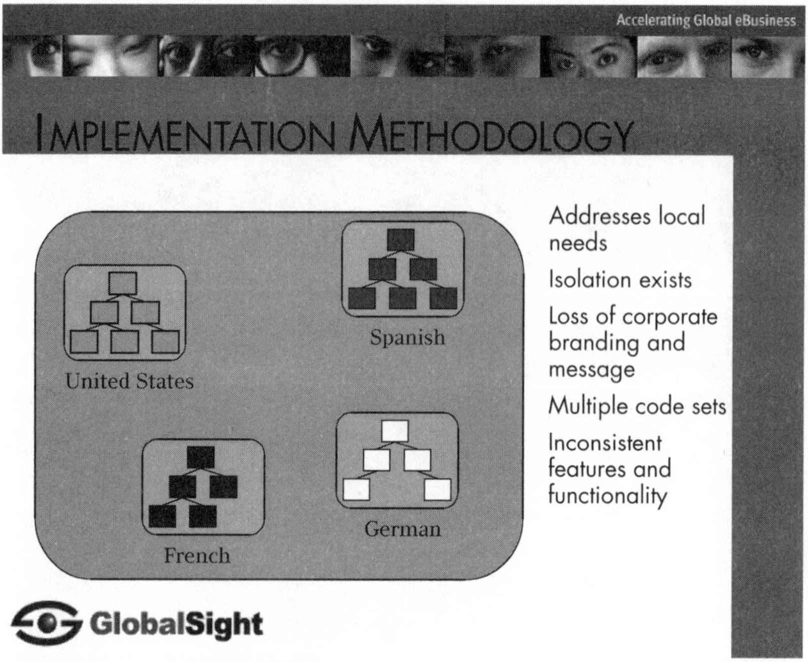

Figure 6.3 Central Control and Local Execution: FastAlliances Tool #13

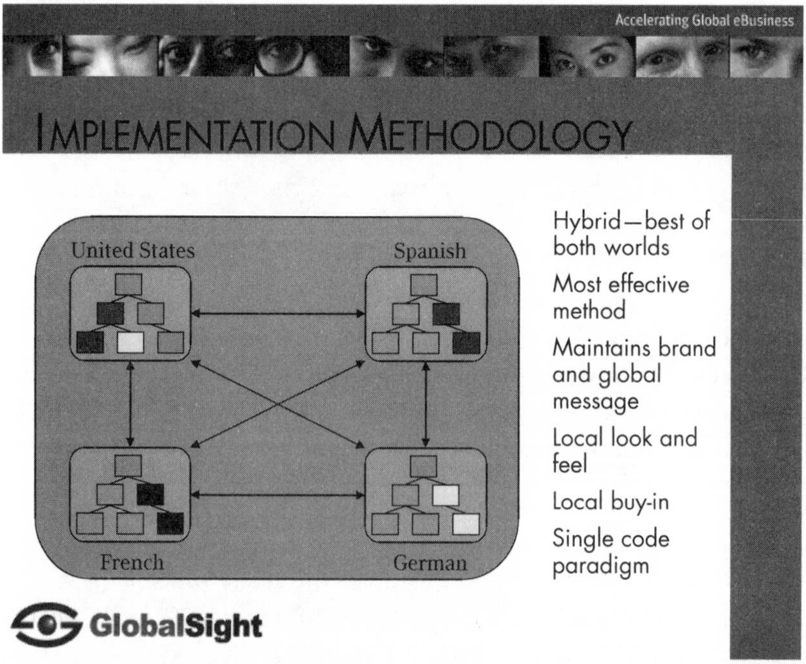

dardization of brand. It is both flexible and able to be changed into 26 languages in over 59 locales. GE's web page for b2b application is in four languages and allows for the leveraging of local content worldwide.

In order to throw off the mantle of the Ugly American (or whatever stereotype applies to your culture), a valiant attempt to be culture-appropriate is in order for all companies doing more than local business (or hoping to).

Whereas large companies generally have the resources to access opinion influencers and intelligence in nonhome markets, smaller companies are challenged in this area. A new company that is filling the information and contact gap is Geomarkets. Founder and president Tom Spargo explains: "We call our company a 'desktop consulate,' where we provide research and access to contacts worldwide to companies who may not know where to turn and in the past might

FastAlli, by Larraine Segil

have contacted the consulate or trade commission." The weekly newsletter from Geomarkets is called *Geoventures,* which gives a bird's-eye view of various parts of the global technology scene.

A key investor in Geomarkets is the Singaporean government, through its Technopreneurship Program.[9] There are many beneficiaries of the Singapore government's venture investments. Its commitment of $1 billion to technopreneurship has been spread among many venture funds, so its influence is widely felt. I spoke with Kian Fai Leong, CEO of Buildfolio.com, which is a supply exchange for building materials in the real estate industry.

> We started in Silicon Valley, even though we came from Singapore, since we did our graduate education here. But we have maintained close connections to Singapore. The Singapore government [through its Science and Technology Board] is an investor and, even more important, has made key introductions for our company in Singapore to add to the list of connections that we already have. This is not unusual for the Singapore government, which is why many of the smaller start-ups that would have left the country have now chosen to stay, or if they have left, have maintained strong connections, seeing Singapore as a viable market and entry point to other parts of Asia.

There are a number of distinct advantages to setting up in the logistics hub of Asia, which Singapore presents itself to be. Ben Lim, CEO of VCHEQ,[10] which is headquartered in Singapore, comes from the traditional banking industry. His company raised money from the Allianz group of insurance companies as well as from J.P. Morgan and the Singapore government. VCHEQ is an international electronic check service that partners with the international payments providers to enable customers (mainly b2b companies) to send money between a number of locations with absolute certainty of the time and date of transfer—sort of like a courier service by wire with guaranteed time of arrival. VCHEQ has had to overcome issues of multiple currencies, restrictions on money transfer, processes, and all sorts of other regulations that change from country to country in Asia. Even though the volume of transfers is far greater in the United States, the complexities are far greater in Asia. If VCHEQ succeeds there, it can succeed anywhere. Ben Lim is confident:

> One of the challenges that we have overcome is the complexity of differences. And we also have another advantage in Asia. That is that the majority of the population in each country is gathered in a couple of major cities. Thus, since we are tying up contacts [Spider Networks!] in those cities, once that is done, we basically have the leading market position in that country and finally in the region. We can do something similar to that in Europe, where the same principle applies. But the United States is very different. Each state in the United States has to be considered as if it were a separate country. It poses a major challenge for us down the line—and we will be starting a U.S. operation shortly.

Ben Lim's sophistication is derived from 17 years as a banker in Asia. He truly understands the major paradigm shift that has to occur throughout the banking industry worldwide in order to take advantage of the e-business wave. "We have to educate bankers to understand that alliances must be nonexclusive. In the e-business world there is no place for exclusive relationships—things move too fast and information is too available. It's more important to be first in time to market than to cut the richest deal—and that may mean leveraging lots of relationships simultaneously and in an open-ended fashion."

Christopher Yeo of Information Fusion Inc.[11] in Singapore agrees:

> We have been in e-business for six years. We were funded privately, have revenues, are profitable, and will be going IPO in the next year (isn't everyone?). We develop e-commerce logistic engines that perform fulfillment processes, inventory management, and global warehouse management. We have partnered with Sun Microsystems, Oracle, and BMC software. Our alliances are fast, but we have a challenge not being physically in the United States in order to get the mindshare of these partners and to contribute our input. Our biggest challenge is the shortage of qualified labor. Here we have an advantage over the United States—we scout for labor worldwide. Compared to the U.S. immigration laws, Singapore is delighted to welcome qualified workers. So if we find them (and the world is our search place) we can easily bring them here, even though as a small island we have limited space.

It's notable that the Singapore government leaves few stones unturned when it comes to exploring opportunities. One approach has been to fund the education of some of Singapore's finest. For example, the Technology Development Fund (TDF) of Singapore funded the education of Max Henry and his partner in the United States. With their newfound skills, they returned to Singapore and founded Private Express, funded by TDF, and another Singaporean venture fund, Transpac International. Private Express is a private messaging service through which one can send private and confidential information across the Internet without concern. It is set up as a kind of FedEx of the Internet, selling services on a monthly subscription basis. Though launched very recently, the company has an office in Silicon Valley. It is yet another example of long-term thinking of a country that is determined to be in the game of e-business.

Labor issues and far-reaching policies of e-business awareness—there is no doubt that these issues will grow in importance for U.S. technology companies and become topics that they will leverage with their congressional representatives. As the e-business cycle ratchets up into hypergrowth (the e-gorilla stage, see Chapter 7), the labor shortage may well become a competitive disadvantage for U.S. companies. This is a cultural difference that could prove to be a major impediment to growth, forcing U.S. companies to take more of their job opportunities offshore.

One area must be mentioned here as a critical failure point for many companies looking to establish themselves in nonhome markets. It is an area in which localization often fails: *advertising.*

Two key elements of advertising in different cultures are (1) user demographics and culture and (2) search behavior. In Japan, for example, users are young and their demands for digital content sales made over cellular telephones are more frivolous in nature.[12] A Dutch Internet marketing research company presents four search methods for determining the extent of brand involvement in a search: area of interest, type of product, name of shop, and brand. When a visitor searches by brand, brand recognition is a nonissue, and the challenge becomes one of increasing brand loyalty—that is what the nature of the communication should target. However, for computers and other technology products, the customer searches by product, so the idea is to be on all the portals that would show such products to potential customers in order to build brand awareness and loyalty. Consumables such as food and entertainment products will be searched for by the names of stores, which means that manufacturers or suppliers must buy into the web real estate on those portals.

There are very different strategies for e-business companies when operating in different countries. E-business tends to use a process of "sell-source-ship" as opposed to the traditional model of "buy-hold-sell."[13] This process was described by Ulf Carlberg, director of Product Strategy at Industri-Matematik International, a supply chain management company headquartered in Sweden and the United States.[14] The problem is that zero inventory can result in zero customers due to the difference in cost structures in these models. High volume under the buy-hold-sell model is generally associated with lower costs, since the marginal costs of delivery of additional units keep falling (assuming that one is managing inventories efficiently). However, under the sell-source-ship model, with multiple sources and delivery points, costs will not necessarily decrease with increased volume. The reason for this is that the major value in a sale on the Internet does not come from the product; rather, it comes from the service that enables the purchaser to choose and order from a customized range of products, anywhere, anytime. The broader the geographic reach of this proposed service, the more complicated and expensive fulfillment can be. These are the supply chain management issues. Then there are the issues of tariffs, shipping, taxes, insurance, and product and delivery tracking.

I recently spoke with Raja Moorthy, CFO and cofounder of eLabs-Europe[15] about the challenges of e-business in Europe:

> You have to localize. We started our aggregator of laboratory products in Germany since it is far more credible to create a pan-European business from Germany than from the United Kingdom, which is another of our main markets. There are many costs associated with doing business here. For example, our customer service representatives earn more than in the United States—they have to be localized and decentralized and knowledgeable regarding different language and currencies, and our people must have industry credibility. Relationships are everything here. In the United States, the economic proposition of, for example, a Chemdex or Sciquest will be enough to interest a participant in trying the auction or the content site Mylabs. But in Europe there is a more holistic approach. Customers and suppli-

> ers look at their internal cost of doing business with us, such as how much time and how many people it will take to digitize their catalogs or teach their people how to do business with us. They also want to feel comfortable with the relationship. Also, there are very different ways of doing distribution. In Germany there is a regional warehouse approach, whereas in the United States you can drop-ship from state to state. Also, there is a higher level of conservatism regarding adoption of e-business in Europe. The opportunity is huge, and so are the challenges!

The bottom line is that creating FastAlliances across borders can be a complex logistical challenge if the promise of anywhere, anytime, and any way is kept. When the FastAlliances is based on services alone, the logistics are people-oriented in terms of cultural sophistication, language abilities, availability, and affability, and in this respect the traditional model of local representatives can be effective. The portal can sell the service, and a local alliance partner can deliver it in culturally acceptable ways. Sometimes, however, due to infrastructure requirements, it may be impossible to take the company global at this point in the Internet revolution.

Brett Smith, CEO of ei3 Corp,[16] a start-up company, has created an online system to manage huge manufacturing projects and plants remotely and to spot and diagnose problems and fix them from thousands of miles away. The company is moving internationally, but is limited to countries where it can get a T1 line (which means the developed countries, not many emerging economies at this point). "For example," Smith told me recently, "we are in China, but there we need a T3 line, which is a satellite connection, and that is very expensive. Of course when you balance the cost of downtime of a manufacturing line that could be producing 850 feet of tape per minute with the cost of the T3 line, it's still worth it." This is a small example of a customer need, a supplier solution, and a cultural adaptation that will allow the two to come together. All of this is relevant to traditional alliances—but the speed and financing required for start-ups to reach this far is different for FastAlliances. The Spider Network that Smith has created includes AT&T as one of ei3 Corp's FastAlliances. AT&T provides all the frame relay networks throughout the United States and cuts through the red tape to get customers new lines so that they can contract with ei3 Corp. No doubt Brett Smith will be looking for European, Asian, and Latin American telecoms as partners to develop his next level of hypergrowth FastAlliances.

Industri-Matematik created a cross-border FastAlliances with Oracle Corporation to market its consumer packaged-goods solution suite of software and has multiple alliances with systems integrators (Oracle Consulting, Cap Gemini, and others) to increase sales and implementation service capabilities.

The key element here is that there is no such thing as a generic, or multicultural, approach. The ultimate in customization takes into account local cultures. That means, for example, not lumping a country like Spain into a single category, but creating different selling approaches for Bilbao versus Madrid versus Granada. It means taking a b2b or a b2c approach that is modular and adapting it according to local preferences (which could be as simple as the color of a web page), then testing it with real-time feedback. For example, a personal online tax-filing program (popular in the United States since many individuals file their own tax returns) makes no sense in Japan, because there tax returns are filed mainly by employers. In addition, although the Japanese are early adopters of electronic gadgetry (hence the huge market penetration of wireless/cellular phones), new management processes or marketing ideas are accepted far more slowly. In China, keyword searches are difficult because the Chinese language depends on characters or phrases—an issue that requires a cultural/language understanding, not just a translation. In addition, at least two main formats are used for programming in China. A simplified character format was introduced into China and Singapore in the 1950s and 1960s, but in many parts of Asia (Taiwan and Hong Kong) traditional complex characters could still be used. If the characters are written in a different format, the search engine will not recognize the keywords or phrases.

Then there are the legal systems. For example, look at the plethora of consumer protection laws[17] in Europe that prevent companies from marketing to Europe as a common market: Italy bans all types of tobacco ads; France requires that all contracts be written in French whether the e-business intends to sell goods or services to France or not; Greece bans ads on toys; Finland bans speed as a feature in car advertising; Sweden bans any TV ads directed at children under 12 and also ads on liquor; Germany bans lifetime guarantees, rebates, and other forms of sales promotion. Basically, posting an offer on an Internet web site is considered de facto cross-border direct marketing, and thus falls afoul of all local consumer protection laws. Although this sorry state of affairs is being challenged in the courts, it is clear that, wherever the application of an e-business strategy is focused, what will *not* work is a thinly disguised, made-over, U.S. (or your country)-centric campaign.

In Latin America, another large market opportunity that is not single-faceted in nature, the Internet economy has developed in multiple parallel applications simultaneously rather than linearly as in the United States.[18] "Everything is happening at once in Latin America—infrastructure development, user growth, corporate web strategy creation, and web entrepreneurship. Investors are therefore likely to see lower returns on their investments in the region and need to take into account a longer-term payback," according to Annika Alford of IDC at a recent conference. International Data Corporation (IDC) estimated an average Internet penetration of 27 percent for the region, with Brazil being the leading market. Overall, however, IDC estimates 47 percent growth in Latin America compared to 40 percent in Asia Pacific, 38 percent in the United States, and 34 percent in Europe.

Other constraints are the lack of online financial payment and transaction facilities, which means that many online purchases have to be made offline as well. Telephony costs are still high (as they are in many parts of the world), and for b2b companies to thrive, *teledensity* (penetration of telephony across the population) and broadband options will have to become more widespread. Nevertheless, Chase Venture Capital has invested over $60 million into Latin Net start-ups and will be adding to that about four new companies every two months. Softbank is there, too (see "The Emperor of the Internet" later in this chapter), and is putting together a $100 million venture fund.

A conclusion for companies not already in Latin America is that their experience in their home markets will help them, but the infrastructure needs may thwart their international success in that region. Many companies would do well to examine cross-border

FastAlliances with local groups who know how to navigate the sometimes tortuous ways of making new and innovative business happen in those areas. Having a knowledgeable (and, more important, well-connected) partner is invaluable.

I am fortunate to have such a person in José Macaya, my partner in Buenos Aires, Argentina, and Santiago, Chile. We spoke about the challenges that alliance partners will face in his region. Here are some of his views:

> There are few original Internet start-ups in Latin America. Most of them are translations of U.S. concepts—online bookstores (like Amazon), auctions (like eBay) and stock brokers (like Schwab). The entrepreneurs who start these companies come from three areas. First, over 50 percent of the young consultants with the large consulting firms are becoming e-business entrepreneurs. For example, BCG lost the manager in charge of Latin America. The second source is MBAs from U.S. universities, especially Harvard[19] and Stanford. Third, graduates from new undergraduate business universities based on the U.S. models, especially from Di Tella and San Andres Universities. About 60 percent of the searches by executive search firms in Argentina are for Internet companies, and compensation is in stock, not cash. Marketing executives are in high demand, as are those in finance (especially ones with U.S. investment banking experience) and technology executives coming from project-related consulting firms. Also in demand are human resource managers with the ability to staff quickly. The management team gets 15 to 20 percent of the company's stock, with 4 to 5 percent going to the CEO. Those with the upper hand are the content companies—newspapers and media who are starting their own Internet companies using U.S. technology in the hopes of selling out to an international company at some point. In fact, Spanish companies are heavily investing in Argentina—Terra (owned by Telefonica) has acquired several portals. Banco Santander Central Hispano purchased of 75 percent of Patagon for $705 million—an Internet broker start-up whose owners were San Andres graduates under 25 years old, Wenceslao Casares and Constancio Larguía.

The e-business real estate grab is global. However, José Macaya draws the distinction: "In Argentina we don't have the right infrastructure to keep the successful Internet start-ups local. Most of the successful ones move their headquarters to Miami where they have better access to local suppliers, Spanish-speaking employees, and more favorable labor laws. This is very worrisome since, although we have the creativity here, it's not translating into long-term and interesting employment for locals."

Patagon.com is a particularly interesting company. It is one of the most popular financial Internet destinations of the Latin American and Spanish markets. Its sites are localized for each country—Brazil, Argentina, Spain, Mexico, Chile, and Venezuela. The company offers banking services, e-commerce payments, access to money markets and online trading through Patagon accounts, and value-added content. U.S. investors Chase Venture Capital and Flatiron Partners added the capital to hire the experienced management required to take the company to sky-high valuations. Patagon.com's marketing strategies were localized to each country within which it operated. Then, in December 1999, the company hit the jackpot with added funding ($53 million) from a variety of investors, including Banco Santander of Spain.

Zsolt T. J. Agardy was one who invested in Patagon.com. He felt that the intensity of entrepreneurs in the region matched those in other parts of the world, with a couple of exceptions: "In Argentina and Chile there is a leapfrog effect taking place in the younger generation, which still has a way to go to catch up with the U.S. consumer culture in purchasing by catalog, mail, and telephone. On the other hand, the common element is in the big egos of Internet management—a phenomenon that seems to be global!" (See more on this in Chapter 5.)

Luis Ramirez Rojas, CEO of Showposition.com, who was introduced to me by José Macaya in Buenos Aires, voiced some optimism regarding his start-up. He felt that he could leverage his substantial industrial experience and reputation to make it successful: "We need as many alliances as we can get. Showposition.com is a company that will allow organizations to track the position of their vehicles through the Internet. Our experience in brick-and-mortar businesses will be what will drive our success on the Internet. It's not an either-or proposition."

It is in this area that traditional businesses will have an advantage if they are already operating in global, culturally sensitive ways.

They can draw on their currency, cultural, transnational, information-sharing experiences and translate them, along with their domestic e-initiatives, into a competitive advantage. The new dot-coms should be aware that they would do well to partner with these traditional companies in many geographic areas—or prepare themselves for some rather unpleasant and delaying surprises (fees, regulations, lack of political connections, permit problems, and other tactics that could make entering that nonhome market an e-nightmare!).

Of course, many dot-coms have already been started by culture-savvy entrepreneurs. I spoke with Ernesto Schmitt (of German, American, and Uruguayan descent), founder and president of of Peoplesound,[20] Europe's largest web company for music discovery. Peoplesound has 3000 artists and is growing daily. It has a three-pronged value proposition:

1. It provides guided discovery and free music for its listeners.
2. It provides a platform for artists so that they can be heard, distributed, and even discovered.
3. It provides a scientific basis for marketing whereby the music industry can test artists on the site before signing them on.

Schmitt is a perfect example of the E-Mindshift start-up entrepreneur (see Chapter 7). He spoke so fast in our interview that thoughts just cascaded out of his mouth. The following is a toned-down, slow-motion version of our conversation:

> When I started in June 1999, the United Kingdom was not yet a major player in e-commerce, and especially in online music. I had a hard time raising money—investors didn't want it. In the last six months of 1999 and the whole of 2000, there has been an explosion in the United Kingdom and Europe. Even the old media are now littered with start-up dot-coms. There is less acceptance in Europe than in the United States. Nevertheless, Europe understands the multicultural needs and multilocal demands really well. To win in Europe, you have to launch in five languages and five markets and cultures right away, and U.S. companies have not done well. For example, a U.K. company, QXL, has beat out eBay over here. Even small start-ups in Europe go immediately for a pan-European launch.

Schmitt's comments are supported by the facts. Timothy Jackson, a 35-year-old *Financial Times* Internet columnist, raised $42 million from Bernard Arnault and Apax[21] for QXL and hired James Rose (an American), who used to run a division of A.C. Nielson in Europe. Rose signed exclusive agreements with Europe's leading portals (Planet Internet in Holland, French Telecom's Wanadoo, and AOL in Germany), rolling out its site in eight countries in local languages and currencies! (In contrast, eBay initially priced everything on its site in dollars when it launched in the United Kingdom and did not make many friends or fans as a result.) The advantage of being the default portal for a wealthy parent (as is Wanadoo for France Telecom) is that a large pot of advertising and brand-building francs goes along with it. The race is on for market dominance.

Such intense competition in the b2c market segment is an early predictor of the b2b and m2m games, which are well under way in Europe, Asia, and Latin America.

Ernesto Schmitt of Peoplesound came from the airline industry and gained his experience there:

> Alliances in the Internet world happen fast and don't need equity. The temptation is to get the big players to invest in you. But most of them tend to fail. Even though the old companies will promise the halo effect[22] and knowledge transfer, it doesn't work very often. What you get is a valuation driver, not a value driver. Traffic and performance have to be measured on a daily basis, so alliances have to work within weeks and, at most, months. And there is no such thing as a defensible business model and barriers to entry. The only things are management insights and skills . . . and content. That is, *proprietary* content.

Peoplesound has 1,000 talent scouts in rehearsal rooms, avenues—wherever artists are found or heard. The talent scouts are paid to bring the artists to Peoplesound, and it is this acquisition method that gives the company defensible content. The artists are not under exclusive contracts, but Peoplesound adds a series of value-added services, such as handing their CDs out at concerts or selling them on its site. The company also has relationship managers working with its top 100 artists to get them record label deals (six are already signed). For every happy artist, Peoplesound claims it gains 200 others. The company has, as Paul Allen would say, "a brave new idea." It has changed the empowerment mechanism so that now the artist is empowered. On the Internet, artists can earn money and be heard without having to sign away their lives.

Peoplesound is also changing the way that the consumer discovers music. Schmitt had this to say when I caught him on the run at his London office:

> Many consumers walk into the store and don't know what they want. Our approach is—you tell us the kind of music you like and through our algorithms we will bring you music you like. Within 10 years there will be no need for CDs. Music will be delivered to the consumer by content aggregators in such a way that you can access a microcommunity that is filled with people who like what you like, and so you can find what you like with little trouble. We are the only place where you can find many of the artists—unlike Amazon where you can go off to Barnes & Noble and get the same product—maybe at a different price, but it's still available. In our industry, people love music and hate the way they have to get it. We are changing that.

The talent scouts that populate Peoplesound with artists are worldwide, culture-specific, and multifaceted. They have created a world community around music and segmented it into microcommunities, which are subsegmented many times by consumer choice into type of music, artist, and language.

E-business Outsourcing Is Happening—Fast

The United States may be the birthplace of e-business, but other places are becoming the preferred centers for web site development due to price considerations. Although many manufacturing activities and software development have beaten a path to countries such as India and China, so has web design. Small entrepreneurial shops are being started by expatriates who have immediate and culturally integrated access to their former homes and can create design shops to connect U.S.-based clients with low-cost web developers.

NetEcho was started by Indian national Sam Gupta and his brother Shobit, both of whom had attended university in the United States, then returned home to India and together started a web design firm that provides services at 90 percent less cost than comparable web design services in the United States.[23] The trends are moving faster in this arena than they did in overseas outsourcing of manufacturing services. Don't be surprised if within 24 months most of the web development is moving offshore, with many larger U.S. development companies outsourcing to keep their costs low, while the mom-and-pop shops in distant locales advertise their wares and services to a global audience like never before.

The Emperor of the Internet

It would be remiss to talk about the international Internet world without mentioning the man whom *Time* magazine calls "The Emperor of the Internet."[24] He is Masayoshi Son (Masa Son), chairman and CEO of Softbank, with a stake in more e-businesses in more countries than any other company in the world—$40 billion in 130 companies.

FastAlliances? "Nonsense," says Masa Son. "Our 300-year plan is the long-term structure we need to fit our goals. . . . Long horizons change your priorities."

He calls his empire a *zaibatsu,* which is a reference to the pre–World War II forerunners of the corporate form known as a *keiretsu*—vertically integrated manufacturing and trading cartels that gave Japan its reputation (and was not constrained by antitrust laws). It was neither a fair game nor played by world rules. Masa Son has changed the rules—somewhat.

I spoke with Ron Fisher (see Chapter 1), CEO of Softbank's operations outside Japan, including Softbank Global Technology Ventures group and start-ups' incubator Hotbank. He said, "Our sense of globalization includes a social responsibility as well as capitalistic involvement. We are working with the World Bank to take the most important brands on the Internet into the next 100 countries beyond the developed world. Not only does this make good economic sense, but it also mitigates the social issues by providing information access to developing countries."

Softbank has created one of the most powerful Spider Networks in history. Masa Son has a deep understanding of the need for a Spider Network. Of Korean descent, he has been an outsider all his life. What joy he must feel now to have created a world that the rich, famous, and powerful are clamoring to join, a world of his own making, where he sets the rules for entry, exit, and dominance—a world where he truly belongs.

Has Masa Son made mistakes? Yes, big ones. The Ziff-Davis acquisition was not an economic marvel, and many of his start-ups have failed. It is the price of admission, according to Masa Son, and only the best will survive. Ron Fisher added, "The Ziff-Davis acquisition was the ticket to play in the game in the United States. It gave huge visibility and access to many of the opportunities that have since evolved."

The acquisition also gave management talent to the enterprise in that the CEO of Ziff-Davis is now the leader of private equity for Softbank internationally.

The Most Advanced Wireless Internet Access Service in the World

DoCoMo is it. How does this company do it? By creating FastAlliances. If anyone has a doubt that the FastAlliances approach is the key strategic device today, the story of DoCoMo will convince them.

Not only has this company been Japan's hottest stock, it is the largest single-country cell phone operator, with a total of 27.1 million Japanese subscribers. Its I-mode phone is the network (the only one for a long time) that allows continuous access to the Internet via a cell phone. Customers are growing by 50,000 per day. However, the way that the company is planning to become a worldwide power in mobile media is through FastAlliances, first with those in Japan who can help the company fend off foreign rivals such as Vodaphone Airtouch, British Telecom, and AT&T. DoCoMo already has a substantial Spider Network of equipment and service suppliers (NTT, which owns 67 percent of DoCoMo, Fujitsu, and Hitachi). It also has the advantage of having been the first totally wireless anytime anywhere technology, which means it has set the standard—low price, high content, and revenue-sharing arrangements with content providers who gain access to their customers from the I-mode menu bar. In its first year in operation, with more than $100 million in revenues and a user base of 5 million, the company projected that within 12 to 18 months DoCoMo's I-mode could exceed America Online's subscription base of 21 million. The reality has far exceeded projections. By the end of 2000, I-mode (interactive, Internet, and independent) has over 17 million subscribers. And the buzz in the industry is that DoCoMo and

AOL are in talks to create an alliance. The company's FastAlliances members include Sun Microsystems for the Java program and a joint venture with Microsoft called Mobimagic to develop wireless data services for Japan. These relationships will help the company deal with hometown rivals DDI Corp. and IDO Corp., which account for 27 percent of the cell phone market. DDI and IDO are merging their cell phone operations in the hopes of competing more effectively with DoCoMo, but the key will be who can create cross-border relationships fast enough to preempt the other players. At the moment, DoCoMo is out in front,[25] and, through widely placed advertisements, is making itself known to U.S. consumers. One of DoCoMo's biggest challenges is breaking away from the bureaucratic culture of its investor, NTT. Another is creating a swift and Cool Decision Process. Let's look at another Japanese company that has made a start in this area.

Breaking the Traditions of the Past to Enable the Future

The traditional way of making decisions in Japan could be seen to hinder the acceleration to the Net for many companies. However, some Japanese companies realize that accommodations must be made. In recent conversations, Peter Clark, president and CEO of Hitachi Semiconductor (America) Inc., revealed to me how quickly certain decisions have been made with respect to e-business opportunities at Hitachi:

> For example, we are involved in a number of consortia-type exchanges. One, called RosettaNet, develops protocols for semiconductor companies to replace EDI and do e-commerce on the Net. Another is the consortium with Compaq and HP. These decisions were made very quickly, by anyone's standards. We are examining our internal as well as our external activities with a view to being e-business-ready and competent. Upper management is very aware of the need for change. Some within middle management are afraid of it, and that is understandable. But it is being driven from the office of the president, because the change is inevitable.

Another major Japanese company that is adapting to the e-business world in a different industry is Toyota.[26] I spoke with Irv Miller, vice president of the office of the web for Toyota Motor Sales, who commented:

> There is no question that in many ways E-GM is further ahead than Toyota in the e-business environment. We are a very traditional company and the office of the web operates within this traditional structure. This poses both an opportunity and a challenge. The opportunity is that our structure is different. Within the office of the web we have five different organizations. One of these is the group charged with b2c operations, working with the dealer network on web page development and to create opportunities for them. We have made a commitment to go through our channels and not around them. Our brands of Lexus and Toyota are our keys to the consumer and are augmented by marketing alliances with Coach and also American Express for their Platinum customers, as well as Barnes & Noble and Dell Computers. Our goal is to lower the age demographic of our buyer, and we are using these alliances to help us do that and to extend to our web strategy as well.

Miller conceded that the traditional way of making decisions in Japan has complicated issues in the e-business environment. However, change is happening.

> TMC [Toyota Motor Corporation] in Japan has realized that business is moving fast and that was their rationale in establishing the office of the web, which will facilitate a speedy decision process. We have many initiatives. One of them is the NETCAR, which is the transition of the automobile into an Internet contact point to web-enable the consumer in their car. This enables the strengthening of the bond with the consumer, since dashboard time is owned by the automaker. If the company has the consumers' permission to deliver valuable ideas while they are driving, and as bandwidth increases, the entertainment companies and ISPs [e.g., AOL, Time Warner] will naturally align with the auto manufacturers—and we will be right there. For Toyota, it is not so important to be the first mover. We are quite pleased to be second, but with a better and improved idea.

I was intrigued. A traditional Japanese company that has changed its decision-making processes? After all, one would expect entrepreneurial moves by a Masa Son, the king of independent thinking, but Toyota? I was not disappointed when I spoke to the father of the idea to create a FastAlliances between Toyota Motor Sales and I2 Technologies in the United States, Doug Formby. Toyota Motor Sales is the marketing, sales, distribution, and customer service arm of Toyota in the United States, which oversees operations for more than 1,400 Toyota, Lexus, and Toyota Industrial Equipment dealerships in 49 states. I2 is a leading global provider of intelligent e-business solutions.

The iStarXchange

The iStarXchange is the first b2b parts and service marketplace to serve the automotive replacement parts market. Toyota has two of the three board members and i2 has one. Formby lived the genesis and evolution of this project. He was in strategic planning in the parts logistics division and was creating a long-range strategy to compete in the new economy. This meant developing not only a market strategy but also a technology strategy. When examining his company's existing internal alliances, Formby saw that it had varying and limited capabilities with its trading partners and could not leverage these and other relationships. A major investment had to be made in enabling technology. In order to leverage the technology investment and create greater total system efficiency, it was necessary to adapt the power of the Internet to improve the Toyota supply chain. That gave birth to the idea for the exchange. The challenge was to make it happen in Internet time. The traditional decision-making process at Toyota would not enable the opportunity to be realized at Internet speed. Figure 6.4 is a schematic of Toyota's traditional decision-making process.[27]

Toyota's traditional decision-making process is based on receiving consensus through a process called *nemawashi* (i.e., each individual involved in the decision is presold and his or her comments incorporated prior to the decision meeting). In effect, the majority of discussion and debate occurs between levels and among management at the same level. Due to the amount of preliminary meetings and idea refinement that occurs between each meeting, the decision process is methodical and often slow.

Figure 6.4 illustrates the typical process. Most ideas are generated and flushed out by the manager/national manager (or this person is asked to prepare an analysis of an idea generated from a higher level). Once the analysis is prepared, it is reviewed with the manager's direct report, usually a corporate manager. The corporate manager's revi-

Figure 6.4 Toyota's Traditional Decision-Making Process

sions are incorporated, and the analysis is reviewed at the next level, working its way up. Of course, an idea can be killed at any time during this process if it is deemed unacceptable. The idea is then reviewed with each member of the executive committee individually. Once all of their comments are incorporated and each member is satisfied with the proposal, it is taken to the executive committee to be approved. If approved, the proposal is then taken to the Toyota Motor Corporation (TMC) in Japan. It is an understatement to say that it is tough to make change happen fast with this system.

After examining the cumbersome traditional decision-making process, what Formby and his colleagues achieved seems remarkable. The approval process to launch iStarXchange, the joint venture between Toyota Motor Sales and i2 Technologies, was much quicker and involved far fewer decision makers. The approval process can be broken into two phases. Phase 1 lasted six weeks, which included a 10-day holiday break, and focused on refining the business concept and thoroughly analyzing the business and financial implications. This phase ended with the signing of a memorandum of understanding (MOU). Phase 2 focused on due diligence of the model and ended after three weeks with the signing of a final agreement. Six weeks for a decision that led to an MOU. Pretty impressive!

Here is how it worked. (See Figures 6.5 and 6.6.)

I2 Technologies was retained by TMS for an internal consulting engagement. The idea for iStarXchange was initially developed during this engagement. The leader of the project, Doug Formby, took the idea to Dave Illingworth, senior vice president for the office of the web, and Barbra Cooper, chief technology officer. The concept appeared to have merit, and Illingworth agreed to formally sponsor the project. The process had to move fast at this point because TMS and i2 had an exclusivity agreement on the concept for only six weeks. Formby and his team reduced the lengthy presentation to one page for Illingworth to review with the executive committee on the

Figure 6.5 The iStarXchange Decision Process within Toyota Motor Sales. (Phase 1: Concept Rationale to Design of Memorandum of Understanding [Four to Six Weeks])

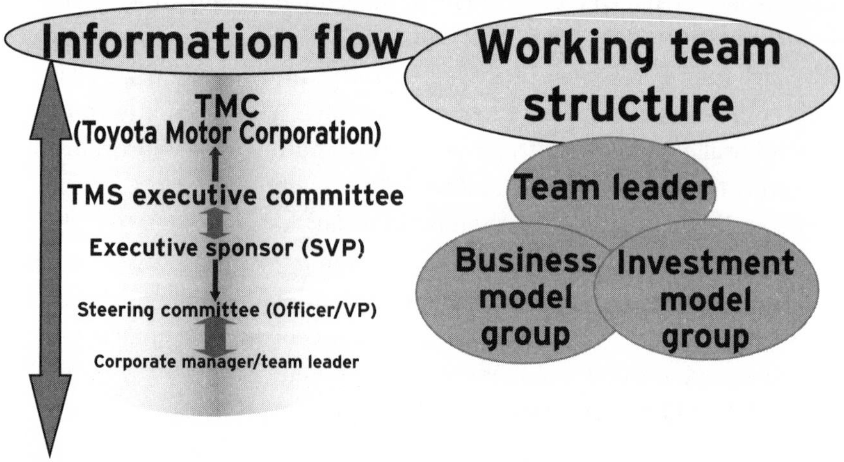

Figure 6.6 The iStarXchange Decision Process within Toyota Motor Sales. (Phase 2: Due Diligence to Final Agreement [Three Weeks])

following day. General interest was created and more detailed reviews followed with each of the executive committee members over the next couple of days.

The executive committee approved the creation of a working team and a steering committee of company officers and VPs to oversee it.

The working team met with the executive sponsor and steering committee during the process at significant action and decision points. The sponsor had the responsibility to communicate with the executive committee. If he was unable to meet with committee members, then a member of the working team would take that role. During this phase, the working team broke into two groups—(1) the business model team, which focused on refining the concept and identifying the business implications, and (2) the investment model team, which focused on refining the financial and legal implications. Based on a recommendation from the working team, the steering committee, and the executive sponsor, the executive committee gave approval to sign an MOU with i2 Technologies. At that point, Yoshi Inaba (CEO of TMS), Dave Illingworth, and Doug Formby met with several senior executives in Japan and received final approval to sign the MOU.

The objectives for phase 2 had changed from model formulation to critical evaluation and refinement. Consequently, the team structure was also changed to include four groups: advocate, risk, finance, and technology.

1. The primary mission of the *advocate group* was to identify and support the reasons that TMS should approve iStarXchange.
2. The *risk group* had to identify the risks associated with approval.
3. The *finance group* was to evaluate the financial model and perform sensitivity analysis.
4. The *technology group* was to evaluate the feasibility of the technology required, whether it was practical to develop what was needed in the proposed time frame, and whether i2 was the best partner.

Each group had a sponsoring officer.

The team leaders and Dave Illingworth met twice a week to discuss and resolve difficult issues. As in phase 1, Illingworth had primary responsibility for updating the executive committee. The working team presented three scenarios to this group, the recommendation was presented to the executive committee, and it was unanimously approved. A member of the executive committee took the recommendation to Japan, where it was approved by TMC.

To say that Illingworth, Formby, and their team were elated would be an understatement. They had achieved a first in the history of the Toyota organization: six weeks for a primary decision and nine weeks for the final commitment.

Doug Formby told me during our interview, "The traditional route would never have worked within this time frame because many in the organization would have been afraid that we would alienate our dealers. The challenge for the company was to create an environment that was able to take risk—a huge culture change, both corporate and country."

Formby is the chief operating officer of the new venture, which as yet has no revenues. The fledgling is building the technology infrastructure and lining up industry participants at this time. The exchange aims to bring together many players in the parts business who have not previously been connected in this way. Doug shared with me two flowcharts describing the new venture. The iStarXchange will enable the current value chain, as seen in Figure 6.7, to operate more efficiently, as seen in Figure 6.8.

At the present time (Figure 6.7), all information about the supply chain is contained in silos and protected by those who have it. The major focus of the OEM at present is toward its suppliers and distributors, who then access the dealers to get to the customer. Suppliers, however, access their own warehouse distributors, who connect with jobbers and installers as well as retailers. It's messy, to say the least. Of course, warehouse distributors can bypass the jobber altogether and go directly to the installer and the retailer. The suppliers can also go to the retailers directly. Methods of communication include snail mail, phone, fax, face-to-face, and some Internet. All the arrows are

Figure 6.7 The Present System

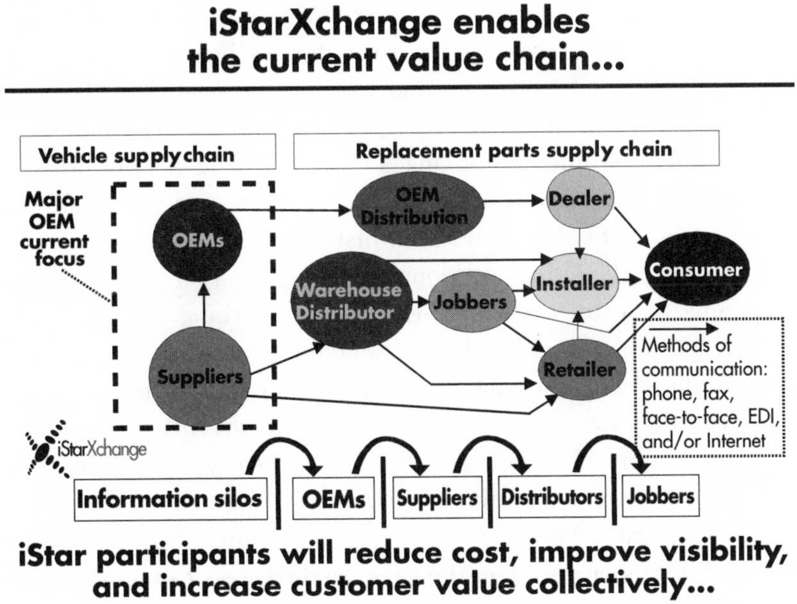

Figure 6.8 The iStarXchange Solution

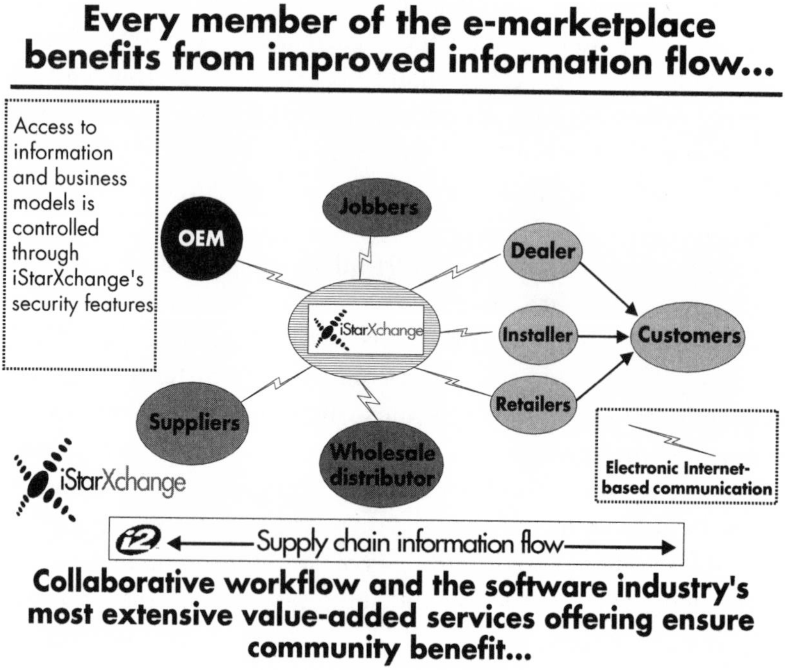

going to the right, and very little information is coming back. Everyone uses rates of return to make estimates on the amount of inventory that is needed—since no one has clear information. There is huge waste in the system.

Figure 6.8 outlines the changes that iStarXchange will bring to the industry. Now the jobbers, OEMs, suppliers, and wholesale distributors connect with the dealers, installers, and retailers to serve the customer. All communications are Internet-based, with information going in all directions. Every time something gets sold, the inventory levels are updated and true demands will be passed back through the system to enable the calculation of real inventory figures. Whereas now every manufacturer has the overhead of huge distribution centers (Toyota's are 400,000 square feet, but others are even larger), with 6 to 7 million square feet of storage space housing 5 to 7 billion parts daily, the new system eliminates the need for the inventory levels presently in the value chain. OEMs can now partner to create master depots for fulfillment, and the dealers can cut 50 days or more out of their systems and convert the space to other uses, thus reducing floor plan cost. Labor costs diminish since there will be no need for employees to tell customers what is in the catalog and at what prices. The jobbers are most at risk. There are 25,000 in the United States alone. At present, they serve the purpose of information flow—but with the new system, their days could be numbered. Now the supplier can look at the whole value chain and see end to end what the product is doing. They can dialogue on line. The rules of the game have changed.

The impact of the iStarXchange has yet to be felt. Some will be delighted, others concerned. As with all FastAlliances in e-business, when rules change, opportunities for some become losses for others. In this case, the jump into the new happened from a most unlikely place—a traditional Japanese company that overcame culture and history. Such is the influence of the new economy.

Create a Common Language and Value Definition

There is an e-business company that deals with many of the challenges faced by traditional companies who are making their first foray into the e-business world of exchanges, as Toyota did. CommerceOne operates on four continents, using FastAlliances with traditional companies. Jeff Smith, vice president of business development and global alliances, gave me the global perspective for his company.

> B2b is not just a U.S. phenomenon. In fact, we are in some ways behind those in Asia in this arena. The reason is that we have been very aggressive in the United States in the b2c area and have the lead—no doubt. Companies in Asia have seen that and have no intention of letting U.S. brands take over their b2b segments—for example, as Yahoo! did when it came into Japan with a U.S. brand. They have come together fast, with the minimum of politics or maneuvering, and have created consortia with us that are tying up the b2b market there. How have we done it? We have partnered with the local players in each major world market. Our partner in the United Kingdom is British Telecom; in Japan our partner is NTT; it's Cable and Wireless in Australia, BANMAX in Mexico. These partners not only give us credibility in the local business

> environment, but they also jump-start the activity using the exchange and consortia for their own cost savings. They automate their own buys and catalog content and then externalize that content, making it available as a service and site for other players who are not part of the consortium for a fee. Our partners help us to adapt to local customs and regulations.

CommerceOne has been approached proactively by Asian consortia rather than having to create the group itself. In addition, the predominance of group rather than individual cultures encourages these arrangements, many of which have existed in *keireitsu* (Japan) and *chaebols* (Korea) in the past.

Global Work Teams

In my monthly e-mail newsletter[28] (which goes out to over 100,000 executives in more than 70 countries), I recently emphasized the need for global work teams. To make FastAlliances work in the e-business enviroment, work teams are a critical success factor. The following elements make FastAlliances global work teams happen and succeed:

1. *Select team members from every country represented in the effort.* This means choosing at least one from each culture that is significant to the project. Regional selections are not good enough (e.g., a German to represent all of Europe, a Japanese to represent all of Asia). We are talking about customization that requires a *real* understanding of cultural differences. The Internet now allows for specificity of application—the nuances and subtleties of subcultures (the Beijing supersophisticates versus Shenzhen cowboys).

2. *Choose the right team leader.* This can be a real challenge because not every culture approaches power and hierarchy the same way. Egalitarian cultures such as the United States and Canada will be uncomfortable with the structured and respectful formality of northern German cultures, or even with the protocol-conscious Parisian French culture. Since these cultures have to work together, some level of cultural adjustment will be necessary, which means discussing and learning different ways of resolving conflict, delegating authority, reporting procedures, and compromising. What will be required is the signing of a psychological contract: "I promise to put

aside my dot-com self-esteem for the moment (which doesn't diminish who I am) in order to work with people I might otherwise offend."

3. *Define success.* This may mean breaking the paradigm—namely, doing a good job of researching, piloting, and proving the strategy over time, reporting back, and so on, which otherwise might constitute prudent and well-trained execution, could be ineffective in the e-business space. To prevent one group (with U.S.-style dot-com self-esteem) from pressuring another group (who may have a consensus-building approach to team work), the team will have to create its own cultural rules. This will cause some discomfort for everyone, but it will evolve into a working understanding that will enable the team to move forward.[29] Team members may come from different corporate cultures or perhaps from different divisions of a single company that are in different life-cycle stages. Hence the diversity of corporate and individual managerial personalities will be a challenge. The ability to proactively diagnose these differences using the E-Mindshift approach (see Chapter 7) will facilitate making this a manageable process.

4. *Align project priorities.* If members of the global team have varying priorities (what I call *project personalities* in the E-Mindshift approach), this imbalance of interests will jeopardize the relationship. It means that timing will be different, resourcing will be unbalanced, and commitment will be challenging. Bitterness and disappointment will often follow since it will appear as if some team members are not pulling their weight. What follows is often cultural stereotyping (Americans are pushy, Brits are stiff, etc.). Again, you must create a *team* culture that brings differences into the open and lets them be negotiated and discussed (even though for nonverbal cultures that may be difficult). After-hours socializing and seeing people out of the work environment can go a long way toward building relationships with more substance.

5. *Even if communicating remotely by e-mail, wireless, or both, at a certain point in time it is critical to have a series of in-person meetings to build the human-to-human contact that will provide the goodwill needed to overcome differences as they arise.* These meetings must include social and bonding experiences that enable different cultures to create relationships that are not just work-related.

Small Is Large

The phenomenon of the Internet age is that small companies can act like large ones from inception. Recently, I spoke with Chris Lyman, CEO and founder of Virtualis, a web-hosting application service provider headquartered in Los Angeles, about this phenomenon.

> We are a small company, about 90 employees at the moment. We were *very* small for a while. I started the company in 1997. Basically, I wanted a way to help web designers help their customers. So I created a program to make them resellers of our web-hosting services, giving them 25 percent of the first customers' fees that they put on the service and an override on the next level so that every month they made money. I printed up 1,000 flyers and asked my sister and my girlfriend to dress up and stand outside a CompUSA store and hand out flyers to all the technogeeks [his term!] as they came out of the store. When the store told us to clear out, we went to the next one we could find, and by the end of that day we were exhausted. The next day when we woke up, there were five resellers on our site. That day we did the same thing, and the next morning we had 35 resellers. We did it one more day—and have never recruited since then. We now have 45,000 resellers, and we are hosting businesses in 96 countries from shoe stores in Zimbabwe to record stores in Italy. Our affiliate program is global, and until we raised our first round of capital, we were profitable for 2.5 years since our customer acquisition costs were very low. Now, of course, our expenditures have gone up a lot, and we are looking to raise serious money, but we can smell profitability again, and we know how that tastes!

Indeed. This also means that competitive analysis for Virtualis is a global effort, since a small mom-and-pop shop in Singapore could be building a worldwide base before it would even have popped up on the traditional radar screen.

The Asian region, cultures, and ruling families are reevaluating their business models. It is clear, after the economic upheavals of the past five years, that property, heavy industry, and retail are not sufficient old-economy supports for new-economy demands. However in combination with e-commerce portals and trade, they create a significant power base. The Lamsam family of Thailand (Thai Farmers Bank and Loxley Industrial Group) now uses a corporate intranet to communicate, bypassing hierarchies and rigid structures of etiquette and relaxing dress codes. Valuable real estate is now also in cyberspace, not only in property. Richard Li, son of billionaire Li Ka-shing, has parlayed his Pacific Century CyberWorks into an Internet power broker in Hong Kong. Peter Lee has created a way to deliver broadband Net access through his family's gas company. Jeffrey Koo is creating an e-commerce strategy for Chinatrust (a private financial group), linking broadband service, online trading, and business portals.[30] Developing a culture of speed, flexibility, and responsiveness is a major culture shift for these large organizations, and it is being driven by the younger generation, some of whom are also bringing new management styles and corporate cultures. However, some of the moves are merely old-economy deals sporting the right lingo, such as the Jakarta Soeryadjaya family's real estate deals in Indonesia.

What's the point? Track the potential power of these conglomerates once they get the formula right. Some are still reluctant to throw themselves headlong into high-risk ventures, but once the new-economy influences catch fire, look out. In much the same way as Masa Son of Softbank created an empire that will soon span the world, the family conglomerates in Asia have the potential to do the same. The rest of us have the choice to create FastAlliances with them or to compete. And the alliance you create may not be able to remain FastAlliances in type. It may take some relationship building, longer negotiations, and many of the processes discussed in my first book, *Intelligent Business Alliances,* which will integrate into traditional alliances. No matter which processes are used, the effort will be worth it. Just as Masa Son imported successful Internet companies to Japan (Yahoo!) and took them public, there is no reason why U.S. and European financiers and entrepreneurs can't do the same in reverse (Asia out, instead of Asia in).

One way into the Asian region, which is also facilitating Asia out, is the portal China.com, which has 1,600 people worldwide. I spoke with its new business development wiz, Chet Hong. China.com is the largest service integrator in Asia and also distributes content through its other portals, Taiwan.com, Hongkong.com, and AOL China through AOL Hong Kong. The company distributes through these various portals and leads visitors into vertical markets in sports, finance, technology, beauty, fashion, and so on. Each portal has its own community and commerce. Revenues come from advertisements, sales, and sponsorships. The company works with Softbank Strategic Ventures and has many alliances that support its business in Asian and Greater China markets. Since Asia represents more than half of the world's population, China.com considers its market grab to be the winning formula. It's hard to argue with the facts—yet the hurdles that must be overcome are resistance to online shopping and a lack of faith that merchants will take the products back or guarantee them. The fact is that credit cards are a debt-facilitating mechanism. For many Asian cultures, the concept of debt is quite different from that of the United States. Hence, many in Japan have created a new kind of business model for e-commerce, whereby consumers order products online but pay for and receive them in convenience stores (*conbini*). In addition, the banks in Asia are becoming an integral part of the consortia with ISPs (formerly monopolistic) and merchants as well as new micropayment upstarts such as San Francisco–based iPIN to create a system where consumers click on the item they want to buy, then on the iPIN logo to confirm the amount with a personal password, after which iPIN applies the amount to their ISP, telcom bill, credit card, or bank account. The system also allows personal iPIN accounts to be allocated to family members with spending limits attached![31]

The bottom line is that partnering in Asia means going with the big guns since the risks are still there, but the market size makes one gasp. Indeed, how can you *not* be there?

The Invisible Invader

Bluetooth, created in the Swedish Laboratories of Ericsson, is a short-range radio hookup that resides on a microchip. A consortium of technology companies worldwide (including Nokia, Sony, Microsoft, Intel, and IBM) are rushing to integrate this hookup into their products. What does Bluetooth mean to the world? Its signal is more powerful than infrared, goes through walls, and can carry voice as well as data. Why is everyone in a fast-forward mode to get this? The consortium is giving it away for free, to set up a world standard, but of course the chip manufacturers will get the revenues from making new chips—which everyone will need. The worldwide application means that if you travel to London and realize you forgot to release the sensors inside your U.S. house (which will cause a repair person to set off your alarm), you can do it through your cell phone while traveling on the London tube. Bluetooth could extend this technology to every appliance and every electronic instrument we use, making the cell phone the "remote control to end all remote controls."

As it applies to the FastAlliances global environment, if you are not in or creating a global Spider Network, you could miss innovations like this until they hit you between the eyes. Constant global competitive scanning is part of the Spider once you achieve Connectivity Velocity (see Chapter 1). Remember, however, that increased access involves privacy issues: Effective Spidering[32] will be limited by the lowest level of security of the least secure member of the network. Should Bluetooth make ubiquitous access a reality, security measures (such as remembering to close off access) will presumably become as habitual as locking the door of your home. Those who are accustomed to living with a level of paranoia will adapt quickly. Those who aren't will have some adjusting to do.

It is risky and inaccurate to create a formalistic approach to anything regarding culture. In addition, the globalization of e-business is in its infancy. My goal has been to raise the issues and to offer some approaches so that the opportunities trickle up and the challenges trickle down! Chapter 8 will get into the nitty-gritty of making FastAlliances work.

CHAPTER 7

Step 7: Employing the E-Mindshift System

In my first book, *Intelligent Business Alliances*, Chapter 2 was devoted to the Mindshift™ system. In this book, I have adapted the approach to apply to e-business organizations and executives and called it E-Mindshift.

E-Mindshift: FastAlliances Tool #14

The Mindshift approach is developed by looking at the life cycles of organizations, whether as a whole, by division, by group, or even by product. The premise is that organizations change their personalities (culture and more) depending on the life-cycle stage that they are in. For a multidivisional organization, this means that each division could be in a different life-cycle stage, thus accounting for the cultural and communication clashes that occur between them. The approach also addresses the individual managerial personalities that tend to change as the life cycle of the organization changes. The final aspect of the methodology is to examine the project personalities by determining differences in priorities for each alliance partner—ranging from bet-the-farm-type projects to middle-of-the-road projects to those that may be experimental. The E-Mindshift approach is based on the same premise. However, there are a number of significant differences in the e-business application, and these are outlined in this chapter.

Why use the E-Mindshift approach, and how is it helpful? It gives you a way to look at the personalities and cultures of the companies that you will be partnering with as well as your own company. By using the charts, you can plot which stage of the life cycle your organization falls into and which stages your partners fall into as well. Understanding the life-cycle stage will enable you to *predict* its behavior by using your judgment, guided by the characteristics that are typical for each stage. Knowing what to expect in most circumstances can be of value. However, use the E-Mindshift approach with discretion because of the potential for exceptions that exists in all human-directed situations.

There is little time for repeating mistakes in the e-business world. You'll gain a distinct advantage by being able to proactively understand or expect a certain type of behavior because this will allow you to design and modify your strategy, your attitude and resources, the people who will best lead or follow the FastAlliances effort, and all the other factors that go into successful FastAlliances based on knowledge about your own company and your partners. Use this approach as a diagnostic and a method of planning how to manage all FastAlliances relationships.

Figures 7.1 and 7.2 show, respectively, the different life-cycle stages for e-business organizations and the individual managerial personalities most commonly found in each life-cycle stage.

The life cycle of FastAlliances is compressed. The start-up stage is closely allied to the high-growth, or hockeystick (on a graph it looks like a hockeystick), stage, although they remain as two separate stages of company or project. Hence, as with the industrycity.com example in Chapter 5, whether a start-up is within a large company or a venture-backed deal as in Stamps.com, it takes more than just capital and an idea to gain growth. Growth can happen fast, however.

Take the example of Napster. This company was started by 19-year-old founder Shawn Fanning in the last few months of 1999. He has been overwhelmed, not only with the attention but also with the negative assaults by the Recording Industry Association of America.

Figure 7.1 E-Mindshift: FastAlliances Tool #14
(Life Cycles of E-Businesses: Corporate and Individual Managerial Personalities)

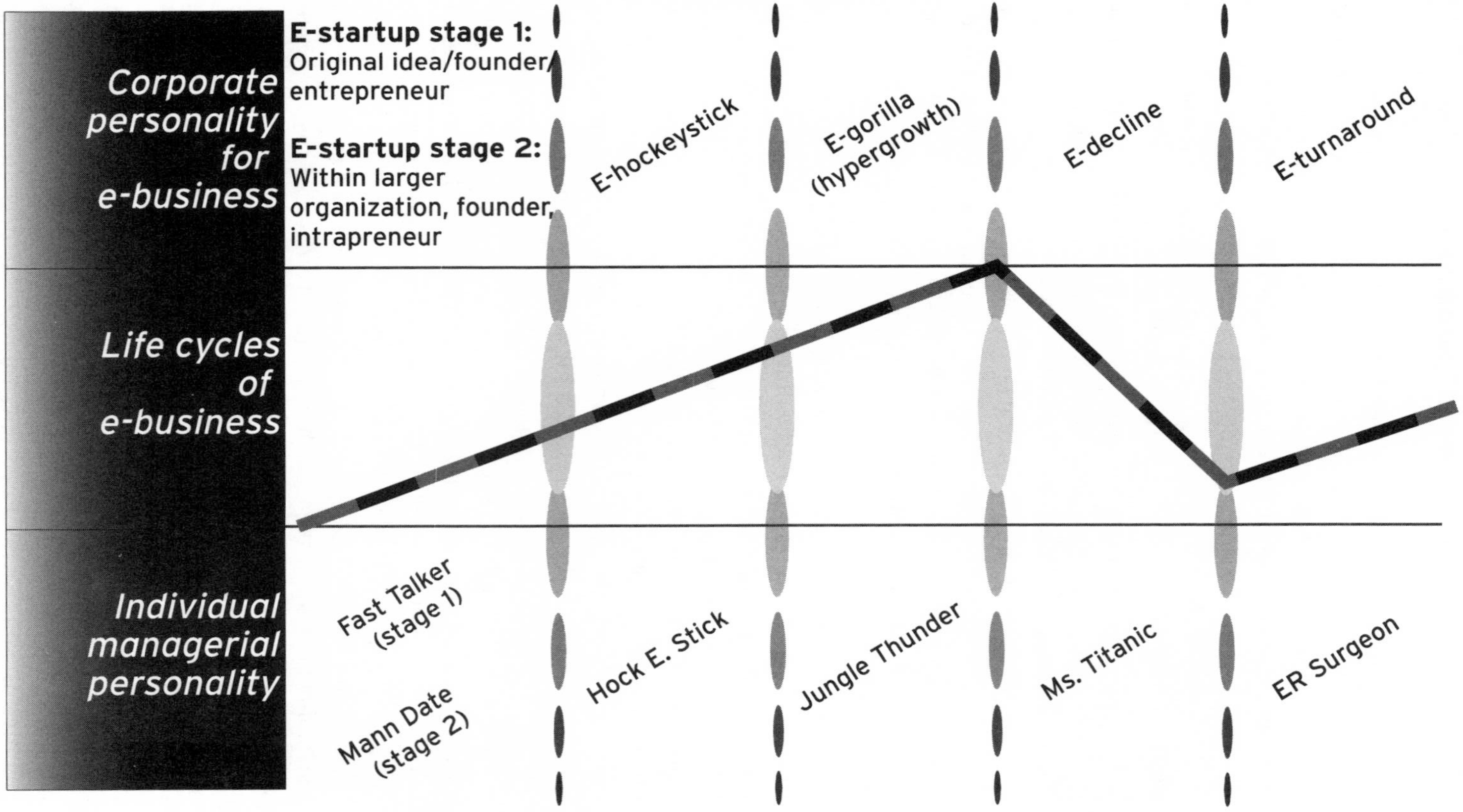

Figure 7.2 E-Mindshift: FastAlliances Tool #14

(Personality Characteristics of E-Business Managers in Each Life-Cycle Stage)

Corporate personality	**E-startup stage 1:** **Original idea/founder/entrepreneur** •Faster•Arrogant and driven•Anyone from anywhere, any age or background•Technology savvy•Starter Spider Network•Promotional•24/7•Outsource everything except consumer contact **E-startup stage 2:** **Within larger organization, founder, intrapreneur** •Understands need to learn dot-com self-esteem•Corporate citizen with urgency for change within the system•Business case developed, approved, seeded by corporate parent•Established industry Spider Network–e-business Spider in development •Slower to start but has resources (capital and industry) for fast leverage•Cherry picks team from inside and outside parent •Outsourcing is cautiously progressive	**E-hockeystick** •Developed Spider Network •Multiple alliances to gain market share/gaps in tech/product/service offerings•Arrogant•Accessible and quick response times•Lack of management depth and training•Management by observation, apprenticeship style•Financing source (parent or VC/corporate VC) looking for professional managers •Spinout optional if in corporate parent or IPO if independent•24-7•Outsourcing well accepted	**E-gorilla (hypergrowth)** •Works in packs•Gorillas lead each corp. function•Not a solo thing–team culture•Coordination and delegation•Aggressive•Territorial–claim, patrol, expand •Not a pure breed–Darwinian best of breed and strongest players survive •Lieutenants of different gorilla packs target new CEOs for e-start-ups and e-hockeysticks•Mercenary feel since market for human capital so acute•Founder often up to chairman of board•Deals come faster than speed of light and can be internally funded	**E-decline** •No or poor leadership–founder departure•Competition perfects/adds value to original idea/business model•VC/parent disillusioned with promises not kept–ceases funding, looks to sell•Lack of focus–jumping from strategy to strategy•Puncturing of dot-com self-esteem–anger, resentment, pushback to authority •Interference in daily operations by politician managers from VC or parent•Outsourcing vendors blamed and often terminated	**E-turnaround** •Acquirer takes over, decimates original team/concept, taking only good parts *or* new CEO with external credibility •Relaunch with new capital, press/analyst communication and fresh team•Short window for success or reverse into decline again•Alliances with big brands reposition company•Like start-up stage, but shorter window–make or break in 60 to 90 days•Back to core business–what is it that we actually do?
Individual managerial personality	**Fast Talker (stage 1)** •Dot-com self-esteem•Fearless and willing to enter snake pit• Absorbent like a sponge •Nonhierarchal and light on metrics•Generates excitement•Huge energy and missionary zeal•Creative and entrepreneurial•Learning e-slang but not fluent **Mann Date (stage 2)** •Respects skinny process•Likes growing company/people•Good leader•High energy •Creative and knows how to maneuver in organizations•Financial skills and good operating experience	**Hock E. Stick** •Frustrated with non-e-speed cultures•Metrics–revenue and market share-related •Problem-solving skills to execute on the vision•Speaks fluent e-slang•Aggressive, can be dismissive•Can-do attitude–can think of way to exit snake pit with gold •Cunning, smooth, and wicked smart•If high priority, instant follow-up•If internal to large co, e-group more open to limited process	**Jungle Thunder** •Professional manager with experience in brick-and-click•Arrogant–it's good to be the king•Knowledgeable •Pressworthy•Platinum Spider Network•Paranoid (rightfully so)•Dismissive if idea doesn't grab him or her in first two minutes	**Ms. Titanic** •Denial•Angry•Brilliant but misguided•Looking for valuation, not value •Desperate•Metrics become confused (or worse, get cooked)•We can do it better ourselves	**ER Surgeon** •Domain expertise•Focused like a laser beam •Upbeat and self-confident•Good financial, controls, managerial, leadership•Solid Spider Network•Focus on the metrics and reward systems for performance•Create sandbox for founder•My way or the highway (no democracy)•New hope–focus on short-term success•SWAT team to implement•Speed/metrics combined•Outsource with caution

He has invented an architecture that makes downloading our favorite tunes incredibly simple. Music is not actually traded through the site; instead, Napster's software, which is free to anyone who wants to download it, allows you to send a piece of music from your computer to another user's hard drive in under a minute.

Until the recording industry prevailed in a lawsuit against the company, teens were rushing to the site. Napster's user base grew anywhere from 5 to 25 percent daily. In March 2000, over 5 million people had downloaded the software. The attacks on Napster's activities (which are alleged to be a form of music piracy) could set a legal precedent in this area. In July 2000, a federal appeals court ordered Napster's site to shut down, and 48 hours later, a federal appeals court issued a reprieve. Whether Napster survives or not, the barn door to being "Napsterized" is open. (The term *Napsterized* refers to an industry policy designed to reduce what customers are willing to pay for a product or service to zero.)

Many e-business companies are still in the hockeystick stage of the e-economy. They have not lived through the stages of maturity or decline. Some, however, have gone directly from hockeystick into decline or have been acquired on the way down or at their peak. Others have entered a new stage of hockeystick, a hyperhockeystick stage, and have remained there. For those who have gone into decline, turnaround will be a management opportunity for executives who have a base of experience in the e-business space and management expertise from traditional businesses. But for many, the next 18 months isn't even on their radar screen. A little later, after discussing E-Mindshift personalities, I will make some predictions for years 2001 to 2005. Let's start with what is happening now.

The E-Mindshift Corporate Personality

1. E-start-up: stage 1 (original idea/founder/entrepreneur)
    - Faster
    - Arrogant and driven
    - Anyone from anywhere, any age, any background
    - Technology/market savvy
    - Starter Spider Network

- Promotional
- 24-7
- Outsource everything except customer contact

2. E-start-up: stage 2 (within larger organization, founder/intrapraneur)
    - Understands need to learn dot-com self-esteem
    - Corporate citizen with urgency for change within the system
    - Business case developed, approved, and seeded by corporate parent
    - Established industry Spider—e-business Spider in development
    - Slower to start but has resources (capital and industry) for fast leverage
    - Picks team from inside and outside parent
    - Outsourcing is cautiously progressive
3. E-hockeystick (both stages of start-up)
    - Developed Spider Network
    - Multiple alliances to gain market share/gaps in tech/product/service offerings
    - Arrogant
    - Accessible and quick response times
    - Lack of management depth and training
    - Management by observation, apprenticeship style
    - Financing source (parent or VC/corporate VC) looking for professional managers
    - Spinout optional if in corporate parent or IPO if independent
    - 24-7
    - Outsourcing well accepted
4. E-gorilla (hypergrowth; both stages of start-up)
    - Work in packs
    - Gorillas lead each function

- Not a solo thing—team culture
- Coordination and delegation
- Aggressive
- Territorial—claim, patrol, and expand
- Not a pure breed—Darwinian best of breed—strongest players
- Lieutenants of different gorilla pack target new CEOs for e-start-ups and e-hockeystick
- Mercenary feel since market for human capital so acute
- Founder often up to chairman of the board
- Deals come faster than speed of light and can be internally funded

5. E-decline (both stages of start-up)
   - No/poor leadership—founder departure
   - Competition perfects/adds value to original idea/business model
   - VC/parent disillusioned with promises not kept—ceases funding, looks to sell
   - Lack of focus—jumping from strategy to strategy
   - Puncturing of dot-com self-esteem—anger, resentment, push-back to authority
   - Interference in daily operations by politician managers (VC/parent)
   - Outsourcing vendors blamed and often terminated
6. E-turnaround (both stages of start-up)
   - Acquirer takes over, decimates original team/concept, taking only good parts,

   or

   - New CEO with external credibility
   - Relaunch with new capital, press/analyst communications, and fresh team
   - Short window for success or reverses into decline again

- Alliances with big brands reposition company
- Like start-up stage 1, but shorter window—make or break 60 to 90 days
- Back to core business—what is it we actually do?

The E-Mindshift Individual Managerial Personalities

1. The Fast Talker (e-start-up stage 1)
    - Dot-com self-esteem
    - Fearless and willing to enter snake pit
    - Absorbent—like a sponge
    - Nonhierarchal and light on metrics
    - Generates excitement
    - Huge energy and missionary zeal
    - Creative and entrepreneurial
    - Learning e-slang but not fluent
2. Mann Date (e-start-up stage 2)
    - Respects skinny process
    - Likes growing companies and people
    - Good leader
    - High energy
    - Creative and knows how to maneuver within organizations
    - Financial skills and good operating experience
3. Hock E. Stick (e-hockeystick)
    - Frustrated with non-e-speed cultures
    - Revenue-driven, metrics revenue- and market share–related
    - Problem-solving skills to execute on the vision
    - Speaks e-slang fluently
    - Aggressive, can be dismissive
    - Can-do attitude—can think of way to exit snake pit with the gold and the girl/guy
    - Cunning, smooth, and wicked smart

- If high priority, instantaneous focus on follow-up—prioritizes quickly
- If internal to large company, e-group more open to limited process, metrics, approval cycles

4. Jungle Thunder (e-gorilla)
   - Professional manager with experience in brick-and-click
   - Arrogant—it's good to be the king
   - Knowledgeable
   - Pressworthy
   - Platinum Spider Network
   - Paranoid (rightfully so)
   - Dismissive if idea doesn't grab him or her in first two minutes
5. Ms. Titanic (e-decline)
   - Denial
   - Angry
   - Brilliant but misguided
   - Looking for valuation, not value
   - Desperate
   - Metrics become confused (or worse, get cooked)
   - We can do it all better ourselves
6. ER surgeon (e-turnaround)
   - Domain expertise
   - Upbeat and self-confident
   - Good financial (accounting) controls, managerial, leadership skills
   - Solid Spider Network for big-brand alliance creation
   - Focus on the metrics and reward systems in alignment with performance
   - Creates a sandbox for founder if still there
   - "My way or the highway" prevails; no democracy in the short term

- Creates new hope and drives for short-term success to reinforce
- Creates SWAT team to implement—clear expectations, quick results
- Speed and metrics are combined
- Outsource with caution and close supervision regarding metrics and quality

On a recent trip to Argentina and Chile, working with my partner in that region, José Macaya, I consulted with the Chilean division of BankBoston. Jorge Ramirez, the head of BankBoston in Santiago, engaged my services to examine BankBoston's internal and external alliances in Chile. He and his senior management did a complete Mindshift analysis[1] of their Chilean organization to determine the areas ripe for change and to predict the cultural and managerial potential of a reorganized management structure. Recently, Ramirez shared with me his perspective on the application of the Mindshift approach to e-business:

FastAlli, by Larraine Segil

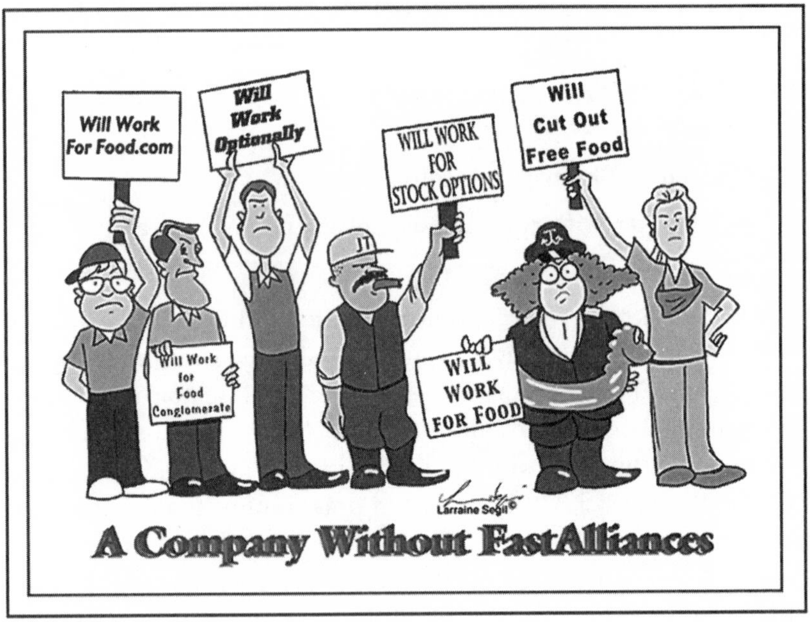

FastAlli, by Larraine Segil

> Our experience with alliances in e-business shows that compatibility and understanding cultural differences are more important than ever, both within the company and externally. So the Mindshift approach applies. There are some differences however.
>
> In most of the cases, you have to deal with start-ups forming alliances with professional or mature companies. However, we've found that there is a new category that describes many of the e-preneurs, which is the *flipper:* Most of the start-ups are looking for alliances in order to get into the hockeystick phase very rapidly and then sell the project either through an IPO or to the alliance partner.

Translating Ramirez's comments—it would seem that the e-hockeystick stage of hypergrowth is the "flipper" he refers to and that the Hock E. Stick, swashbuckling entrepreneurs of e-business are everywhere. Their greatest desire is that Jungle Thunder of the e-gorilla company will come along and sweep them off their feet into hog heaven—in other words, financial freedom!

The third part of the E-Mindshift approach is the e-project personalities. (See Figure 7.3.) I have kept them very similar to those

Figure 7.3 E-Mindshift: FastAlliances Tool #14 (The E-Project Personalities [Priorities])

The E-Project Personalities (Priorities)

•Bet the Farm•

~A market share grab, technology move, or preemptive strike
~A FastAlliance that is critically important to the participant
~Well financed (or stock as currency), with top management involvement

•Middle of the Road•

~On the second tier (of lower importance for management)
~Will tend to slide down to experimental fast if there are no impressive short-term results
~It is difficult at the early stage of the e-business economy to maintain interest in this level of project priority
~Move it higher as soon as possible or it will die from neglect

•Experimental•

~Is a FastAlliance—barely. Could be a press release type at the lowest end
~Could be a genuine commitment of resources for limited time until proven or until alliance managers migrate the project to a higher level of importance
~Won't linger if no results
~Don't confuse with Bet-the-Farm projects that are in beta test

described for traditional alliances in my first book. What's different is the volume and predominance of alliances in each category. Whereas in traditional alliances all three categories tend to get a well-distributed weighting of alliance projects, in FastAlliances there is a predominance of bet-the-farm projects and/or experimental ones. There are far fewer in the middle-of-the-road category. The reason is that time is of the essence as never before, and resources for most e-business companies in terms of people-hours and expertise are in short supply (not to mention attention spans, which seem to decrease by the moment in these early stages of the Internet economy). The alliance is either really important or not—nothing in the middle.

When looking at the project personality or priorities for e-business companies Ramirez's insights were very specific:

> Most important in e-business alliances, the personality of the project differs dramatically. Normally, you would expect these projects to be bet the farm for the start-up and middle of the road or experimental for the larger company. It's a completely new ball game, and old-economy companies are trying to decide what the personality of the project is for them. In my opinion, it is experimental in nature, but to succeed you have to have a bet-the-farm approach.

This draws an interesting distinction. Even if the project is an experiment—it may be one that is so important that it is a bet-the-farm project for the company. In that case, it would be classified as the highest-priority project—a bet-the-farm project.

Future Predictions for Years 2001 to 2005

The two life-cycle stages that are not included in the first category of life-cycle stages are those in the professional and mature stages. Interestingly, the professional stage (when growth is still happening but nowhere near the levels of the hockeystick phase), as I found in my former research,[2] is the most effective for traditional partnering. It is notable that few companies have entered or stayed in that stage in the FastAlliances e-business world at this early stage of the new-economy development cycle. Most are either still in the hockeystick stage or have gone directly into decline. It's either high growth or bust. I expect that will change within two years as the new becomes old. But at this point there is no in-between stage bridging high growth and decline. However, I offer you a future predictive analysis—put it on the shelf and then reread this book in about 18 months. You will be the one in your group with the prescient insight! The E-Mindshift approach will include two more life cycles, as follows:

E-professional: Revenues Increasing but Not at the Hockeystick Rate

- Brick-and-mortar realities setting in—earnings valuations, not revenues valuations
- Traditional alliances intersect with FastAlliances[3]
- Longer-term relationships are recognized as valuable
- Aggressive search for innovation and refresh of business model, products, and services
- Acquisitions
- Reinvention of the organization—could be completely different industry/business (more common in latter stage of this cycle)
- Change of team—more outsiders, often founder is booted out (with pot of gold, bruised ego, determination never to do it that way again)

E-mature

- Team changes again—more consultants
- Outsourcing of some, in-sourcing of other services—some lack of strategy/cohesion
- Finance and legal departments have stronghold on management
- Attrition of good people—dot-commers abandon ship
- Potential acquisition target
- If already acquired—business model or brand may disappear soon,

or

- Founder buys it back—and does it different next time (maybe)

The e-professional stage generally follows on the heels of the e-hockeystick phase, which then moves into the e-mature phase (said fast sounds like immature—no pun intended). Then it cycles into e-decline.

Now let's look at the e-personalities of the individual managers who are attracted to (or detract from) each particular life-cycle stage. (See Figure 7.4.)

Figure 7.4 **E-Mindshift: FastAlliances Tool #14**
(Life Cycles of E-Businesses: Corporate and Individual Managerial Personalities, Years 2001 to 2005)

Corporate personality types	E-startup stage 1: Original idea/ founder/ entrepreneur	E-hockeystick	E-gorilla (hypergrowth)	E-professional •Brick-and-mortar realities setting in—earnings valuations, not revenue valuation •Traditional alliances intersect, longer term relationships valued •Innovation and refresh of business model/products •Acquisitions•Reinventing organization •Change of team—outsiders in, founder out—bruised ego	E-mature •Team changes again—more consultants •Outsourcing and in-sourcing—lack of strategy, cohesion •Finance/legal is strong•Attrition of good people—dot-commers abandon ship•Potential acquisition target •If acquired, brand or business model changes, *or* founder buys it back and does it differently this time	E-decline E-turnaround
	E-startup stage 2: Within larger organization, founder, intrapreneur	SAME	SAME			SAME
Life cycles of e-business						
Individual managerial personality	Fast Talker (stage 1)	Hock E. Stick	Jungle Thunder	Prof. Realist •Experience in old and new economies•School of hard knocks—used to anticipating problems •Ethical but stretched to max on thin red line •Good people person—schmoozes Spider Network•Dot-com self-esteem modified by need for group communication•Off-site planning/budgeting adds reality check•Training•Innovation	NIMBY (not in my backyard) •Territorial and self-protective•NIH personality is new issue •Old-boy network brings in investment bankers and large-firm consultants•Pressure from old-boy crowd for acquisitions—as acquiree•Golden handshake agreements top priority for senior management•Legal is strong	Ms. Titanic ER Surgeon
	Mann Date (stage 2)	SAME	SAME			SAME

Prof. Realist: E-professional

- Experience in old and new economies
- School of hard knocks—used to anticipating problems
- Ethical but stretched to the max on thin red line
- Good people person, used to schmoozing in Spider Network
- Dot-com self-esteem being modified by need for group communication
- Off-site planning sessions and budgeting adds necessary reality check
- Training and education become mandates
- Creating an innovation drive is important focus

Not in My Backyard (NIMBY): E-mature

- Territorial and self-protective
- Not-invented-here (NIH) personality evolves as new issue
- Old-boy network brings in the investment bankers and consultants (large firms)
- Pressure from old-boy crowd for acquisitions—more likely as acquiree than acquiror
- Golden-handshake agreements top priority for senior management
- Legal plays stronger role

The e-project categories will remain the same—however, the importance and volume of activities that can be categorized as middle-of-the-road in FastAlliances will increase to parallel those in traditional alliances.

Who Is Michael Marks?

Let me give you an example of a Mann Date (e-start-up stage 2) in a most unlikely place. His name is Michael Marks—not exactly a household name . . . yet. Remember Michael—his profile is rising like a rocket. Why? Because he runs a stealth b2b player that is participating hugely in the e-business phenomenon. What does this Mann Date personality do?

Michael Marks is chairman and CEO of Flextronics International, the premiere contract electronics manufacturer in the world, chosen by *Industry Week* magazine as one of the top 100 companies in the world in 1999–2000.[4] When Michael took over the company in 1993 it was in decline—$93 million in annual revenues and on the verge of bankruptcy. Michael is living proof of the Spider Network theory. Before he undertook the major task of overhauling Flextronics, he put together a network of influential venture capitalists in Silicon Valley. Kleiner Perkins and Sequoia Capital were among those who acquired a controlling interest in the company for $12 million. Flextronics today has exceeded $9 billion in annual revenues and for the past six years has maintained a growth rate of over 60 percent. Not too shabby, even for VC-expected returns! The company has plants in Malaysia, China, Mexico, Hungary, Germany, and Sweden—over 5.1 million square feet on four continents. Its manufacturing partners are Ericsson, Cisco, Hewlett-Packard, Lucent, Philips, Motorola, Microsoft, and on and on—a veritable who's who of corporate muscle. They are the operations management solution for the world's largest product manufacturing companies, since most of the OEM firms are outsourcing their entire manufacturing operations (e.g., Nortel will do so within two years). Whereas in the past, OEM customers would ask the company to build a small part of their manufacturing activities, now they are asking for Flextronics to actually take their orders directly off the Internet and integrate and manage every part of the supply chain. As a result, Flextronics is growing aggressively both internally and through acquisitions. Its approach is so streamlined that the company is integrating five acquisitions at the same time.

Marks shows all the characteristics of a Mann Date personality. But what is most remarkable is that he has created an organization in his image—one that he is convinced can and will thrive even without his presence one day (not that he has any present plans to leave).

Mann Date: E-startup Stage 2

- Respects Skinny Process
- Likes growing companies and people
- Good leader
- High energy

- Creative and knows how to maneuver within large organizations
- Financial skills and good operating experience

A *Skinny Process* is process that is short, transparent, and flexible—but most of all *speedy!* A fat process is what exists in most organizations and is what people groan at mentally when thinking of process—a long, drawn-out, bureaucratic method of multiple steps that slows things down. Skinny Process is best illustrated with a story.

The 14-Day Factory

A potential Flextronics customer whose company had a $75 million piece of repeatable business to award called Michael Marks, Flextronics' CEO. Since at that time Flextronics had only $200 million in annual revenues, this could be a huge chunk of business.

"Michael, we have a problem—can you solve it?" the customer said. "Here's the situation. We need a factory capability in Nowheresville—you know, that area deep in the south of the fourteenth continent? Well, anyway, we need it in 14 days. That is, on day 15 we need to have the capability to produce 80,000 units a week. Can you do it?"

Marks loves a challenge—especially one that is way out of the box. "Give me eight hours and I'll have an answer for you," he said. Then he and his team got to work. He pulled in all the members of his Spider Network of contractors. At that moment, there was no team on the ground, no building, no equipment on order, and no people.

Marks knew building trade people from his past. He plugged into their Spider Networks and gave them the parameters: "Guys, here it is—we need a factory, fully operational, within 13 days. Can you do it? Whatever it takes?" The Spider Network went to work. Through their connections they found local contacts, searched until they located a building in the area specified, and started the project. In the meantime, every other contractor Marks spoke with committed to do the project, drawing people from other projects all over the world. Marks was there, too. He noticed something interesting, and pulled one of the contractors aside.

"How is it that everyone here has a new truck?" he asked. The contractor laughed. "Because everyone here is a foreman, supervisor, or the owner of the companies you called to get involved in this job. They knew that the only people they could trust to get it done on time and in budget was themselves."

In 14 days, the factory was operational, and on day 15, as promised, Flextronics shipped 16,000 units.

There are many such stories in Flextronics. New-employee orientation disusses the folklore of how the company turned around and how things get done there—people are fast, flexible, and empowered. Marks does the new-employee opening sessions himself. His senior management team has the same energy—Mike McNamara (president Americas), Ron Keith who reports to him, and many others. I asked Marks how the culture has evolved and what it has to do with his personality and beliefs:

> Our company is very responsive. In many ways, we do have the mentality of an e-business company. Our headquarters is in Silicon Valley, so we are in the middle of it. It would be impossible not to be affected by the speed of change. We are always looking at how to use new tools. We are a traditional brick-and-mortar company, but we do operate with many of the principles of the click companies. Click companies are customers of ours. If not for us, many of them could not fulfill what they promise. Someone has to actually build this stuff.

Marks is creative and knows how to maneuver within organizations. He has run other organizations (a chip processing equipment manufacturer) and worked for other companies (including his father's air-conditioning and heating equipment distribution company in St. Louis as a young man). He has achieved an unusual goal. He explained it to me when I asked him what would happen if he left the company, whether the culture would persist.

> There is over $100 million of capital spending per quarter at Flextronics—and none of it gets to me. Everyone is empowered—we have *no* budget cycles. A plant manager can make a decision to

> spend $2 million. Obviously, we have to do cash-flow forecasting. However, the system is set up in such a way that people are empowered. My philosophy is that once you have more than one signature for sign-off there is no value added. People wait for others to make the decision, and effort goes into following up to see whether they have. This is part of the culture. So if I am not here, nothing changes—people still keep on making their own decisions. It is critical when running a multibillion-dollar enterprise that it operate fast without a bunch of approvals. We don't believe in a lot of meetings, either. People move fast and are not bogged down. My experience with meetings is that for the first 15 minutes everyone is talking about the project and the next 45 minutes are spent talking about how to get sign-off to do it. We don't do that. We are fast-moving and highly flexible, and that's what our customers love about us.

The Mann Date personality in Marks will not put up with stultifying bureaucracy. Although he has experienced and knows how the system works in traditional organizations, he will not stand for it at Flextronics.

All four of the following characteristics are present in proven form in Michael Marks—his record is self-evident:

- Likes Growing Companies and People
- Good Leader
- High Energy
- Financial skills and good operating experience

The E-Mindshift method does not put people in boxes. The world doesn't work that way. And people change (thank goodness). The ability to see the world through others' eyes is an integral part of being a leader. Not everyone will have the same personality as yourself. My next book will address leadership characteristics that make sense in e-business.[5]

For now, let's turn to another example.

Who Makes the Aeron Chair?

Herman Miller Inc., Zeeland, Michigan, is one of the hottest manufacturers of well-designed furniture. President and CEO Michael Volkema realized that product differentiation wasn't going to do it for the future. His company needed more.

When I spoke to Volkema, I got the impression of an understated but very determined person. He is youthful and fit and gives an impression of calm confidence. When I examined the recent history of the metamorphosis of his company, I understood how he was able to make it happen. He embraced technology in order to reengineer the design process as well as the manufacturing and order-entry systems in the company. Even more impressive was his ability to sell the idea to a very reluctant board (proposed expenditures would increase to $500 million or more) and then to his dealers and salespeople, who felt extremely threatened by the potential channel conflict of customers ordering directly from the company through the Internet. It is here that the best characteristics of Prof. Realist (e-professional) managerial personality are demonstrated.

Prof. Realist (E-professional)

- Experience in old and new economies
- School of hard knocks—used to anticipating problems
- Ethical but stretched to the max on thin red line
- Good people person, used to schmoozing in Spider Network
- Dot-com self-esteem being modified by need for group communication
- Off-site planning sessions and budgeting adds necessary reality check
- Training and education become mandates
- Creating an innovation drive is important focus

After winning over his board for the proposed spending, Volkema spent many weeks meeting with his dealers and salespeople to reassure them. He was been proven right—many dealers have seen their business increase. Volkema is spreading the word into every part of the Herman Miller organization, reducing build and delivery times, boosting on-time shipments, equipping all his salespeople and suppliers with the software, and creating dedicated web sites for the company's best customers. Volkema has created and sustained the innovation drive of a plant built five years ago whose success is now permeating the entire business. All of the preceding characteristics, plus training, interpersonal skills, and experience in new and old economies have served him well.[6]

E-airlines

The airline industry is not one that you would normally describe as an e-business. However, like every industry, e-business change has come to airlines—not only in the way their customers access and use their services, but also in the way they enable themselves to function and compete. Only leaders who can wear the hats of many E-Mindshift personality profiles will be able to accomplish this goal. One of these leaders is Leo Mullin, CEO of Delta Airlines.

Mullin is at once Prof. Realist and Mann Date, with a healthy dose of Hock E. Stick and the clear vision and swift hand of ER Surgeon. He welcomes and understands fast-talkers and, early on in his tenure at Delta, recognized those politician-managers who must be dealt with in order to take Delta into the new economy. He cut them out of Delta with a sure incision. His leadership, management, and financial skills have stood him in good stead. When Mullin took over the helm of Delta, things were pretty bad—and Delta's technology was under par.

I met Mullin when he asked me to deliver a keynote on alliances at a New York summit for Delta's airline partners. His style is low key, personal, and passionate. It became clear from our various quiet conversations that this was a person with more than a corporate vision for Delta. He had a personal interest in Delta's employees and their futures. Mullin is a man with his own ego under control who can understand the many different personalities that make up his world and the world of Delta. He focused on fixing the problems with a number of good moves. A deal with Priceline generated $775 million in addition to over $280 million annually in Priceline ticket sales. Mullin also created over 40 Internet-related programs with customers, alliance partners, and employees. He launched a web-based travel service (Orbitz) with other airline partners to compete with Travelocity. And he created an online exchange for supply purchases.

The most prescient move, however, was a recent announcement by Mullin that every single Delta employee (over 75,000) would receive a free computer and free Internet access by the end of 2000—a gift from Delta as a good corporate citizen and, as Mullin put it, "to be sure that all Delta employees overcome the Digital Divide." Leo Mullin is an example of a leader who understands and can manage each of the individual managerial personalities reflected in both the Mindshift and the E-Mindshift approaches.

Use these approaches to understand the resource and people issues of traditional as well as FastAlliances. They are not trivial, whether VC, corporate parent, entrepreneur, intrapreneur, or traditional company in mid-metamorphosis to e-business. This understanding will facilitate communication and speed of information transfer—essential success factors for all organizations in the new economy.

CHAPTER 8

Step 8: The Deals—Making, Managing, Adding Value, and Terminating Them

As a former operating manager I know the value of pragmatic tools that can be applied immediately. That has been the focus of this book. This chapter will drill deeper into more of the tools that assist not only in the FastStrategy application, but also, and with more focus, on the operating stages of the FastAlliances. Keep in mind, however, that since the time between strategy and implementation is truncated and overlapping in these speedy relationships, the line between doing strategy and implementing has been blurred. Some tools will be applicable to both the strategy development and the execution stages of the alliance.

The Pyramid of Planet CAD: FastAlliances Tool #15

There is another tool that will give good practical results. I call it FastAlliances Tool #15, the Pyramid of Planet CAD. Yes, there really is a company called Planet CAD. I spoke with its general manager and vice president, Isaac Kato. His company was acquired by Spatial in 1999. Planet CAD sells 3D technology to large companies like

Autodesk and provides the modeling kernels that go under the hood of computer-aided design (CAD) technology. One of the key attributes of its products is enabling manufacturing design engineers to move data from one CAD application to another, meaning that engineers who receive a model in one software program can use this technology to translate it into another software program so that they can work on it there, too. Lots of other software vendors were interested in wrapping this technology into their offerings. So, in January 2000, Planet CAD set up a new division to offer its software on the web. As I was speaking with Kato, a new model for analyzing the different variables that go into FastAlliances coalesced into a schematic, which I call the Pyramid of Planet CAD (see Figure 8.1).

The three variables that go into the pyramid are these: *skin in the game* (risk), *time* (which drives the build/buy decision), *capabilities* (of the players).

Planet CAD Base Level

The lowest level of the pyramid includes the following: banner advertising, cross-bannering, comarketing, affiliate, copromotion, joint dis-

Figure 8.1 Pyramid of Planet CAD: FastAlliances Tool #15

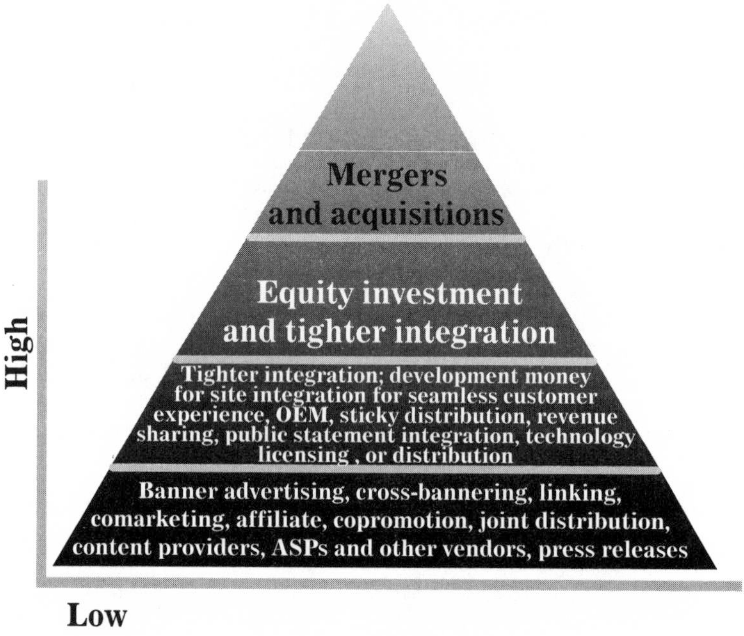

tribution, content providers, application service providers, other vendor relationships, and press release relationships. This level can fall into the category of a FastAlliances, but for many it does not reach the level of intimacy for an alliance. Nevertheless, this level can be divided into gradations of intimacy—from the basic press release, which is essentially all there is, to copromotion and marketing or other kinds of deals with content providers, application service providers (such as web-hosting companies), and those multifaceted affiliate programs that permeate many e-business companies. Scott Dorman, now COO of Silicon Planet, formerly headed production affairs for two different divisions of Disney, then went to DoubleClick Inc., where he created the strategic alliances group. He recently told me,

> The strength of the company [DoubleClick] is that it answers the fundamental question, which is, "I am paying for advertising; what am I getting for my money?" DoubleClick can tell you what banner ads are effective and then you can target your ads so that you can display another banner to those who buy. Of course, in addition to buying and selling of banners, DoubleClick has a huge business in data mining. Our goal in our alliances was to utilize as many of the DoubleClick services as possible. For example, in an alliance with a company like Unilever [traditional offline company], our goal was to show them that our entire line of services would increase their sales beyond the traditional advertising market. We did pilots to establish the needs and show our solutions to them. For example, for a packaged product like food—not only would we want to target a specific market (perhaps women) as traditional advertising does, but we would want to use the power of the Internet to get people to start talking about it. We could do this as part of an alliance with iVillage about cooking and what the product means and the effect it would have on people's lives, which creates loyalty to the product and context within which the product was used. It's viral marketing, not a company-sponsored or -directed communication system.

Another company has benefited greatly from the concept of viral marketing. Virtualis Inc, mentioned in Chapter 6, has created a series of 45,000 affiliates. As of March 2000, the company was growing at a rate of 25 percent monthly. Virtualis has based its whole business model on the affiliate alliance approach. You may remember from Chapter 6, CEO Chris Lyman was 26 years old, with only a high school education but innate street smarts and technical wizardry, when he founded the company. He began as a consultant offering software development to web designers. From that he built a web-hosting company with software that made it easier for new and experienced web designers to create web pages for small and midsized businesses. Based on a subscription fee with upgrades, he created a small service company that was first in web hosting for the small-business marketplace. Lyman raised money from premier VCs, Knight Ridder, Adobe, Hambrecht and Quist, and others. We spoke about the change in his evolution from the e-start-up stage of fast talker to where he is now.

> I'm learning all the time. I know what I want, but there is a problem now in being an Internet CEO. The position is one almost of idolization. The reason is that no one really knows what to do in this space; everyone is making it up as they go along. The CEO is seen as the visionary, and the employees put a lot of faith in the fact that the CEO knows where he or she is going and what to do next. The CEO represents the dream, the vision. And you can't make that vision happen unless you have a really good operating person and CTO [chief technology officer] or all you will have is vision and no action. There are lots of deals being made by people who are afraid—fear is a major driver. That is, fear of being left behind. Lots of traditional offline businesses are giving up rights they don't have to, such as exclusive access, in order to be part of the dot-com space. I am not driven by fear. Don't have much of that at all in fact.

Lyman at 26 has already been through huge learning curves that many his age have not. He has been in some negotiations that would make your hair stand on end, and he has strong feelings on the new economy:

> The Internet has wiped out two of the three constraints that drive business—time, location, and money. Time and location are now nonissues in our business. We have created a recurring revenue model for technogeeks (of which I have been one) worldwide. Most of the expansion in this market is still coming from viral marketing: "Hey, have you heard about this site?" The industry is in its infancy and most of the offline dot-coms are not really Internet companies at all. They are struggling to create the business model

that works. The one thing that is certain is that the Internet represents mass consciousness. It moves at the speed of mass consciousness, at the same speed as human thoughts and feelings. The viral nature of the medium means the global effect is almost immediate. As a small company, you are in the world even if you didn't plan to be. It is both thrilling and overwhelming at the same time."

Lyman is talking about a trend that I call the *gossip factor* of the web.[1] Tens of thousands (soon millions) of kids talk up and trade the cool stuff they find on the web, and companies are now leveraging these gossip sessions and tendencies. Companies visit popular Internet chat rooms for groups or special-interest bulletin boards, find the kids (or techies) who gossip away, and offer them freebies (for kids it's free CDs or movie passes, for techies it's free downloads, tips, or other barter of value) to spread the word online about specific sites or products. No payment changes hands. Virtualis has taken this idea one step further and offers the web designer a way to make money—but the designer is the one who finds the customer, signs the deal, and services the client. Virtualis services the web designer and creates shared revenues streams. In addition to being fearless, Lyman is a very quick learner. He fits perfectly into the e-start-up fast-talker group and knows he needs a Prof. Realist on his team:

> We are looking for professional management. Virtualis is one of the 1,800 [this is not a typo] companies in California that are looking for a professional CEO. I am a start-up guy, not a professional manager. In addition, we are looking for a corporate partner to do a FastAlliances with, a company that has eyeballs [a large base of web visitors]. We have the hosting model and a revenue model as well as a deep understanding of easy-to-use proprietary software that makes the web designer's life much simpler with tools—for example, survey tools to let him as a small company survey his customer, bulletin boards—we have 24-7 support and data centers that we control. And our market is the globe. Quite incredible when you think about how it all started![2]

The next variable in the Pyramid of Planet CAD is "skin in the game." At this, the lowest level of the pyramid, there is some skin in the game, but not so much that the participants would feel the loss if the FastAlliances didn't work out. These deals can come together very quickly—overnight if necessary, and on a handshake. Some of them never really progress further than the press release and some initial investor excitement, but not a whole lot more. I still classify them as FastAlliances since they can transition equally fast up (or off) the pyramid. Integration on the upper level of this stage of the pyramid can be fairly intense, or it can be extremely loose (as is press release only) on the lowest part of this level.

One large equipment supplier in the mobile phone business told me that vendors who sell products to this company are always asking for joint press releases in order to leverage off its brand. This supplier's stock answer is, "We have thousands of suppliers, so if we did it with one we would have to do it with all, and such announcements would have no meaning."

Planet CAD Second Level

The next level up on the pyramid is a more integrated version of the lowest level: tighter integration, development money for seamless customer experience and site integration, sticky distribution, revenue sharing, public statements of integration, distribution of technology, technology licensing, and ingredient branding. There is more *skin in the game* (risk) and some commitment of capital to either develop programs or build connectivity between sites so that customers have a seamless experience moving from one site to the other and possibly returning to the site at which they entered in order to complete their transaction or activity. That will create what I call *sticky distribution*, which means that even though one company may be distributing the software or products/services of another, the site that pulled the customer in retains that customer's eyeballs throughout the transaction or at its conclusion. The technology distribution could be by visualization (seeing it on the site), by downloading it from the home site, or by some form of technology licensing whereby the technology is embedded in another product or service. There is, however, some kind of payment that takes place—revenue sharing, license fees, or development cost. In addition, there are public statements and joint marketing of activities, beyond just press releases to commitment of actual site or technology integration. In this way, a failure would have more serious negative effects than in the lower levels of integration of the pyramid due to brand value damage and public/analyst/customer perceptions.

Ingredient branding is the highest level of integration in this level of the pyramid. It means that every time one partner's brand is shown, the other partner's brand is also shown. The classic example of ingredient branding is "Intel Inside." Few companies will agree to this unless the brand valuation is made with other considerations in mind.

A few words on channel conflict: It is here to stay (for a while at least). Most manufacturers are too afraid to jeopardize relationships with their traditional retail outlets by creating web pages that actually allow customers to buy products/services. Rubbermaid, for example, has a web site that looks great, but customers cannot buy products on it. How long can companies do this without losing customers altogether? At this time there are customers who will research products on the web and then go to the brick-and-mortar facility to actually purchase. Manufacturers may keep that kind of customer with their info-only approach, but the e-customer will go elsewhere—maybe even to the retailer's e-site and buy the product there. Wal-Mart has been quite clear: "A supplier that e-tails will be treated as a rival."[3]

There is a compromise approach, however. GE Appliances doesn't sell from its own site, but it does sell via a site called xoom.com, which relies on GE to stock product, box it, and ship it to customers. Unified Marine (a Naples, Florida, maker of boating products) has become a fulfillment house for other web sites selling boating products. It inventories and ships both its own products and those of competitors to online merchants. Its web revenues have already surpassed those from its dealer networks.

This issue will not go away. For very large manufacturers, it will not be easily solved. The irony is that although their brands are a large part of their market worth, they have to create another brand (or in fact a nonbrand) in order to sell their products on the web. The good news for these companies is that the web is still focused on viral marketing. Creating a network of chat rooms and bulletin boards, along with some enticing freebies or entertaining add-ons to essentially boring products, may be the solution for getting the message out that they are really in the online business even though they look different. For example, Procter & Gamble has created a web site for products that are not branded with the company brand. The company created a brand specifically for web sales called reflect.com. For small manufacturers it is already a nonissue, since most retailers could not care less whether they sell the same product on the web (because they take up so little shelf space anyway).

Planet CAD Third Level: Equity Investment and Tighter Integration

This level of the pyramid is the investment of equity, thus ensuring an even tighter level of integration and commitment. The skin in the game and risks go up, since now it is not only brand and development money, it is also equity sharing or investment. The payoffs are also greater—and, considering the valuations over the past 24 months, hardly seem sustainable. However, many venture and corporate investors find it necessary to reach this level. Compaq, for example, has created a system of investing in start-ups that takes only three weeks from beginning to end (from investigation of opportunity to investment of funds). Compaq has a formula that works: mostly minority positions, opportunities relevant to its strategies, and a Cool Decision Process that makes it all happen. Jeff Clarke, vice president of finance and strategy for worldwide sales and marketing, is one of those remarkable fast-track executives clearly meant for huge things, a can-do Mann Date personality. Leigh Morrison, vice president for the western region of Compaq and a veteran of the company from its early days, embodies Compaq's initial entrepreneurial approach to making things happen. When Clarke or Morrison say they'll do something, they do it—and *fast.* They are both typical of the proactive culture that CEO Michael Capellas has infused into Compaq over the past year.

Another talented Compaq executive who has been involved in structuring a trading community or high-tech exchange for Compaq in the electronics industry is Wendy Caswell, formerly vice president of corporate strategy, technology, and corporate development and now running the exchange she helped to create. The exchange in which Compaq plays a key role includes other high-powered companies such as Hewlett-Packard, Gateway, Hitachi, NEC, AMD, and Samsung. This FastAlliances came together at lightning speed and with huge effort as a trading community for the buying and selling of electronic components online. There are huge amounts of these products with continually changing prices—two characteristics that lend themselves well to the electronic marketplace environment.

The 12 founding partners in the alliance will be joined by another 8 companies, bringing the total to 20 companies or more. As with all exchanges, the preemptive nature of grabbing the right partners in the beginning will only bear fruit when the operation actually gets going. Stay tuned.

Planet CAD Highest Level: Mergers and Acquisitions

This is not a subject that needs explanation. Everyone seems to be doing it and it is by far the most common subject discussed in the business press. The point of the pyramid, however, is to understand the motivations of the players in the FastAlliances. If you were the fly on the wall in a roomful of FastAlliances participants, this might be what you would hear:

FAST-TALKER: Hey, good to see you guys—whassup???

MANN DATE: You, too. Looking good—cool outfit! Okay, where are we?

FAST-TALKER'S THOUGHTS: *Wow, this is really cool. Look at this huge conference room—can't believe I'm really here and all these old guys from this huge company are paying me respect. Have to pinch myself under the table. Wow, if the homeboys could see me now!*

FAST-TALKER: Well, we're right into the growth curve now, moving up fast. Do you guys want to come along for the ride? And if so, how?

MANN DATE: We are certainly impressed with your performance and are considering some sort of comarketing and cross-licensing as part of the quid pro quo.

FAST-TALKER'S THOUGHTS: *Uh-oh—whoops, that wasn't in our last discussion. Our software wasn't part of that deal. What do these guys really want?*

FAST-TALKER: Sounds interesting. What did you have in mind for cross-licensing?

MANN DATE'S THOUGHTS: *They really need us—our brand is golden even though our web site sucks. Kind of arrogant kid—smart though. Don't underestimate his smarts. I gotta sell this internally. Now that's going to be interesting—he doesn't know what interesting is!*

MANN DATE: You guys have been really successful in your space. We applaud what you have done. I am sure we have a lot to learn from you. . . .

FAST-TALKER'S THOUGHTS: *Wow. . . .*

MANN DATE: What do you really want from us? Comarketing? License your technology? Equity?

FAST-TALKER'S THOUGHTS: *Here it is—do I go for it now or later? Help! Someone tell me what to do!*

FAST-TALKER: Now that's an interesting idea—not one we've actually considered yet. That will require some interface with my team, the board, you know. What were you offering?

MANN DATE'S THOUGHTS: *Finally, it's on the table—these kids think they're so smart. I've been around this track before—a lot. Oh well, let's do it.*

MANN DATE: Well, what we normally do is take a minority share in your company. In fact, we really are not interested in comarketing unless we can take a minority share. Our brand is too valuable, and as we add value to yours we want to share in your increased valuation, not pay twice for it later.

FAST-TALKER'S THOUGHTS: *I am totally over the edge—this guy is wicked smart. Have to check with my board on this one. Licensing, equity, comarketing—soon they'll be talking acquisition. Whew, could this be cash-out time? On the other hand, could we just get the value of their brand by co-associating with it and* ***not*** *sell out to them but to someone else who wants the value of their brand with ours and puts our valuation up even higher? Might it be smarter* ***not*** *to sell to these guys but to use them to go public. . . .*

FAST-TALKER: You know, this is great. We have covered a lot—a really good meeting. I need to think about it all. How about if I get back to you, uh, let's say, Monday?

MANN DATE: Sounds good. Let me see you out. Thanks for coming by.

MANN DATE'S THOUGHTS: *Hope I didn't blow him out. I'll call him tomorrow and repeat our enthusiasm for a comarketing arrangement first. Then maybe we can step it up.*

Although small- and large-company FastAlliances have their own challenges in terms of culture and personalities, large-company acquisitions are no less complex, maybe even more so. The various stakeholders are many—management, employees, shareholders, customers, other alliance partners, and community. If the two companies who are merging are both hockeystick companies growing at aggressive rates, one of the potential risk factors is in not accelerating their combined growth, but stalling both of them. The integration process is arduous (if the companies consider themselves equals, it's even worse), and there is a consequent loss of momentum.

Other challenges lie in overlapping or conflicting partner relationships and channel conflict. And don't forget the merging of two high-ego management teams. Regardless of capability, egos will be a huge factor. (Imagine two Jungle Thunders and three Hock E. Sticks—need I say more?) Clearly, many acquisitions fail due to culture and personality.

The speed factor has also changed the ability to win in acquisitions. Shareholders (as well as employees) must see some quick wins, or their disappointment will be reflected in their actions (sell, sell, sell). Other stakeholders also need to see quick wins. If the companies merged have different perceptions and visions of the market (and in e-business few companies really know where they are going), the rationalization of these views will take time and will slow down the integration and hoped-for growth.

Probably the most important quality of leadership in acquisitions (which require intense negotiations regarding integration) is the ability to walk away from a potential deal. If there is little alignment with all the aforementioned factors, the risks of the acquisition will rise dramatically. Not going forward may be the smartest decision.

Unfortunately, without tools to work with, there may be too few or too many assumptions in FastAlliances discussions. The tools assist in the clarification of intent and, ultimately, of partner expectations. Transitioning up the pyramid (or down it) may be perfectly acceptable. However, using a visual tool from the inception can ensure at least some kind of reality check in the Wild West of e-business deal making.

A business development perspective has to consider all structures for FastAlliances relationships, no matter the level on the pyramid. If acquisition is the approach chosen, the key to value and the realization of the business development goals (whether they be increased revenues, transferred technology, intellectual property, or geographic expansion) is an appropriate acquisition integration process that takes into account culture, learning opportunities, and quality. Although it would seem at first glance that the integration of an acquisition is hardly the responsibility of business development, in FastAlliances the speed of deal flow is such that unless a finely tuned approach is created, the value of the relationship will not be reached, thus impacting the business development decision. The potential disconnect between acquisition integration and business development will cause both activities to be less than effective.

One company that has created an excellent acquisition integration process is Flextronics International. I spoke with Ron Keith, vice president, who gave me the approach depicted in Figure 8.2.

Clearly, there is a lot more to an acquisition—compensation issues (rationalization of differences between them), redundancies, and issues of brand, as well as the financial underpinnings of the deal. Nevertheless, Flextronics has crystallized the issues. With lightning speed after the deal is closed, the company implements the streamlined approach shown in Figure 8.2. There is little doubt that Flextronics knows exactly how to make a world-class manufacturing facility come about, no matter what the local constraints or resistance. The most impressive part of its approach, however, is the fact that the company willingly acknowledges that it does not know everything. The recent acquisition from Siemens of some manufacturing operations led to intense knowledge acquisition for Flextronics. The company was able to take the best from the Siemens experience and spread it throughout the company without a whimper of the not-invented-here (NIH) factor. Flextronics acquires companies for capability as well as geographical reach. Many organizations do the same. However, few are as effective as Flextronics in transferring that knowledge to those who can benefit from it within their companies.

Cisco and *acquisitions* are becoming synonymous terms. And much has been written on the company and its approach. What is notable, however, is the strategy behind the acquisition process—a FastAlliances strategy that has been extremely successful. For Cisco, acquisitions have been the most viable way to acquire first-class engineering talent, the gold standard of the Internet infrastructure world. Spending huge amounts of money and stock to buy companies that are stars in their technology market segments is the fastest and, amazingly, most cost-effective way to enter those markets in a lead position. When Cisco comes calling, it's hard to refuse the golden carrots and the opportunity to be part of a company that is one of the premier stock and Internet players in the world. For companies that may not have the pizzazz of a Cisco, their challenges are to be sure

Figure 8.2 Acquisition Integration Process of Flextronics: FastAlliances Tool #16

The 15 steps to a Flex factory

1. Common financial and operational indicators, common display format and standardized operations reviews
2. All factory floors taped out with Flextronics simple visual indicators for basic shop-floor control
3. Same look and feel for all employee smocks and badges
4. ISO 9002 certification within 6 months
5. Automated shop-floor quality management system
6. Demand flow technology processes and training in all operations
7. Failure-mode effects analysis in all operations
8. Standardized graphical manufacturing process instructions
9. Standardized new-product introduction processes
10. Flextronics housekeeping system in place
11. Bar coding installed throughout factory
12. Virtual factory implemented (web-based data exchange tool)
13. Customer satisfaction survey process in place
14. Probe audit quarterly
15. BAAN ERP system (and whole IT infrastructure) to implement within 6 weeks—e.g., do 2-day closing of books monthly

Integration of learning that ensures achieving acquisition goals

1. Benchmarking excellence that company acquires—sharing it across the company through the general managers' meetings
2. Key operational indicators (42) are the same worldwide for all operations and are reported weekly, published on company intranet, and discussed and benchmarked by everyone—part of general manager get-togethers

All general managers get together 3 times annually, review 15 steps, benchmark internally and externally

15 Steps to Flex factory implementation

Culture seminars by president at acquiree

Senior operations team, personally meet at company

The FastAlliances Culture of Flextronics

1. Storytelling—the 14-day factory
2. Empowerment stories (plant manager can spend $2 million with no sign-off needed)
3. No bureaucracy; no meetings; do it, don't talk about it
4. Move people around across company worldwide
5. Financial incentives are high for operational excellence and sharing information—awards, recognition, team bonuses (majority), and individual bonuses
6. No organization chart (putting name in box is limiting); do whatever the customer needs

that the knowledge they have developed internally or acquired externally actually translates into the working culture and intelligence of the whole organization.

There is a company that does a good job in this area of internal knowledge transfer (what I call *internal* FastAlliances), which has to do with the relationships between divisions or groups within the same company as well as the integration of new learning from acquired companies. That company is CEMEX, the third largest cement manufacturer in the world, after Dutch Holderbank and French LaFarge.

How did a relatively small Mexican company become the third largest in the world? It took a while, but acquisitions were the route it took. Being in Mexico added another dimension to CEMEX's strategy: The cost of capital was high because of concern about credit risk in Mexico. This meant that any acquisition made by CEMEX would have to reap benefits sooner rather than later. (Although the acquisition price was the same as for other acquirees, the overall cost was higher due to the increased cost of capital.) I met with executive vice president for finance, strategy, and business development Hector Medina, who commented, "We have to make acquisitions pay off faster than anyone else. This approach is also helping us in our e-business strategy. The need for speed is recognized up front."

Working with Medina, I developed the schematic in Figure 8.3 showing CEMEX's acquisition integration process. Let's expand on the concepts shown there.

1. *The integration process:*

- CEMEX makes clear that it is an acquisition, not a merger of equals.
- CEMEX identifies and targets the areas where it wants to make profound changes in the acquired company.
- The integration team is in place early on. Team members take control of the management, make the changes, and implement them fast. They don't beat around the bush. They want the acquired company to become integrated into the CEMEX family—*fast.*
- They take the best people from the acquired company and make them part of the integration team. If they carry their weight, they stay. This has created a circle where key man-

Figure 8.3 Acquisition Integration Process of CEMEX (Mexico): FastAlliances Tool #17

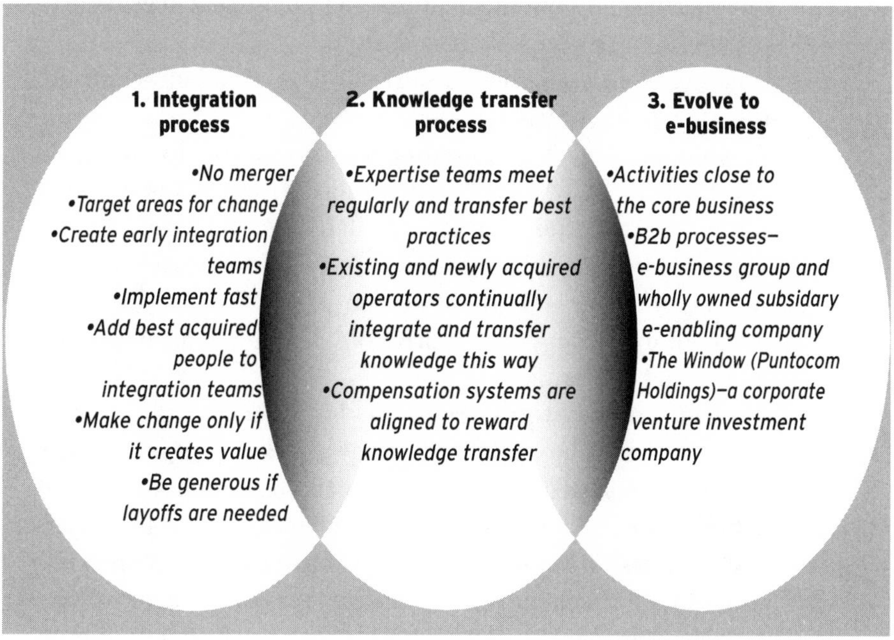
1. Integration process
•No merger
•Target areas for change
•Create early integration teams
•Implement fast
•Add best acquired people to integration teams
•Make change only if it creates value
•Be generous if layoffs are needed
2. Knowledge transfer process
•Expertise teams meet regularly and transfer best practices
•Existing and newly acquired operators continually integrate and transfer knowledge this way
•Compensation systems are aligned to reward knowledge transfer
3. Evolve to e-business
•Activities close to the core business
•B2b processes–e-business group and wholly owned subsidary e-enabling company
•The Window (Puntocom Holdings)–a corporate venture investment company

agement people from the acquired companies become part of the integration teams for the next acquisitions. They have been there and done it, so they bring real empathy, understanding, and a no-nonsense attitude to the process. They understand how to work through the local issues with respect for the local culture. They want to make change that creates value—not just change for the sake of it.

- Sometimes acquisitions create the need for reduction of the workforce. Although that is a challenge for the integration team, workforce reduction has taken place on a number of occasions without major labor problems. The reason is that CEMEX is generous, very generous, and treats people with respect. It's expensive, but it pays off because changes are made faster. Being generous is a good investment.

2. *The knowledge transfer process:* The integration teams learn what is valuable in the acquired company and transfer it into the rest of CEMEX through a number of methods.

- Specific groups called *expertise teams* meet twice a year or more to discuss new and best practices (e.g., practices used in the high-temperature furnaces).
- Ongoing communications between team members continue the knowledge sharing globally.
- Existing and newly acquired operators continually integrate and transfer knowledge to each other through this method. For example, accounting is a challenging area since it operates in many emerging markets, and inflationary accounting (where inflation is 30 to 80 percent *per month*) is very complicated; marketing is similarly complex due to local requirements and preferences
- Compensation systems are particularly important, and after acquisition they are equalized worldwide. For example, country managers' compensation is 60 percent fixed and 40 percent variable; total compensation is divided according to performance, with 70 percent for local performance and 30 percent corporate performance. This ensures that knowledge transfer contributions are recognized both on a local and a corporate level. Regional managers are similarly compensated, as are local managers (with a greater focus on local performance).

3. *Evolve to e-business:* CEMEX is not new to the concepts behind e-business. As early as 1988, its worldwide operations were connected via a satellite network so that anyone at corporate could read what was happening in any market and determine the status of inventories, the amount of energy being used, and so on. In the 1990s CEMEX included its distributors in that network in order to rationalize their requests. Now the company's e-business strategy is evolving in three ways, and newly acquired companies are immediately integrated into this process.

- *Activities close to the core business.* This is the internal activity of the company, which is evolving to a networked and e-business model of intranets—24-7 worldwide, streamlined operations and decision processes (Cool Decision Process, Chapter 2). In addition, as of September 2000, CEMEX began to sell cement on the web. Information about these online orders will enable CEMEX to speed delivery and trim inventory for distributors and customers.

- *B2b processes.* CEMEX has a separate group that reports to the CEO, whose mission is to look at all operations and to develop e-procurement and potential construction and building materials protocols. In addition, an enabling group of 500 people in a wholly owned subsidiary founded nine years ago provides software developed for CEMEX. This so-called e-enabling arm has many fast and traditional alliances within Latin America. It is an area distributor for Lotus, IBM, Cisco, and Oracle and has several contracts with large manufacturers.
- *The Window.* This corporate venture group, or business accelerator, called Puntocom Holdings can invest in any e-businesses that it considers of value. Puntocom is capitalized at $50 million by CEMEX, with other partners contemplated. Management people are young, recruited from e-businesses and consulting.

It is hoped that the dot-com self-esteem will rub off on the part of CEMEX that is more traditional (thus slower), while at the same time preserving the cultural parts of the company that are valuable. CEMEX calls it the click-and-mortar revolution, not inappropriate for a cement manufacturer!

A company that does a good job of technology knowledge transfer is General Electric. Gary Reiner, GE's CIO, spends lots of his time looking at the various companies within the GE family to see what they are doing to develop solutions to tech problems.[4] Quarterly, he gathers together the information chiefs of all the divisions of GE for a day and a half of comparing notes. Then the divisions borrow each other's employees to help transfer learning. Doing it at e-speed means that knowledge discovery and transfer must happen within the quarter, in accordance with GE's new grow-your-business (GYB) mandate to all divisions to create and implement the company's Internet strategy.

Freebie or Sell: FastAlliances Tool #18

Another helpful tool is the FastAlliances Freebie or Sell analysis. (See Figure 8.4.) In the era of commoditization (see Chapter 1), unless value is added to a readily available product or service, the price will fall to the level of the lowest-priced supplier. The Internet provides such huge and varied access to information that a diligent search by a determined buyer will dig up a plethora of price comparisons. So the decision for a seller is, "Do I give this product away for free on my site in order to keep the customers *sticky* [keeping them at the site for as long as it takes to convert an eyeball visit to actual transactions], or do I sell the product and/or service?" That decision must be seen within a continuum, because *time* is the critical element behind the decision. With the speed of change and the democratization of information (i.e., it's accessible to everyone on the Internet), product life cycles are shorter than ever before. Thus, it is logical to assume that sooner rather than later everything will be in the public domain. The question is, *how long will you wait?*

THQ may not be a name that jumps immediately to your mind when you think of the entertainment world, but I would hazard a guess that you'll find this company in your home somewhere. It is a leading company in the home video games business and one of the top 10 publishers of the console platforms on which they compete—Sony PlayStation, Nintendo 64, and Game Boy. Most of THQ's PC titles are played over the Internet, and it owns a number of mega-hot franchise titles—World Wrestling Federation, Sinistar, and Rugrats, to name a few. THQ calls itself content-driven, multiplatform entertainment. I sit on the board of the Price Centre for Entrepreneurship at UCLA's Anderson School of Management with Brian Farrell, THQ's president and CEO. He is energetic, thoughtful, and visionary:

> We have told our customer that they don't have to pay for things. We are providing an online game where the customer has to download the trading cards in order to play the game. The business model is based on the Pokéman approach. The first game is based on the World Wrestling Federation Franchise. The cards have different powers and you buy them in packs that are random. On every deck you download, there are good cards and not-so-good ones. These cards are downloadable only and are not available anywhere else. The marketing strategy is to have a point of sale at a checkout counter (for example at a Best Buy store) that is a starter kit. This is not a retail version but is meant to entice the consumer to download the cards. This is just one of our product strategies to

Figure 8.4 Freebie or Sell: FastAlliances Tool #18

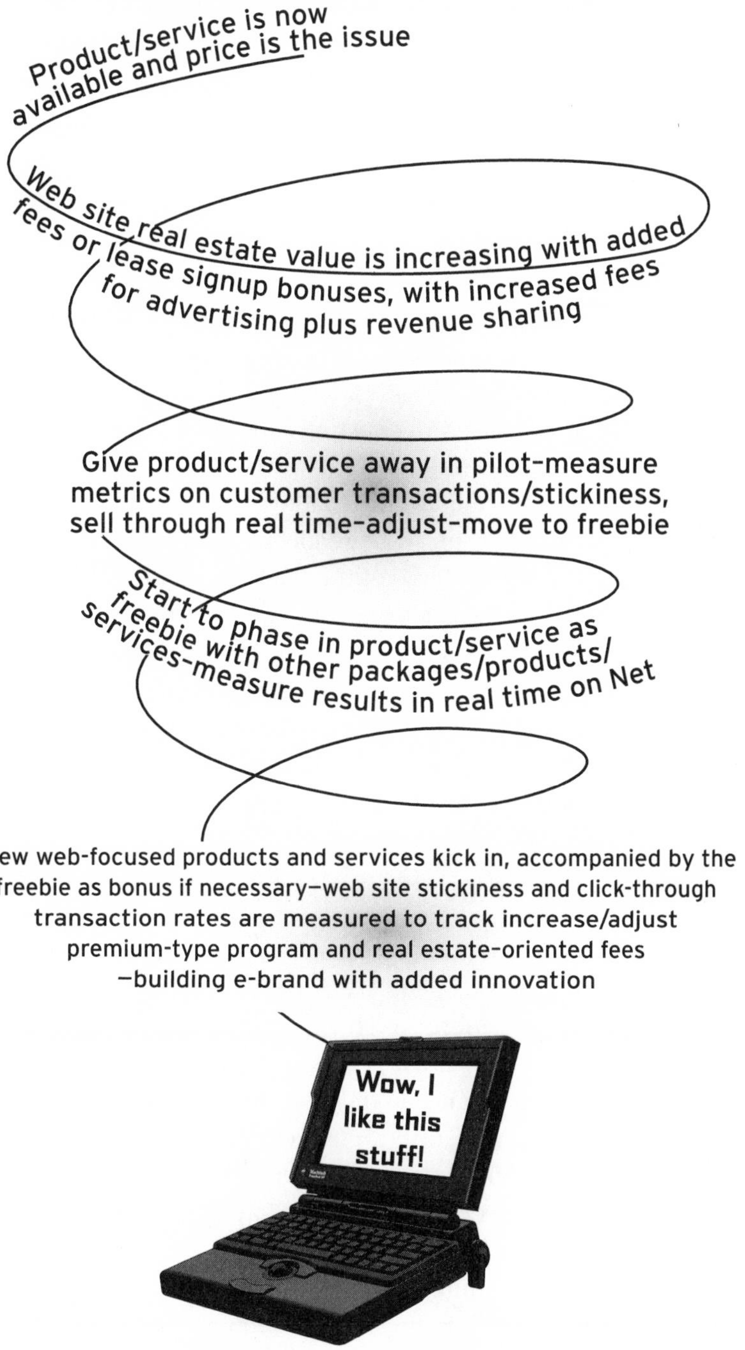

Product/service is now available and price is the issue
Web site real estate value is increasing with added fees or lease signup bonuses, with increased fees for advertising plus revenue sharing
Give product/service away in pilot–measure metrics on customer transactions/stickiness, sell through real time–adjust–move to freebie
Start to phase in product/service as freebie with other packages/products/ services–measure results in real time on Net
New web-focused products and services kick in, accompanied by the freebie as bonus if necessary—web site stickiness and click-through transaction rates are measured to track increase/adjust premium-type program and real estate-oriented fees —building e-brand with added innovation
Wow, I like this stuff!

encompass the Internet. We are a young company in a young industry. Innovation must be who we are continually, and building our franchise is part of that.

Clearly, the customer will visit and stay for some time on THQ's web site[5] in order to download the cards, thereby building the brand and adding revenues.

There is customer-loyalty value in giving something away (i.e., the currency of your site is now its *real estate value* instead of the product or service). So stop worrying about the price pressure on the product and hike up the value of the buttons[6] on your web site. To help you decide when to do this, think of all your products and services as being timed out. Create pilot tests on the web to see what happens to your web-based transaction rate when product prices are dropping (offer it at a lower price or free). Do this analysis with every product and create a schedule that enables you to see the product and service *time-out* (when their value reduces to 0). Doing this will allow you to anticipate your schedule of time-outs so that the value of your site increases as your product price decreases. Then you can attach the site value increase as a real estate fee to the anchor tenants and those less integrated (lower) on the Pyramid of Planet CAD. In essence, you are adding a web real estate division to your company while some of your competitors' products and services are being taken to a less-than-cost level.

The Synthesizer (Ninth House): FastAlliances Tool #19

One of the most fascinating competencies evolving in the new economy is the integration of people from multiple industries into the same team. Its hugely energizing to hear and learn new ways of looking at the world—and for most people with dot-com self-esteem, the opportunity to learn is one of the most influential hooks to keep them in the job. Employee retention is a key challenge for every company, traditional or e-business, so it is critical to find a way to integrate the best from every area without having one contingent feel underappreciated while another is overvalued.

Ninth House Learning Network[7] is an angel- and VC-funded e-business located in San Francisco. Started just a few years ago, the company has attracted talented people from publishing, game design, web development, enterprise software, instructional design, broadband delivery, television broadcasting, and knowledge management. All have varying degrees of dot-com self-esteem, high energy, great capabilities, and creativity in their own fields. The challenge has been twofold:

1. How do we leverage everyone's strengths into a structure that is greater than the sum of its parts?
2. How do we bring that structure to our partners and influence them to work with it in the operation of our alliances?

In a number of intense sessions, an approach was developed to provide solutions. First, the role of senior management must be clear. If it is not, the operational structure and its ultimate integration with alliance partners will fail. The senior management contributions are laid out in Figures 8.5 and 8.6.

At Ninth House, one gets the impression of intense energy and creativity. The environment has been designed by Gensler (see Chapter 1), and the team process is supported by flexible work spaces, creative structures, and innovative seating that create an atmosphere of total learning, information transfer, and access to both content provider and customer needs and added value. Long hours and an intermittent sense of chaos and deadlines simulate the movie/television industry with the systems and metrics of instructional design and executive education mandates.

Organized chaos? The bottom line is that the company has created a FastStrategy FastAlliances implementation model that synthesizes the best from all its internal alliance partners (valuable resources within the organization who could easily have become encapsulated and ultimately lost to the company). When Ninth House has implemented this approach with its partners, it has had varying results. For some of the larger companies, the time demands of the new economy are uncomfortable—their old-economy decision cycles are slow and cumbersome. Over the past six months, the company has discarded some partner opportunities for this very reason, even though the business propositions could be positive. The market changes too fast to allow for decision-related delay. Ninth House has used the preceding process to evaluate potential partners. If the rapid-design, prototype, FastStrategy, flexible process and execution approach cannot be

Figure 8.5 Schematic 1—The Synthesizer (Ninth House): Fast-Alliances Tool #19

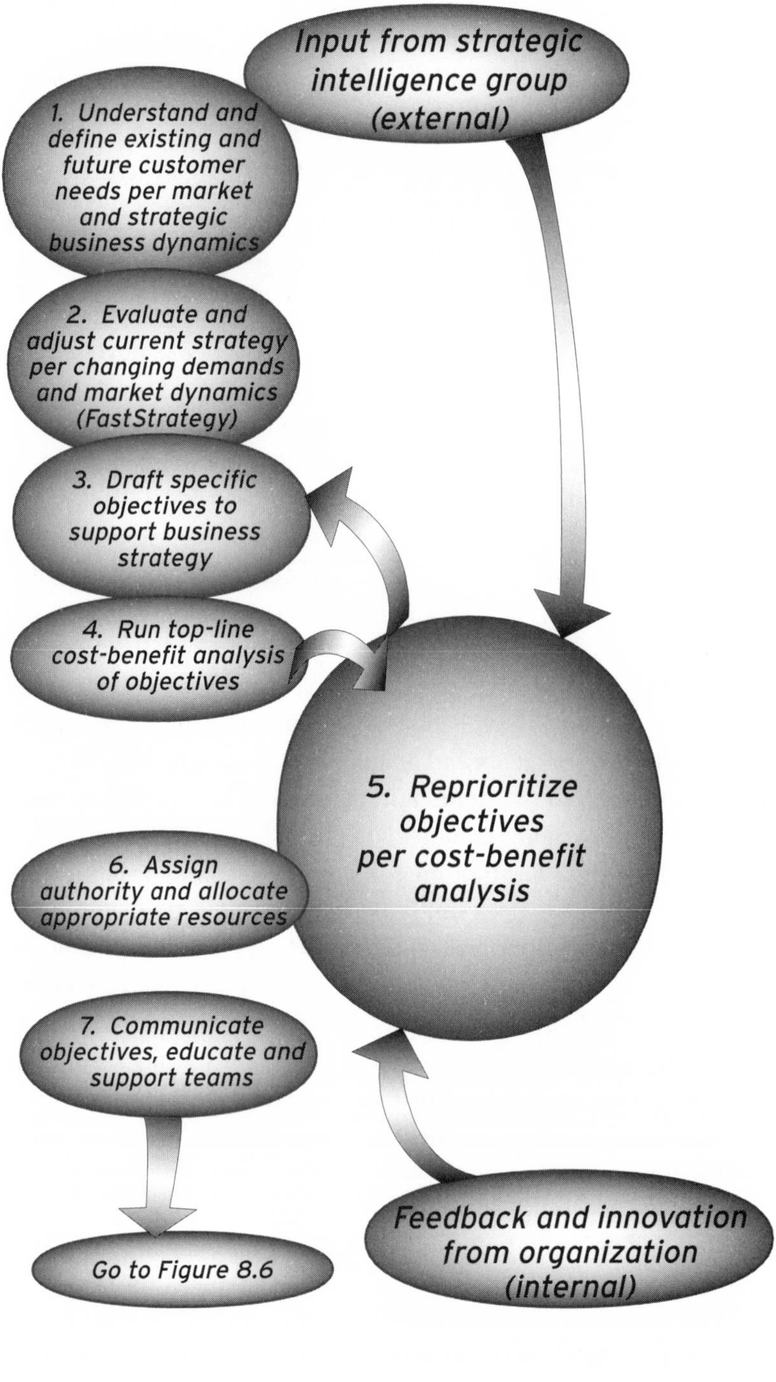

Figure 8.6 Schematic 2–The Synthesizer (Ninth House): FastAlliances Tool #19

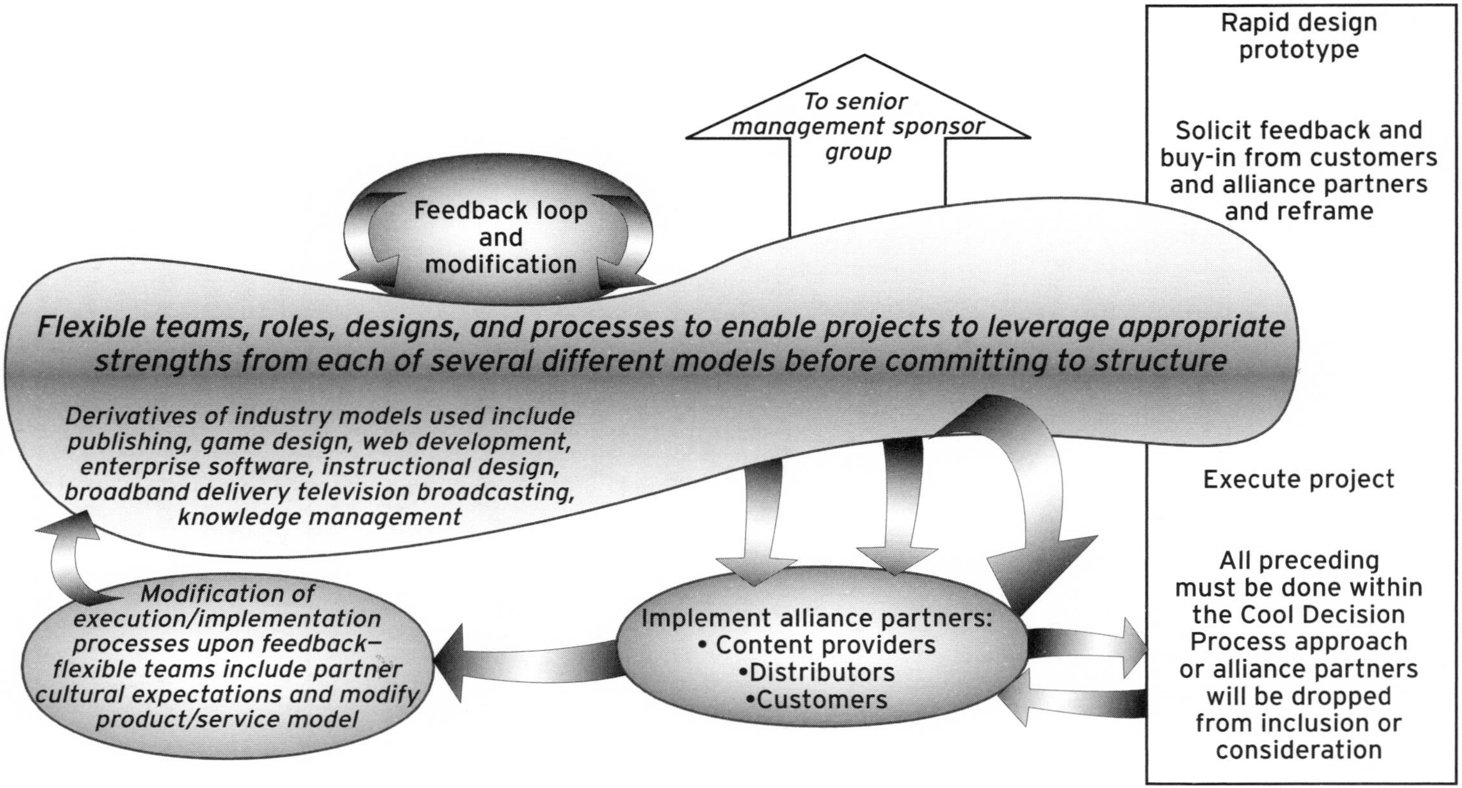
Rapid design prototype
Solicit feedback and buy-in from customers and alliance partners and reframe
To senior management sponsor group
Feedback loop and modification
Flexible teams, roles, designs, and processes to enable projects to leverage appropriate strengths from each of several different models before committing to structure
Derivatives of industry models used include publishing, game design, web development, enterprise software, instructional design, broadband delivery television broadcasting, knowledge management
Execute project
Modification of execution/implementation processes upon feedback– flexible teams include partner cultural expectations and modify product/service model
Implement alliance partners:
• Content providers
•Distributors
•Customers
All preceding must be done within the Cool Decision Process approach or alliance partners will be dropped from inclusion or consideration

implemented with compatible partners, then those partners will ultimately not be able to participate in the growth cycle.

At this point, Ninth House has more partners than it can handle, so using the FastAlliances Synthesizer approach in the selection process is very valuable. This tool can also be used midstream in an alliance that is encountering difficulties, because it can isolate the areas of dissonance. For example, when used as a diagnostic tool, the following issues could be uncovered:

- Lack of flexibility of team processes
- Divergence in understanding of how to do things
- The prototype, testing, and launch cycle
- Input and commitment of sponsor/senior management

Sometimes, start-ups in the e-space are not as inexperienced as their name implies. One company that has a fairly well-developed process more often found in companies at a more advanced stage of growth is e-Frenzy. Chatri Trisirpisal, who is in business development there, had this to say: "We have created an online marketplace for buyers and sellers of all kinds of services (tennis lessons, web design, massage, etc.). The key to e-Frenzy's success is creating many FastAlliances with all sorts of brick-and-mortar, traditional companies. We need *fast* deals with quality brands in order to fill our database quickly. So we have created a FastAlliances process." I have adapted Trisirpisal's process, which follows.

Fire, Aim, Steady (E-Frenzy): FastAlliances Tool #20

Assumptions

- Many traditional partners don't understand the business development process or alliances the same way the Internet world does (where alliances are a competitive advantage).
- Traditional partners don't move as fast as e-companies do. Therefore all deals for e-Frenzy have to be made at the partner's senior management level in order to speed things up.
- Contracts may be no more than two pages long.
- The focus of the business development group is to make the deal. They hand it off to the strategic alliances group, who implement it.

Process

Research. Select an industry and use competitors against each other to bid for the best partner.

The sales process. This means making a traditional company feel good about the deal with e-Frenzy. The process has four steps:

1. Establish the credibility of e-Frenzy. The company is a world-class company backed by IXL Corporation. It has a top-gun CEO and high-quality partners.
2. Demonstrate the value proposition. Why does it make sense to partner with e-Frenzy? Because it is a media company linking buyers and sellers. It presents itself as a local business with the eyeballs of local consumers in local markets. It sells advertisements, and its pages are only as valuable as the number of readers in that segment. Metrics include page views (how many are generated) and revenues.
3. Create a sense of urgency. Big companies move slowly as a rule, so e-Frenzy tries to tap into three to five sources within a large company in order to create a buzz within the potential partner company.
4. Create a sense of scarcity. This positions e-Frenzy as the best single solution to the problem.

These four steps are part of the strategy to strike the deal. Clearly, there has to be an internal organizational process for any deal to succeed.

Negotiations include lots of off-the-table work, which refers to discussions of mutuality, opportunity cost, and wins for all parties. This is often not included in the contract, but is part of the relationship building.

Signing the documents by senior management—do it fast.

The handoff team comes in early in the deal. The partner's team is added only after the deal is negotiated. The handoff team has to coordinate the representatives from marketing, technology, and product (domain) expertise.

The challenges? There are many. Some of the key ones are as follows:

1. *Uncertainty factor is high.* You may be doing deals with companies that could be competitors.
2. *Sheer volume is an issue.* The more deals that are done, the higher the visibility and the less likelihood of being left behind.
3. *PR value is large.* Many alliances may happen for perception reasons rather than added value. This will add drag to the speed of growth if not strategically sensible or valuable. Rigorous analysis, synergies, cost savings, and potential must be part of the considerations.
4. *Economic model is useful.* Whereas 75 percent of Internet startups don't know how to build an economic model, e-Frenzy has a professional CEO and two investment bankers in business development. Their mandate is to do models on traditional cost and benefit over the deal's lifetime, determine how much the customer is worth to e-Frenzy, and evaluate the PR aspect of the deal in attracting financial and human capital.
5. *Preemptive deal making is necessary.* There is more downside to being conservative in deal making than in being aggressive. Preemptive deal making is key—if you don't do a deal, your competitor will. There is no point in singling out one or two companies. Do deals with everyone and look for some to stick and some to fail.

In fact, e-Frenzy did a deal with the Tribune Company—a large, traditional company in the newspaper, radio, and TV business who recently bought *Times Mirror.* Tribune has agreed that all of its web properties will be powered by e-Frenzy. Now people can search the Yellow Pages, place a request under e-Frenzy, and the seller can respond in real time—thus creating a *captive* exchange (meaning that customers have to go through the Tribune site, whose sales force will be used to aggregate requests through its own site). Trisirpisal explained why the deal came together:

> The Tribune is really a media company, and the people within the company who negotiated the deal are in the new media group. They really get it. They understand what it takes to succeed in this space, and it was amazing dealing with them. They have done

> deals before—and that also helped. We spent a lot of time talking about what a partnership was, how we could each deliver value to each other. And senior management at the CEO and CTO level were involved in the merger right along with the new media deal-making team.

Sounds a lot like traditional alliances, doesn't it? The big difference was that it happened *fast*. The partners were *very* different in personality and size, but the negotiations were done by managers who were sharp, young, and clued into each other's needs. Of course, implementation is key—and so far the FastAlliances is working well. The handoff team is *making* it work.

The Tiering Process (Siebel): FastAlliances Tool #21

Other tools are also used for organizing FastAlliances. One in particular is impressive. It is the creation of Bruce Cleveland, vice president of Siebel Systems, a company started a few short years ago in Silicon Valley and now approaching $1 billion in revenues. Its focus is entirely e-business and includes customer acquisition and management technology. Siebel Systems has created a way to provide this to companies in exchange for equity. Siebel wants to demonstrate that it has a large customer base that uses its e-business technology to run electronic commerce. No matter the size of the company or the differences in their business models, all of the companies that partner with Siebel need customers they can retain. And dot-com start-ups don't have much internal infrastructure to do the customer acquisition. Siebel's partnering solution packages the infrastructure to get the technology to work and marries that to the access to the customer and partners. The result is what the company calls its Siebel Venture Program.

Siebel offers two options. One is the software-only option. The other is a completely hosted site with software and services. Siebel finds out what the start-up needs to run its business. Examples of those needs might be web site services, call centers, fax/e-mail, or marketing. Siebel determines the start-up's needs for a two-year period and offers software packages (plus outsources of the hosting of the site) at a reduced cost—with equity as part of the payment. This is then integrated into the Siebel Alliance Program, which is highly focused on the partner's success, and an alliance manager is designated to work with the start-up. He or she writes the business plan that enables the start-up to gain access to the Siebel customer base, which includes how Siebel will help the company gain new business through that base. In other words, Siebel don't just throw the contacts to its partners, but actually facilitates their leveraging of those contacts (both internal and external)—the equivalent of a guided tour plus real services and benefits.

The Siebel Alliance Program is impressive. The partners are tiered in order of integration. I have created a tool adapted from the excellent Siebel tiering[8] process, which can be used in FastAlliances. (See Figure 8.7.)

This tool should be used in conjunction with all the other tools and should be overlaid over the Pyramid of Planet CAD in order to understand the skin in the game, the timing, and the level of integration necessary. If the wrong tier is chosen for a FastAlliances (i.e., if the FastAlliances is philosophically on a higher or lower level of the pyramid), there will be dissatisfaction as the outcome fails to meet the expectations of the relationship. Using this tiering process with the pyramid analytical tool will ensure placement in a category that fits the FastStrategy you have chosen and your short- and long-term goals for the relationship. Keep in mind that due to the time/speed constraints of many FastAlliances, failure is not an option. And preventable failure is especially not an option. Understanding where you and your partners are on the pyramid and developing a tiering strategy as a consequence will be time well spent.

The horizontal tiers are the areas for partners to define their relationship with your company. There are also vertical tiers that can overlay those—for example, each horizontal tier could involve a number of vertical tiers. Let's say that a technical consultant wants to partner. He or she could sign up online under the baseline partner tier and then also be categorized as a vertical participant within that tier, grouped with other technical consultants. Or a software designer could be listed as part of the horizontal baseline (lowest) tier and also in the software developers' vertical category. Benefits for each vertical category could be designed to best fit that group's interests and

Figure 8.7 FastAlliances Tool #21: The Tiering Process (Siebel)

Kinds of partners

•Consulting (vertical industry such as e-automotive) •Content •Software (with solution-type partners such as call center monitoring) •Global (regional worldwide) •Platform

Tiers of Relationships

Global Strategic Partner

•Team + agent selling, reselling •Major financial commitment •Codevelopment globally •Meet various minimum training and selling commitments

Partner Portal

•Available to all partners but with firewalls between them and case-sensitive passwords for access to specific pages

Strategic or Premier Partner Management

•Alliance manager appointed •Responsibility is to ensure both companies meet their agreed-upon business objectives in revenue, product delivery, and market share •Manages daily activities related to alliance, revenue generation, review product/service delivery forecasts, manage the capital investments for projects, manage engineering/technology sharing, definition/execution of marketing programs, joint implementations, quarterly written progress, and board reports •Partner must meet minimum training, implementation, market development, and dedicated alliance managers/resources for each level of strategic or premier (strategic could be higher than premier) •Benefits include brand sharing and public relations, joint selling and information sharing, education and licenses

Base-Level Partner Management

•E-mail link to company that will create a service request to be handled by team members to document hundreds of partner communications daily and route questions to the right people •E-mails become part of permanent record •No designated alliance manager for these partners •Certain minimum requirements, including fees and education/market development •Create subverticals from this level for partner categories (consultants, developers, etc.)

still be covered by the horizontal tier's qualification and registration requirements. And so on.

As of the first half of 2000, the Siebel Venture Program (which is proprietary to Siebel and not described here) combined with the Siebel Alliance Program has been integrated into 5 companies, with 5 more pending and 25 more on the horizon. Needless to say, Siebel has close relationships with some of the key venture capital firms.

Throughout the world, this concept has caught on in the form of incubators—for example, Garage.com (see Chapter 4) in California, iCocoon in Europe (a division of Protégé, the U.K. Internet business development group whose Spider Network includes Citria, which is also a division of Protégé and a leading professional service firm in the Internet), and Global Retail Partners (a European VC firm). Another incubator joint venture is eVentures—Softbank and e-Partners, GorillaPark in the Netherlands. However, the Siebel approach goes beyond the concept of an incubator. It creates a competitive advantage by incorporating the company's unique and well-proven alliance management processes.

Siebel is now operating in a market where demand is huge—not only for alliances with the company, but for its capital and market access. When a market is so new that it is hardly developed and the players have yet to place their stakes in the ground, the approach has to be somewhat different.

My meetings and interviews with two outstanding companies that are very different from each other yet leaders in their own industries yielded a common perspective that I have drawn into a process I call the Circle of Influence. The companies are Qualcomm and Roche Pharmaceuticals.

Circle of Influence: FastAlliances Tool #22

Qualcomm in San Diego has been thrilling investors and techies for a number of years as it comes up with new technologies and approaches to the telecommunications market. The company has undertaken a mission to have the Code Division Multiple Access (CDMA) technology accepted as the world's digital wireless standard. With increasing acceptance of digital voice and wireless data, Qualcomm's timing could not have been better. The CDMA standard is perfect for all kinds of wireless appliances, from phones to handheld devices to every environment that could accept the communications we have become addicted to—even the Netcar described by Toyota. CDMA can pack a much higher volume of calls onto systems than can the competing TDMA system, which has been dominant in the United States. In 1999, Qualcomm created an alliance that set the standard for third-generation (3G) phone and networks—the 3G accord with Ericsson and other major European wireless carriers. Since Qualcomm collects a royalty for every CDMA phone sold, there is huge upside for the company in creating a ubiquitous CDMA environment. Fortunately, CDMA is the third most widely used system in the world, behind TDMA (number one in the United States) and the global system for mobile communications (GSM), which is used mainly in Europe.

So how does a company create a worldwide standard? What are the dynamics of Qualcomm's Spider Network that enable this to happen?

Qualcomm has created a brilliant process that I call the Circle of Influence. I explored this concept with Anthony Thornley, CFO of Qualcomm. Thornley is a low-key, unusually strategic CFO. He sees his role as far more than financial:

> My role encompasses the alliance arena, but not just the financial aspect. I am pretty much a people-person and contribute to the cultural issues of alliances, which are critical for success [he is singing my song!]. Our biggest strategic challenge is in growing the markets for our CDMA technology, since we do not have the direct capability to manufacture and produce end products that use it—nor do we want to. Our goal is to encourage other companies to do so. Certainly this has influenced many of the alliances we have developed, especially those where investment is appropriate—because when we have a minority position, we can clearly influence the direction of the company as quickly as possible. The more companies that sell products with our technology, the more chips and software we sell. We really don't have an investment process—rather, we look where we will have the most leverage. For example, China. Our goal is to have China adopt our technology. We have met with some resistance by the Chinese government. Our approach has had to be very strategic.

The process that Qualcomm has executed has influenced the market that it wants to see happen in the present and future—without accessing the ultimate consumer of the products and services to be sold in that market. In addition to the hundreds of patents that the company has in place and pending, I believe that this is one of the most important aspects of what makes Qualcomm valuable. (See Figure 8.8.)

What steps must be taken in order to create a Circle of Influence?

Step 1: Who are the stakeholders (immediate as well as long term)? Move fast to preempt decisions that would prevent your positive positioning with them, even if that means developing pre-FastAlliances contacts and conversations. Use your Spider Network

Figure 8.8 Circle of Influence (Qualcomm): FastAlliances Tool #22

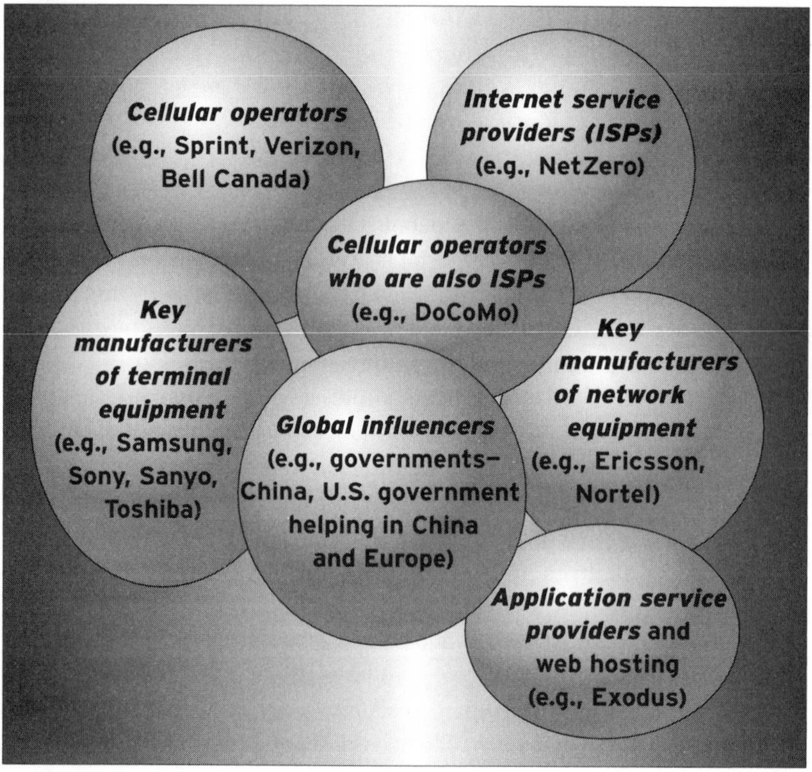

FastAlli, by Larraine Segil

to find the specific opinion influencers within each stakeholder—and pull out all the stops in order to get their attention. The stakeholders must be prioritized with an action plan for contact that places them strategically into the Circle of Influence, first as organizations, then as individuals within those organizations who must be co-opted. Again co-option can be direct or indirect (through third parties who have influence on them, for example). This is not unlike the *guanxi* method of interconnecting and cross-benefiting favors that exist in Chinese societies. To review, create a mapping process so that team effort can be deployed:

1. *Research* the stakeholders.
2. *Identify* the specific strategic interest they might have—their hot buttons that will enable you to get their attention.

3. *Investigate* the Spider Network for each target and determine how they interconnect within your Spider Network so you can understand how to approach them with "influencers."
4. *Prepare* the pitch—succinct and clear, easy to understand.
5. *Couch* it in culturally acceptable terms, analogies, and context in order to position yourself as a desirable and appropriate partner.
6. *Do* it all within the FastAlliances concept of Cool Decision Processes, E-Mindshift understanding, and the FastAlliances Gantt chart to plan and interrelate these activities.

Step 2: This involves education on your technology and advantages. Qualcomm's mission was to convince operators that they should adopt its technology and to start developing the product even before the market was established for it. This is no easy task. How did Qualcomm do it? Well I would love to say through eloquent conversation and rational argument, but, although I am sure that played a part, the reality is that money and influence together are a powerful combination. Qualcomm contributed development dollars for a variety of programs. For example, Qualcomm invested $200 million (as did a Canadian pension fund and Microsoft) in Korea Telecom. The Korean company wanted to go public but needed to pay off its debt beforehand. This investment helped Korea Telecom achieve its goals and establish a high-speed wireless technology competence. Another player in this Circle of Influence was KT Freetel, a cellular company. Once the product is launched, Qualcomm will play a different role, which is explained in the next step. This step involves the following:

1. *Educate* the stakeholders.
2. *Find* their hot buttons and needs and take care of them—leveraging off your Spider Network to increase theirs if you have to.
3. *Co-opt* their Spider Network to be sure that they feel comfortable with the level and credibility of players in the game with them.
4. *Invest,* and be willing to continue to invest for the long term.

Step 3. Once the initial catalyst is in place with credible stakeholders who have their needs identified and met (at least in part), step back and let the relationship evolve. If it is embedded in the local environment well enough, further action may not be needed, except to provide continuing support and education. If, however, it has not taken hold, return to step 2 and invest in encouraging other operators to adopt the technology. Invest until you bridge the gap between the *expectation* and the *actual accomplishment* of adopting the technology and establishing the market. Qualcomm in Korea is prepared to continue to invest in high-speed wireless, knowing that the market is not yet well understood, which means a heavy commitment to step 2.

In step 3, however, the activity moves to account management—on many different levels of the organization—and continues to be a priority at the executive level as well. The processes of market trials and technology beta tests mean that close working relationships are needed, and relationship managers will continue to roll the ball of the Circle of Influence onto multiple points of interface within the organizations concerned. To review:

1. *Step back* from pressurized influence creation and persuasion if the market is developing.
2. *Move* the management of the relationship to the account level.
3. *Develop* multiple points of interface within the organizations so that the relationship is diffused and does not stand or fall on the personalities of particular managers or their activities.
4. *Maintain* close executive commitment even though day-to-day activity will be at lower levels in the organizations.
5. *Expect* the unexpected.

The unexpected happened for Qualcomm in the latter part of 2000. The South Korean government announced it would lower its mobile-phone subsidies, and various Korean telecom providers indicated they would adopt WCDMA technology rather than Qualcomm's CDMA2000 technology. Another unexpected happening was that the deal to license CDMA to China Unicom appeared to be in trouble. Although the company licenses both technologies, its chipset business is focused on CDMA2000 sales. Nevertheless Qualcomm makes money no matter which standard is adopted, and its leadership remains convinced that CDMA will be the dominant platform.

Without doubt the Circle of Influence strategy and approach is one that is iterative, continuing, and greatly affected by the Spider

Network members of each player. As the Spider Network members change, the players in the Circle of Influence will, too. Perhaps Qualcomm will look for another addition to its Spider Network, seeking partnership with a company with WCDMA technology, who will then be plugged into the Circle of Influence three-step process. And the game continues.

Another company has taken the same approach as Qualcomm. The company is Roche. I met with the president of Roche Colorado Corporation and Syntex, Eric Lodewijk.

Roche has divested itself over the past few years of many companies that, although successful, were not necessarily in sync with Roche's competency and comfort level. Its core competency is related to the health care industry and designing new drugs. Roche sells primarily to hospitals and wholesalers. However, e-business is changing that. Many pharmaceutical companies are now driving the hospitals and medical providers by stimulating patient demand. Notice the proliferation of prescription drug commercials on U.S. television (e.g., Prilosec for heartburn that "could be something more serious," various cholesterol-reducing drugs that encourage patients to recognize symptoms and call their doctors). Television advertising for pharmaceuticals in the United States amounts to over $2 billion annually. However, nationalized health systems in many European countries have precluded the advertising of drugs directly to patients through commercial means. (Simply put, since governments pay for the patients' increased demand for prescription drugs, this would be counterproductive.)

What is the Circle of Influence for Roche? It is somewhat more subtle than for Qualcomm, but the process is very similar. From this example you can create your own Circle of Influence.

From my conversation with Lodewijk, I've identified the stakeholders and developed a brief application of the FastAlliances Circle of Influence tool:

Step 1. Who are the stakeholders? For most pharmaceutical companies in the United States they include the following.

1. Medicare and Medicaid.
2. U.S. government—FDA and a variety of other agencies of the government.

3. Hospitals.
4. Wholesalers like McKesson or Cardinal Health, who buy the drugs and distribute them to the hospitals, doctors, and pharmacies.
5. Physicians.
6. Patients—accessible directly through television as well as indirectly through the other stakeholders.
7. Other companies—small and large for joint development, equity investment, licensing, and royalty arrangements. Roche is masterful in its management of the development and approval process as well as its manufacturing technology/processes (and in bringing this competency to smaller companies who may have innovative technologies).

Step 2. Roche develops a number of relationships with each of the stakeholders, a huge investment of time and effort. Although the details of such activities are confidential, the depth of understanding of the needs of the various stakeholders is part of what makes the company a sterling player in the pharmaceutical marketplace. When analyzing your step 2, the FastAlliances Gantt will help you structure your strategy—as Roche has done in what can be decade-long development cycles.

Step 3. In many ways, this is the implementation of the investment in education and influencers that have come before—whether it be the beta sites of hospitals and centers of excellence or the physician providers who have run the clinical trials. But the ultimate sales and service that continue to keep products on the market for their life cycle is where the wholesalers and distributors earn their stripes, backed up by the credibility, research, and support of the pharmaceutical companies. Of course, the dance continues between reimbursement issues and availability of drugs, which means that steps 1 and 2 in this industry are never really done.

The preceding examples will help you focus on your Circle of Influence processes, which will add to the leverage of the Spider Network and FastAlliances Gantt tools in hand.

By now you are thoroughly "tooled out." However, you also have a menu of options to draw from as your FastAlliances evolve. Chapter 9 addresses some of the final issues that should be part of your portfolio of FastAlliances management skills. When should you use the FastAlliances approach? When is the traditional alliance approach more relevant? How can you operate using both approaches in parallel?

CHAPTER 9

Step 9: Pitfalls and Opportunities—Summing Up

The strategies and tools that have been presented in the first eight chapters require constant adaptation. There is no definitive way to construct FastAlliances, or indeed traditional ones—only methodologies that must be adapted to your particular situation. Ultimately, this is about growing the company and adding value. The approach must fit the goal. Becoming truly competent requires running the alliance activity for traditional and FastAlliances in parallel.

Federal Express (FedEx) has been a consulting client of the Lared Group, and a number of its executives (Laurie Tucker, David Payton, and David Roussain) have been integrally involved in the alliances of the organization. David Roussain, now vice president of e-commerce marketing, explained how the FedEx of the past and the present have come together to create the future:

> This is a major cultural challenge for FedEx since their origins came from a culture where they have everything under control. The nature of their success has been that there is not a second in the processes of the organization that they did not know where every package, parcel, and letter was, anywhere in the world. That

> was their promise and they fulfilled it brilliantly. The problem with the Internet is that no one really knows much about anything. I came from HP, and our way was that when we didn't know what to do, first we acknowledged that we didn't know what to do, then we went and researched it and learned what to do or made it up.

David Payton, a long-term employee of FedEx, really knows the ins and outs of the organization:

> We invented the overnight shipping business, and over the past 10 years we have personalized and customized our relationships and increased the bond between our customers and ourselves. We have automated the customers' business processes and put in shipping devices to make shipping easier. Now customers have lots of technology and are asking us to integrate into their business so that they have proactive information on their shipping. We are adding more all the time—labeling, address verification, visibility, notification—the customer wants a number of services from us through a single pipeline. Now customers in e-business are not just looking for shipping—they want solutions on how we at FedEx can make their processes work better. Now the customers are more valuable than the products and services we give them. This means that we have to become highly competent at all kinds of alliances.

Payton has found the Spider Network to be an excellent tool for describing the variety of alliances that the company has built, especially where the clusters of alliances differ from region to region:

> For example, we will not even enter into a memorandum of understanding or a letter of intent in Asia unless we have someone on the ground in the area. These relationships are very important, and having someone with local presence and knowledge is part of what FedEx is all about. We have also avoided exclusive relationships for alliances of all kinds, and that is a reciprocal request. But there is a huge amount of energy and human bandwidth that is necessary to make these relationships happen.

FedEx is still working through the need for custodial control of everything that has driven the company for its lifetime and enabled it to become the world leader in their market. This is antithetical to the concept of alliances, which require a corporate mind-set that is collaborative and involves risk sharing. FedEx is making the transition by bringing in new employees, younger people who have grown up with the Internet and who think graphically.

Companies like FedEx, who are successful at what they do and have created a whole industry, are coming to the Internet world with two challenges:

1. A culture that evolves from a job done well in the past—which now has to be done another way
2. A commitment to alliances—which must speed up considerably as FastAlliances become the norm

Just as the FedEx culture has started to accept the approach used for traditional, slower, and more sequential alliances, the pressure is on to create FastAlliances. David Payton explains:

> We have made more equity alliances, since we find that they are easier to do than nonequity—the partner feels that we have more skin in the game. And we are now doing FastAlliances—with shorter negotiation times and higher payback for our risk. Our main focus, however, is not the ROI, although that's still important. It is how to leverage the operating company and whether the alliance will have a technology that will be important for FedEx's future. We have to know how to do both kinds.

This is no different from the approach of the Walt Disney Internet group and is a solid method for traditional companies to leverage their brand and past history with new structures and relationships that can catapult them into e-business. With the use of the Cool Decision Process to break through the bureaucracy, success is more likely.

What elements go into deciding whether an alliance opportunity is a traditional one or a FastAlliances candidate?

The following seven-part approach is a good model which I have used. Remember, all the tools in this book need adaptation to your particular circumstances. One size does not fit all.

The Right Choice: FastAlliances Tool #23

1. Evaluate whether the alliance opportunity has FastAlliances characteristics:
   - Internet-related is its primary vehicle.
   - Competition is operating in an Internet model.

- Customer wants value, and the Internet online model is the best solution to deliver this value.
- It has to happen fast (within days/weeks, not months/years).

2. Apply the tools to create the environment for success in FastAlliances (see index of tools at back of book), especially FastStrategy and Cool Decision Process.
3. Start the Spider Network development. You may already have one in process or in place. Start to chart it, make the team aware of its importance, and add their contributions to it.
4. Use the E-Mindshift approach to understand the personalities and organizational cultures you will be dealing with, both within your own company and externally. Match your presentation/communication/data analysis style to those with whom you will be interfacing. Speak in the language of the receiver of information.
5. Choose tools relevant to the FastAlliances application.
6. Create a FastAlliances Gantt chart, prioritizing the relevant tools with the action items, estimated time to completion, and so forth.
7. Evaluate the following in order to make a decision about whether to transition the FastAlliance into a longer-term one:
   - Is this relationship penetrating a variety of areas within the organization?
   - Are the stakeholders changing to include those not primarily within e-business activities?
   - Are the resources (people and financial) expanding into longer-term and/or larger commitments than originally projected?
   - Is the impact of the alliance increasing for related partners in your/their Spider Network?
   - Is the project priority increasing for one, both, or all partners?

For these and many other reasons that will be relevant on a case-by-case basis, the decision may be made to transition into a traditional alliance.

The following stakeholders may not have been involved, but they will become part of the implementation process:

1. CFO
2. Other divisions

3. Corporate alliances group
4. Traditional business development group/acquisition team
5. Research and development
6. Marketing and marketing analysis/research
7. Corporate planning

In other words, many of the slower yet detail-oriented activities that traditional alliances encompass (either before or during the alliance) could become involved in the postalliance implementation as the effect of the FastAlliances spreads throughout the organization.

Issues that may arise are the not-invented-here (NIH) factor and the need for continuous internal selling to enlist widespread buy-in. A rather complex issue to resolve at this time may be a new look at the business model. Is it working? Is the FastAlliances approach now appropriate for a widespread, longer-term alliance? Or does the business model require revisiting, which could call for a complete reinvention of the e-business portion of the activity?

Scalability of the Organization

One of the building blocks that seems to come contemporaneously with the decision to convert a FastAlliances into a traditional one is the issue of scalability. However, scalability is also a separate issue. Here's the question:

How can you get bigger yet retain what made you good to start with?

Can you scale up for growth without adding bureaucracy and excessive process? Jerry Yang, cofounder of Yahoo!, says "Building an organization that scales smoothly is the true test of an entrepreneur. Often what it comes down to is how well the founders continue to scale themselves."[1]

Growing the e-business through alliances, whether fast or traditional, will ultimately depend on whether you can scale up the management of these relationships so that you can deal with multiples of them, adding to their value over time. The E-Mindshift approach will assist you in putting the right human resources into the job, but it will not prevent the alliance from falling in priority as a new and more exciting deal comes along. Thus it is necessary to create an alliances group (part of the traditional alliances model) that can be at both the corporate and the division level. This group should consist of the following.

The Alliances Group: Fast and Traditional Alliance Management

1. A database of alliances in place/development
2. A knowledge-capture system that is integrated throughout the organization
3. A VP- or senior vice president (SVP)–level executive who reports to the CEO/COO and has both power and credibility within the ranks—but no desire to build a fiefdom
4. Alliance management processes—metrics, conflict-resolution tools, communication protocols, termination processes
5. Education methods

Database of Alliances in Place/Development

Amazing as it seems, many organizations actually have no idea of all the alliances that are in effect throughout their companies. This means that their negotiating positions are weak in discussions with partners with whom they are already in partnerships, but don't know it. The Internet makes recording this data so much easier that it's frankly incomprehensible why companies would not have this available. How to do it? Create a one-page online form as the FastAlliances or traditional alliance is being created, input the relevant data, and there it is. The alliances group can monitor and input commentary into the database, adding value to it, but the operating managers or those close to the information about the alliance should be inputting data continually.

Knowledge-Capture System

This is a critical tool for four reasons:

1. When employees leave, they take their knowledge and experiences with them.
2. When meetings take place with potential partners, the information that is transferred by conversation can be extremely valuable. Unless it is captured, only the participants gain that value.

3. Interdivisional learning is difficult. Time is short, calendars for meetings to share knowledge are unavailable, silo mentality can prevail (reluctance to share), and memories fade.
4. The corporate memory is only as good as the memories of those who remain. Downsizing, dot-com fever, and demographics all contribute to the brain drain that depletes the corporate memory.

How do you capture knowledge? Many contact-capture sales software programs could be adapted to this purpose, but the general idea is to capture it online.

It can be painless, not tiresome. Recently, as I was addressing a group of senior executives, one executive was entering the knowledge he was capturing from the presentation into his Palm Pilot. Then he beamed it to all the other participants' Palm Pilots at the end of the meeting and downloaded it into the company knowledge-capture database system when he returned to his office. Data can be captured by entering the following information:

1. Date and time of meeting/project/discussion
2. Who was there (company, person, title)
3. Project name and manager
4. Key subject
5. Key knowledge/thought
6. Keyword for search
7. Immediately related topics/companies that come to the mind of the entry person

Imagine that every time you want to call Digital Virtual (a fictitious company), you search under its name or subject and find not only how Digital interacts with your company, but also with its competitors; then, to your excitement, you find that someone in R&D is working on something that could augment your own program; and so on. (I have simplified both the system and its applications, but you get the idea.)

Context Integration Systems has developed a good tool for internal knowledge capture that is somewhat more of a commitment than the simplistic approach I have described. (I just couldn't write a chapter without another tool for you!) This company is a b2b provider and builder of high-end integration systems and solutions for financial services and entertainment clients. Context Integration Systems has created an internal system called Intellectual Assets Network (IAN). The system has enabled the company to capture the knowledge developed internally among its own employees in nine offices, as well as from client activities, and to share it effectively. In addition, it has made a substantial commitment to keep the system relevant and working efficiently by dedicating full-time resources to its maintenance and upgrading. I spoke at length with Steve Sharp, CEO of Context Integration, and Bruce Strong, company founder and creator of IAN, and we are now working together to adapt their IAN program to fit an alliance knowledge-capture role in addition to other intellectual assets of the organization. (See Figure 9.1.)

"IAN works very well," Sharp reports. "We have more work than we can handle, and we had to have a shortcut to accessing the tremendous amount of knowledge that is developed every day by our internal consultant experts. IAN enables the flow of information across cultures and disciplines." Bruce Strong, creator of IAN and cofounder of the company, saw the added value of IAN in the context of alliances: "The relationships internally and externally, which any company has, generate a huge amount of knowledge, which most organizations fail to leverage to its fullest extent."

Working with Context Integration, I have adapted IAN for FastAlliances (called IAN/FASTAL) to add an aspect of the IAN constellation relevant to *all* alliances—traditional as well as FastAlliances. IAN and FASTAL will include information about the alliance relationships, the names of champions (alliance leaders) and their teams, names of companies, the stages of investigation, first contact, development, nondisclosure agreements (NDAs) signed, who was present at the meetings, embedded knowledge desired (theirs), embedded knowledge at risk or intended to be transferred (ours), and a myriad of other data including that regarding the Spider Network. Keyword access is deliberately designed to be flexible in order to access this data from a number of angles.

The IAN/FASTAL approach is immensely adaptable for a variety of organizations—whether hierarchical or flat from a power-structure point of view. It does, however, require a commitment from management and a reward system (e.g., vacation trips, bonuses, gifts) to incen-

Figure 9.1 IAN and FASTAL Knowledge-Capture System (Context Integration): FastAlliances Tool #24

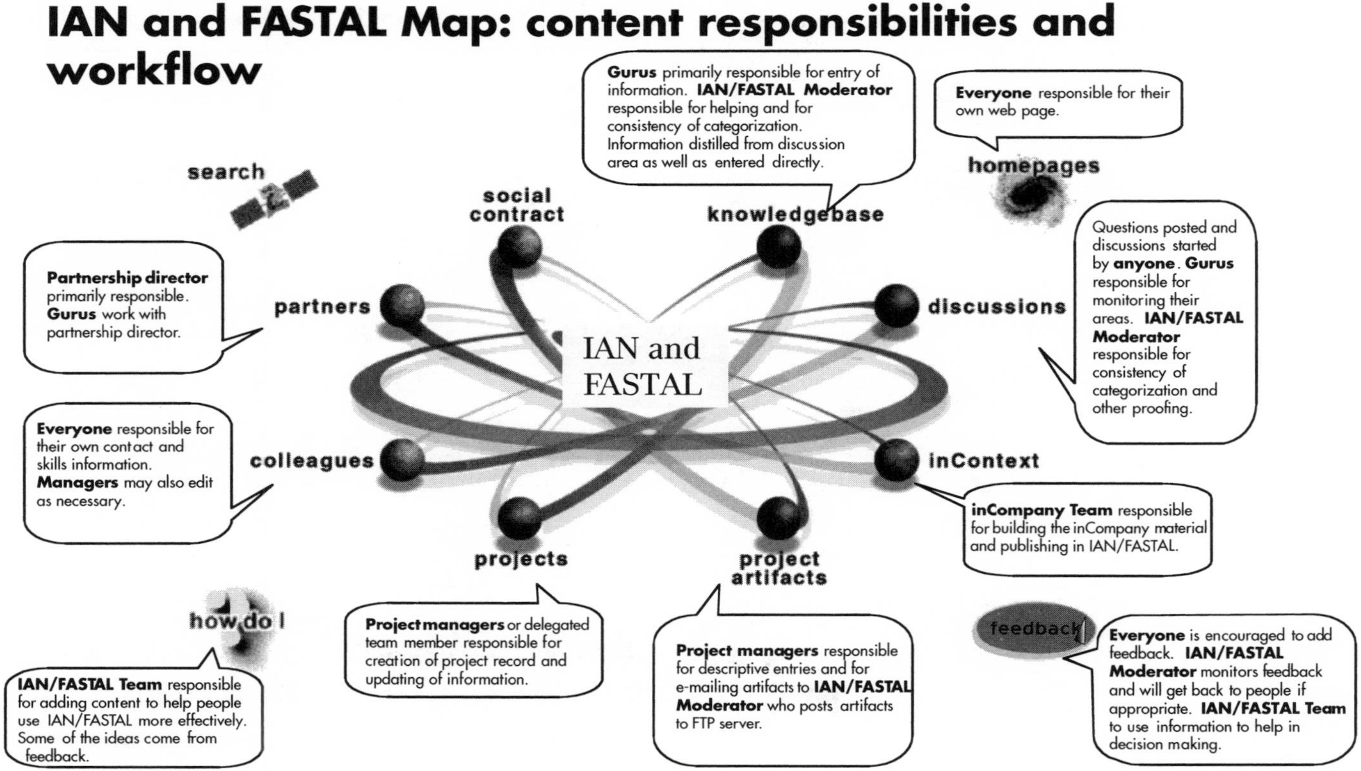

IAN and FASTAL Map: content responsibilities and workflow
Gurus primarily responsible for entry of information. IAN/FASTAL Moderator responsible for helping and for consistency of categorization. Information distilled from discussion area as well as entered directly.
Everyone responsible for their own web page.
homepages
search
social contract
knowledgebase
Partnership director primarily responsible. Gurus work with partnership director.
partners
IAN and FASTAL
discussions
Questions posted and discussions started by anyone. Gurus responsible for monitoring their areas. IAN/FASTAL Moderator responsible for consistency of categorization and other proofing.
Everyone responsible for their own contact and skills information. Managers may also edit as necessary.
colleagues
inContext
inCompany Team responsible for building the inCompany material and publishing in IAN/FASTAL.
projects
project artifacts
how do I
Project managers or delegated team member responsible for creation of project record and updating of information.
Project managers responsible for descriptive entries and for e-mailing artifacts to IAN/FASTAL Moderator who posts artifacts to FTP server.
feedback
Everyone is encouraged to add feedback. IAN/FASTAL Moderator monitors feedback and will get back to people if appropriate. IAN/FASTAL Team to use information to help in decision making.
IAN/FASTAL Team responsible for adding content to help people use IAN/FASTAL more effectively. Some of the ideas come from feedback.

(continued)

Figure 9.1 FastAlliances Tool #24 (Continued)

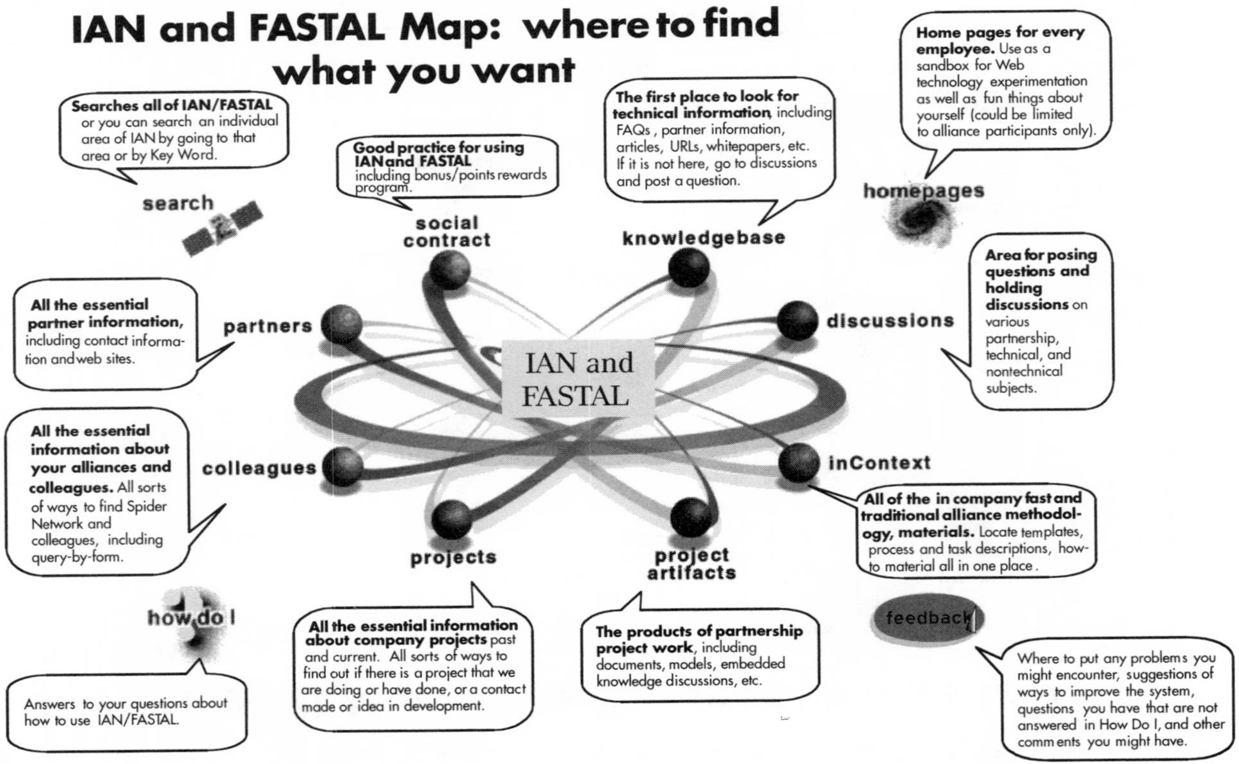

IAN and FASTAL Map: where to find what you want
Searches all of IAN/FASTAL or you can search an individual area of IAN by going to that area or by Key Word.
search
Good practice for using IAN and FASTAL including bonus/points rewards program.
social contract
The first place to look for technical information, including FAQs, partner information, articles, URLs, whitepapers, etc. If it is not here, go to discussions and post a question.
knowledgebase
Home pages for every employee. Use as a sandbox for Web technology experimentation as well as fun things about yourself (could be limited to alliance participants only).
homepages
All the essential partner information, including contact information and web sites.
partners
IAN and FASTAL
discussions
Area for posing questions and holding discussions on various partnership, technical, and nontechnical subjects.
All the essential information about your alliances and colleagues. All sorts of ways to find Spider Network and colleagues, including query-by-form.
colleagues
inContext
All of the in company fast and traditional alliance methodology, materials. Locate templates, process and task descriptions, how-to material all in one place.
projects
project artifacts
how do I
Answers to your questions about how to use IAN/FASTAL.
All the essential information about company projects past and current. All sorts of ways to find out if there is a project that we are doing or have done, or a contact made or idea in development.
The products of partnership project work, including documents, models, embedded knowledge discussions, etc.
feedback
Where to put any problems you might encounter, suggestions of ways to improve the system, questions you have that are not answered in How Do I, and other comments you might have.

FastAlli, by Larraine Segil

tivize its use. After people have used the system for a while, its intrinsic benefits will be clear and contributions will be easier to corral.[2]

The next requirement for effective FastAlliances is known as *position power.*

Position Power

Any alliances group needs a VP- or SVP-level executive who reports to the CEO/COO and has a position senior enough to garner respect and to add weight to the alliance concept. He or she must also have experience and credibility within the ranks of middle or entry-level management.

If you are serious about alliances, put your money where your mouth is. Appoint a senior officer with direct access to the top of the organization and the resources to launch your alliance and make it grow. This does not mean creating multiple layers of corporate staff. Alliance managers who report in a matrixed fashion to the alliances group could be scattered within the divisions of the company, and the alliances group could be rather small. But there has to be a key group of people who provide the internal services for alliance management and training and who offer insights and added value for knowledge capture and database management. That is the job of the alliances group—dual roles as business development experts and internal service providers. These functions can also be split, with the alliances group providing tools, skills, and services to the divisional business development activities, but not building their own empire or fiefdom.

Alliance Management Processes

These include metrics, conflict-resolution tools, communication protocols, and termination processes. All are covered in my first book, *Intelligent Business Alliances,* and in my courses. They are the normal processes for alliance management. Let me add some metrics here that I've recently developed.

What is value worth measuring?

In FastAlliances, value has been extended to include more than financial returns. Although traditional alliances included these deliverables as added value, measuring them has always been difficult. I am referring to value such as the increase or decrease in customer numbers, knowledge transfer between Spider partners, and more. Nevertheless, it is important to have a series of measurements that establish a baseline of value, followed by increases or decreases over time (no matter how short the time) and an evaluation decision that says,

This FastAlliances is working for us since the value added is greater than the cost, so we will continue with it [or not].

The following are metrics I recommend adding to your "value added or not" approach, which should be incorporated into a regular review (weekly, monthly, quarterly, and annually). Set up the metrics so they coordinate with those targets presented in your FastAlliances rollout plan (or, at the very least, use the business opportunity analysis as their baseline). Adjustments should be made to these targets as market realities dictate.

Of course, I would not be happy unless this was contained in another tool for quick reference: See Figure 9.2 for the Metric to End All Metrics Tool.

Education

There are many ways to be educated about alliances: live programs, web-based programs, satellite programs, seminars, articles, books,

Figure 9.2 Metric to End All Metrics: FastAlliances Tool #25

Financial

What is the financial impact of this FastAlliance?

On revenues, earnings, capital invested, margins, or other financial measures such as economic value added (EVA)?

Relationship

What is the impact on the relationship issues?

- **Competency-level increase**—training hours, cross-fertilization of multiple alliance types by alliance managers
- **Conflict-resolution challenges**—where, how often, resolution, or status
- **Process adherence to alliance processes** and tools as outlined in this book and those applicable to traditional alliances
- **Reward and compensation alignment** of alliance managers with process of alliances (e.g., number of bonuses received) to measure effectiveness of system
- **Churn rate of alliance managers**—new hires, burnout
- **Job preference rate**—related to recruiting difficulty or preferences, measuring whether this is more or less desirable as a career choice over time

Nonfinancial

What is the impact on other barometers of value that are not directly financial?

- **Customer-related issues** (if relevant)—customer acquisition cost at regular intervals (including both customer increase as well as churn rate or decrease), customer value potential over time (upselling, integration into customer alliances through joint development, etc.), and the effect of the alliance on this metric, customer communication intimacy levels (how often and in what depth customers are surveyed regarding issues of concern), customer service cost (increase or decrease)
- **Development-related issues**—increase or decrease in development time, increase or decrease in staffing and resource allocation to the development process or activity, intellectual property issues (number of patents pending or approved), and the prioritizing of these development activities according to how these measures evolve
- **Manufacturing-related issues**—defect rate increase or decrease, quality impact rate
- **Knowledge transfer sessions**—how often, what was transferred, still outstanding, and adherence to knowledge transfer schedule or plan

and so on.[3] The alliances group has the responsibility for making sure that all the interested people in the organization (and even those who are not interested but need to know about it!) have access to these resources so that their knowledge can be shared.

Security

This is a big issue—maybe bigger than you think. Not to be alarmist, but this is a good place to share some of the insights I learned from those who know about cybercrime—the FBI. I spoke with Special Agent Chris Buechneri, who is a member of the Computer Intrusion Squad. He referred me to Director Louis Freeh's comments on the subject.[4] His recent presentation in March 2000 to a Senate committee on technology and terrorism will knock your socks off. Read it, I implore you, and look once again at your own actions and those of your business. Here is a summary of some of the facts:

Categories of Cyberthreats Using Computers as Weapons or Targets

1. *Insiders.* This group includes terminated employees. Forbes and the National Library of Medicine (relied on by medical professionals worldwide) both suffered attacks.
2. *Hackers.* Also known as crackers, these people use readily available tools to disrupt systems (witness the denial-of-service attacks that hit CNN, Yahoo!, Amazon.com, and others). The FBI has developed its own FastAlliances with multiple law enforcement agencies worldwide to combat the problem (a recent example is the arrest of two suspects in Wales who had stolen credit card numbers in multiple countries). In addition, "hacktivism" attributes bigoted speeches to those who didn't make them. Other examples abound.
3. *Virus writers.* Melissa, Love Bug, and many more present constant threats.
4. *Criminal groups.* An international group of criminals commit cybercrime for money. The same old tricks actually still work (asking people for passwords, etc.).
5. *Terrorists.* These people use computerized files, e-mail, and encryption to support their activities. The mastermind of the

World Trade Center bombing stored detailed plans to destroy U.S. airliners in encrypted files on his laptop.

6. *Foreign intelligence services.* They now view computer intrusions as a useful tool for acquiring sensitive government information.
7. *Information warfare.* Foreign militaries try to manipulate our critical infrastructures.

Internet fraud is also coming from other directions, such as selling securities over the Net in stock-manipulation schemes. In addition, theft of intellectual property has become such a problem that a projected loss in 1997 of $2 billion a month has now exceeded that number by a substantial amount.

The laws have not kept up with the technology. Nor has enforcement. The bottom line: *Caveat* web user. Your security and that of your company and the security of your traditional and FastAlliances partners is almost entirely in your hands. I am not suggesting that vigilante groups arm themselves to protect what is theirs. However, I am suggesting that vigilance is essential, laced with a healthy dose of paranoia. Your personal and corporate security on the web is only as good as the least secure member of your Spider Network.

Final Thoughts

Throughout this book I have used the terms *traditional* (for *old*) and *new economies* to describe how people view the e-business world. Because this is a chapter of looking forward, I want to take this opportunity to throw those terms out *now.* There is no old and new. There is only what works and what doesn't. Many so-called old-economy issues such as good old earnings and sound management principles are becoming more relevant as the e-business world faces the harsh reality of "what goes up must come down." Lots of so-called new-economy aspects are now being integrated into the old bricks-and-mortar economy to make it more efficient and effective. Bottom line? *Please* don't get stuck on the terminology. Fast-talkers of the click world love all the buzzwords that make them sound different, and managers from traditional manufacturing firms either get depressed when exposed to it (because it makes them feel old and different) or grab onto the e-slang with a vengeance, outtalking the most voluble fast-talkers. It's all about what works and what doesn't—don't let the words separate you from success.

What will count in the decade that follows is endurance, resource management, responsiveness, and dependability. Sound like those reliable values of the past? They are, and the great shakeout of 2002 to 2005 will see many e-business companies fall away, be acquired, or grow. Continuity, global sophistication, and management competency will become more important. The time for the seasoned managers will return.

A recent study[5] found that by 2003, 20 percent of large businesses (over $1 billion in revenues) expect their online business to be above 20 percent of total revenues, whereas 18.8 percent felt that online business would be under 5 percent, and the remaining 56.2 percent felt their online business would be between 5 and 20 percent of their total annual revenues. At the moment, the majority of offline businesses with over $1 billion in revenues are moving slowly. However, if that survey were done at the end of each consecutive year, I believe that the percentages would go up.

When online transactions outnumber those offline, we are talking about a major consolidation of e-business, because megacompanies not seriously into e-business will face price cutting, cutthroat competition, and shakeouts that can hardly be imagined. The security of your Spider Network will be sorely tested, and the preemptive moves you make now to claim your place in the game with FastAlliances will prove themselves over and over again. The good news is that, knowing this, you can be a much more effective FastAlliances player. Just don't let your competition read this book!

AFTERWORD

It is the nature of the e-business world that everything changes and evolves at incredible speed. However, the nature of the publishing process is snail-like in its execution. When the final manuscript for this book was given to the publisher, everything contained in it was fresh and relevant. However, there is no doubt in my mind that a certain percentage of the contents will need refurbishing and updating on a continuous basis. I have created a web site specifically for that purpose. On it, I will place updates on FastAlliances and access to the suite of over 24 software processes that comprise the *Larraine Segil Partner Relationship Management (PRM) System.* To gain access, please log on to www.lsegil.com, where you will be asked for the following:

- Your e-mail address
- Fax and phone numbers
- Your name and title
- The name of your organization
- Your geographical address

We will give you a pass code and access number to the FastAlliances software and updates' secure web site and information on our privacy policy. You may then register as a subscriber by entering your credit card number online.

I look forward to a continuing relationship with you, the reader and customer, and with the community of those who are energized by FastAlliances and their relevance in our world. My e-mail address: lsegil@lsegil.com.

APPENDIX A
FastAlliances Toolkit

Chapter 1

The Spider Network: FastAlliances Tool #1
Brick-to-Click Culture Change Process: FastAlliances Tool #2

Chapter 2

The FastStrategy: FastAlliances Tool #3
Creating the E-business Exchange (CommerceOne): FastAlliances Tool #4
Brand Positioning Castle: FastAlliances Tool #5
The FastStrategy Playbook (Compaq): FastAlliances Tool #6
The Cool Decision Process (Office Depot Online): FastAlliances Tool #7
The E-business Consortium (Praxair): FastAlliances Tool #8

Chapter 3

Capability Quiz: FastAlliances Tool #9
Gantt Chart: FastAlliances Tool #10

Chapter 4

The Lawyers' Checklist: FastAlliances Tool #11

Chapter 5

Vertical Portal Quicktest: FastAlliances Tool #12

Chapter 6

Web Culture Integration: FastAlliances Tool #13

Chapter 7

E-Mindshift: FastAlliances Tool #14

Chapter 8

Pyramid of Planet CAD: FastAlliances Tool #15
Acquisition Integration Process of Flextronics: FastAlliances Tool #16
Acquisition Integration Process of CEMEX: FastAlliances Tool #17
Freebie or Sell: FastAlliances Tool #18
The Synthesizer (Ninth House): FastAlliances Tool #19
Fire, Aim, Steady (E-Frenzy): FastAlliances Tool #20
The Tiering Process (Siebel): FastAlliances Tool #21
Circle of Influence: FastAlliances Tool #22

Chapter 9

The Right Choice: FastAlliances Tool #23
IAN/FASTAL Knowledge Capture Tool Context Integration: FastAlliances Tool #24
Metric to End All Metrics: FastAlliances Tool #25

APPENDIX B

Companies Supplying Weapons and Countermeasures in the War for Web Customers

The following information came from *Forbes* magazine (January 24, 2000).

Company	Weapon	Countermeasures
Ichoose	Pop-up window guides consumers to better deals elsewhere	Contract with Ichoose to show consumer even better deal
Liaison	Automatic agent grabs prices and other data from thousands of web sites	Block Internet protocol address of agent from accessing site
Auctionwatch.com	Agent compiles price and product data from online auction sites	Block IP addresses; litigation
ClicktheButton.com	Comparable price data for consumers in real time	None known
IQOrder.com	In-store price comparisons via cellular telephone	Frisk customers for cell phones

GLOSSARY OF PRIVACY TERMS

The following terms, related to online privacy, have been adapted from an article in *Business Week* magazine.*

advertising networks The Net equivalent of advertising agencies, like DoubleClick, which amass millions of profiles of web surfers based on their online habits. Ads are then targeted toward those most likely to buy whatever is being pitched.

cookies Text files of user data that help e-tailers personalize web pages for specific users and identify online customers' shopping habits. A cookie resides in the browser memory, but when the browser is closed, the information is written to a file on the user's hard drive. Bottom line? These software programs keep a log of where you click, thus allowing sites to track your habits. The spooky thing is that a cookie gets placed on your computer the first time you visit a site or use online calendars, new services, or shopping carts. You can find cookie-blocking programs to put on your computer.

IP address A number automatically assigned to your computer whenever you connect to the Net so that the network can send data. It can also be used for profiling and targeting.

online profiling By using cookies combined with personal information, sites build profiles about what customers buy and do.

opt in and opt out Privacy choices that some web sites offer to visitors. The site may be free to use the information unless you forbid it by clicking on a button.

* Adapted from *Business Week*, March 20, 2000, page 85.

personally identifiable information Your address, name, and other details (credit card) linked to your identity.

privacy policies Notices on a web site explaining how a company collects and uses your data.

referers Information that your web browser passes along when you move from site to site or use a search engine or e-mail. Referers can be collected and used to target advertising.

registrations Any forms or sites in which you fill out personal information. This data can be sold or shared with other web sites or advertisers.

third-party databases Companies like Acxiom stockpile information about most U.S. households to sell to other web sites and software makers.

WAP Wireless application protocol, a standard for wireless data delivery. WAP is on the next generation of handheld communication devices, making it easier to access the Internet from wireless machines such as portable phones and personal digital assistants.

ACKNOWLEDGMENTS

Although this book is dedicated to my son, James Segil, he must also be my first and most important acknowledgment.

The idea for the book came from James. He was the first to read it, edit the first complete manuscript, and the resource I turned to when frustrated by concepts I could not communicate clearly, or even enunciate at all.

James is an officer of a dot-com company, an Internet executive who left the security and promise of the fast track to a senior executive position in a traditional large Fortune 500 consumer-products company. He exemplifies many of those I interviewed for this book. His Spider Network and mine have now intertwined, gaining benefit for each of us and all our network members. Surely there can be no greater pleasure for a parent than to become the mentee, while the child becomes the mentor. I have quoted James only occasionally in the book, although his thoughts are reflected in many places. He has huge wisdom (heaven only knows where it comes from at his tender age of 29) and a sense of humor that will not stop. I did not include him as often as I wanted in order not to appear subject to nepotism. But he has been (and continues to be) my greatest inspiration (and if you hadn't realized by now) my continuing source of pride. Thank you, James.

A very special thanks goes to my husband, Clive—so many dinners, functions, concerts, events, and even trips that he has attended alone, as my writing has consumed 17 to 18 hours a day for the 60 days in which I put the first draft of this book together and the nine months within which I have written it. Your support, love, and patience helped me create it all.

Continuing thanks to Flo Dunagan, personal assistant and mom-in-residence, who tells me where to go and when, for fielding my life and giving up all time off while I hid away to write.

Thanks to Nancy Ellis for her never-ending belief in me and my myriad books, to Linda Mead for starting the process that has brought us all so much success, and to Hershey Felder for his original call to Millie.

Thanks to Airié Dekidjiev, whose enthusiasm is more than I could have hoped for—and with whom I will work again and again—and to her colleagues and the incredible team at Wiley (especially Jeanne Glasser, who made sure that Wiley would be my publisher). What a class act!

Thanks to my partner in The Lared Group, Emilio Fontana, whose good cheer has helped us to weather the stress of busy schedules that have kept us on the phone and e-mail at night and on weekends (which we vowed not to do in former lives).

And my heartfelt thanks to the hundreds of executives who shared their time, insights, processes, feelings, and hopes with me in the pursuit of a definitive tome on alliances for the e-business world.

NOTES

Introduction

1. *Real estate* in the Internet means the eyes of people who look at the site, their numbers, and the purchases they make. These things add value to that site (increase the real estate value of the site).
2. The first term applied to those with familiarity with and competency in the Internet.
3. *Click* is the commonly mentioned term for Internet and web-based environments and space, with *bricks* referring to the old-line buildings and physical space of the non-web-based environments. However, companies in both spaces now need competency in each environment in order to succeed in either.

Chapter 1

1. Yes, this is my son, mentioned in the dedication of this book, and I think the saying goes "the apple does not fall far from the tree. . . ."
2. Corporate Executive Board, Working Council for Chief Financial Officers, report titled *Stand and Deliver,* 1999.
3. Refer to Internet addresses www.sun.com and www.mysun.com.
4. These activities have been done through The Lared Group, which I cofounded with partner Emilio Fontana. It is a consulting group, headquartered in Los Angeles, specializing in alliances. In addition, speaking services are provided through Larraine Segil Productions Inc. See appendix for further information.

5. Larraine Segil, *Intelligent Business Alliances* (New York: Times Business, Random House, 1996), www.lsegil.com.
6. Doreen Carvajal, "Leading Bertelsmann's Role to the Future," *The New York Times* (January 30, 2000).
7. Frank Gibney Jr., "Emperor of the Internet," *Time* (December 6, 1999): 70–71.
8. The giant and the gazelle are based on real companies. I have created the story to protect their confidentiality.
9. The Larraine Segil FastAlliances Partner Relationship Management (PRM) software programs are available for all the tools in this book. See page 283 for further information, or download them from www.lsegil.com.
10. See Larraine Segil, *Intelligent Business Alliances* (New York: Times Books, Random House, 1996).
11. Ninth House has launched a partnering program called "Partnering for Profit," based on *Intelligent Business Alliances,* which is web-based and interactive, as part of its learning network. See www.ninthhouse.com.
12. Literally, SWAT is an acronym for Special Weapons and Tactics, a term used by police departments in the United States for the special teams that are brought in to resolve highly dangerous situations.
13. Gensler Architecture, Design and Planning Worldwide (www.gensler.com, jordan_goldstein@gensler.com, walter_trujillo@gensler.com).
14. See Larraine Segil, *Intelligent Business Alliances* (New York: Times Books, Random House, 1996).
15. Andrew Pollack, "After Space, Hughes Battles Time," *The New York Times,* Business Section (Sunday February 27, 2000).

Chapter 2

1. Primedia Satellite Television is the network on which I had my distance learning programs for Executive education. Similar content is now contained in my video series, *Larraine Segil, One on One*, seen on www.lsegil.com.
2. See www.commerceone.com.
3. Russ Banham, "Don't Let Branding Burn You," *CFO Magazine,* February 2000, page 91.
4. See www.compaq.com. In 2000, Compaq posted approximately $44 billion in annual revenues.

5. From a personal interview with Brian Bonazzoli at Compaq Silicon Valley.
6. Praxair's web address is www.praxair.com.

Chapter 3

1. See Larraine Segil, *Intelligent Business Alliances* (New York: Times Books, Random House, 1996), for traditional processes.
2. Jim Mocarski, a superb aeronautical engineering executive with Lared client Northrop Grumman, shared his business analysis and program management expertise with me, and I adapted his Gantt charts. See jmocarski2@aol.com.

Chapter 4

1. These remarks are from my interview with Brian Bonazzoli and Adrienne Higashi at Compaq Silicon Valley.
2. I am a Senior Research Fellow for the IC2 institute.
3. I am a board member of LARTA.
4. Luisa Kroll, "Mad Hatchery Sundrome," *Forbes* (April 17, 2000): page 132.
5. http://56.0.78.92/pdf/subm0799.pdf; http://56.0.78.92/
6. See www.interforum.org, the quasi-government body created to provide an objective channel of information exchange between IT vendors, Internet service providers, and purchasers of systems. The forum develops common standards and provides the framework to assist legislators in areas such as the use of digital signatures.
7. John R. Kasich, "The Great Internet Tax Debate," *Business Week* (March 27, 2000): page 228.
8. Hart-Scott-Rodino Antitrust Improvement Act of 1976 gives the Federal Trade Commission (FTC) and Department of Justice (among other rights) notice of and time-limited opportunity to review all large mergers and acquisitions before they are consummated.
9. In my book *Intelligent Business Alliances,* Chapter 2 outlines a methodology to proactively analyze and predict different cultural behavior and individual managerial personalities.
10. He is singing my song. See Larraine Segil, *Intelligent Business Alliances* (New York: Times Books, Random House, 1996): Chapters 2 and 5.

11. MaryAnne Murray Buechner, "Gray Is Good," *Time* (April 10, 2000).
12. MP3.com is in litigation and settlement discussions with a number of record companies, and as this book goes to press these matters remain unresolved.
13. VerticalNet operates 57+ business portals with trade news for market sectors as well as auctions.
14. See Larraine Segil *Intelligent Business Alliances* (New York: Times Books, Random House, 1996): Chapter 2.
15. Published by American Productivity and Quality Center, Houston, Texas, the first "Benchmarking Study on Sales and Marketing Alliances, 1998," designed by Larraine Segil as the subject matter expert on alliances.
16. "Is the Street Lowballing IPOs?" *Business Week E-Biz* (April 3, 2000): page EB 112.
17. Catherine Yang, "Earth to Dot-Com Accountants," *Business Week* (April 3, 2000): page 40.
18. See www.mcfd.com. The firm advises companies from all industries on recapitalizations, raising private equity, working with investment bankers, analysts, and companies under $1 billion in revenues.

Chapter 5

1. See www.berglas.com.
2. Richard Behar, "The Bigger They Are, the Harder They Fall," *Time* (November 4, 1999): pages 14–16.

Chapter 6

1. Richard Tomlinson, "Europe's New Business Elite," *Fortune* (April 3, 2000): page 182.
2. International Data Corporation (1999), European Internet and eCommerce—Ready for 2000?
3. An Australian-founded company, Talisman, created technology that enables this to happen.
4. Henry Muller, "Europe Closes the Gap," *Time* (March 13, 2000): pages B18–23.
5. David Fairlamb and Gail Edmondson, "Work in Progress," *Business Week* Special Report (January 31, 2000): pages 80–87.

6. Michael Manden, "The New Economy," *Business Week* Special Report (January 31, 2000): page 77.
7. Moon Ihlwan, "The Latest Chaebol Startup Game Plan: Stalking Cyber Startups," *Business Week,* International Edition (April 10, 2000): page 170E2.
8. Moon Ihlwan, "Shopping at the Chaebol Cybermall," *Business Week,* International Edition (March 27, 2000): page 58E6.
9. See www.geomarkets.com.
10. See www.vcheq.com.
11. See www.1-fusion.com.
12. See Japan Internet Report, www.jir.net.
13. See geoventures@geomarkets.com, vol. 1, no. 8, page 7.
14. See www.im.se/.
15. See elabseurope.com.
16. See ei3corp.com.
17. Brandon Mitchener, "Border Crossings," *Wall Street Journal,* Special Section on E-Commerce (November 22, 1999).
18. Presentation by Annika Alford, International Data Corporation, "The Challenges Ahead: Good and Bad surrounding Latin America's Internet Market," at January 17 conference organized by Silicon Valley World Internet Center, Palo Alto, California.
19. José Macaya is a Harvard alum and past president of the Harvard Alumni Association in Argentina.
20. See www.peoplesound.com.
21. Apax is a venture capital company that manages over $5.6 billion in institutional money. It was created in 1977 by Alan Patricof (New York), Ronald Cohen (London), and Maurice Tchenio (Paris).
22. *Halo effect* refers to the effect of the Spider Network and the credibility that goes along with those associations.
23. Lee Gomes, "*(Not)* Made in America," *Wall Street Journal,* Special Section: E-Commerce (November 22, 1999).
24. Frank Gibney, Jr., "The Emperor of the Internet," *Time* (December 6, 1999): pages 70–72.
25. Irene M. Kunii and Stephen Baker, "Japan's Mobile Marvel," *Business Week* (January 17, 2000): page 88–90.

26. See www.toyota.com.
27. I am most grateful to Kerry Racanelli on Doug Formby's staff for her speedy response to my requests.
28. To subscribe (it's free), please register at www.lsegil.com.
29. I have a team game for global work teams that enables people to create fictional cultures with made-up rules and then resolve conflict in those cultures so that everyone has the experience of feeling like a minority or a stranger who is misunderstood.
30. Mark Clifford, Bruce Einham, Frederik Balfour, and Jack Ewing, "The Dealmakers," *Business Week* (February 28, 2000): page 102.
31. See www.geoventures.com.
32. *Spidering* is the capability of creating, measuring, and managing a Spider Network.

Chapter 7

1. See Larraine Segil, *Intelligent Business Alliances* (New York: Times Books, Random House, 1996): Chapter 2.
2. See Larraine Segil, *Intelligent Business Alliances* (New York: Times Books, Random House, 1996), and my web page at www.lsegil.com regarding processes, planning, and metrics.
3. See Larraine Segil, *Intelligent Business Alliances* (New York: Times Books, Random House, 1996), and my web page at www.lsegil.com regarding processes, planning, and metrics.
4. I sit on the *Industry Week* panel of experts who select the Top 100 Companies each year.
5. See my web page at www.lsegil.com for publication date.
6. David Rocks, "Reinventing Herman Miller," *Business Week E-Biz* (April 3, 2000): page EB93. Certain facts were taken from the article to support the in-person meeting.

Chapter 8

1. Philip Kafka, "Talk Is Cheap," *Forbes* (April 17, 2000): page 150.
2. As of October 16, 2000, Virtualis Inc. has been acquired by Allegiance, a telecommunications company, and will become its web-hosting division.
3. Neil Weinberg, "Not.coms," *Forbes* (April 17, 2000): page 424.

4. Srikumar S. Rao, "General Electric, Software Vendor," *Forbes* (January 24, 2000): 144.
5. See www.THQ.com.
6. These are the areas on your site where you permit alliance partners to place icons that take the customer to their sites or allow for a sell-through transaction to take place with revenue sharing to your company—the lowest or second lowest level of the Pyramid of Planet CAD.
7. From interviews with Jeff Snipes, CEO of Ninth House, and Tom Fischman, cofounder and vice president of marketing.
8. See www.siebel.com/alliances.

Chapter 9

1. Brent Schlender, "The Customer Is the Decision Maker," *Fortune* (March 6, 2000): page F85.
2. A software program is available for this system. See www.lsegil.com.
3. I present programs on traditional alliances (*Intelligent Business Alliances*) and e-business alliances (*FastAlliances for E-business*). They range from keynotes to two-day programs. I've written books by the same titles. In addition, I have web-based programs and live satellite programs on both subjects. Finally, I offer a video series on all these programs. Please contact the following address for online purchase or pricing: www.lsegil.com.
4. See www.fbi.gov.
5. Chart in *Business Week* (April 17, 2000): page 10.

INDEX